(ISBN : 2.7118.2714.3 French edition)
Translated into English by Anthony Roberts

Caroline Mathieu, curator at the musée d'Orsay

Guide to the Musée d'Orsay

List of the principal donations and bequests to the Musée d'Orsay

1881	Gift of Juliette Courbet: Courbet, *Un enterrement à Ornans (A Burial at Ornans)*
1890	Gift by subscription following an initiative by Monet: Manet, *L'Olympia*
	Gift of Mme Pommery: Millet, *Les glaneuses (The Gleaners)*
1896	Bequest Caillebotte: Manet, *Le balcon (The Balcony)* Renoir, *Le Moulin de la Galette (The "Moulin de la Galette"* Monet, Cézanne, Pissarro, Sisley, etc.
1906	Donation Etienne Moreau-Nélaton: Daumier, *La République (The Republic)* Fantin-Latour, *Hommage à Delacroix* Manet, *Le déjeuner sur l'herbe (Lunch on the Grass)* Monet, *Les coquelicots, (The Poppies), Le pont d'Argenteuil, (The bridge of Argenteuil)*, etc.
1909	Donation Chauchard: Millet, *L'Angélus (The Angelus)* Daubigny, Rousseau, Dupré, Meissonier
1911	Bequest Camondo: Degas, *Répétition d'un ballet, (Ballet Rehearsal), L'absinthe (Absinth) Les repasseuses (Women Ironing)* Manet, *Lola de Valence, Le fifre (The Fife-Player)* Monet, Cathédrale de Rouen *Rouen Cathedrals)* Sisley, *Inondation à Port-Marly (Flooding at Port-Marley)* Cézanne, *La maison du pendu*, etc. (The House of the Hanged Man), etc.
1916	Donation Auguste Rodin: Rodin, *Balzac, La porte de l'Enfer (The Gate of Hell)*
1920	Gift by public subscription: Courbet, *L'atelier (The Studio)*
1927	Bequest John Quinn: Seurat, *Le cirque (The Circus)*
1929	Bequest Jacques Doucet: Douanier Rousseau, *La charmeuse de serpents (The Snake-charmer)*
1937	Bequest Personnaz: Cassat, Guillaumin, Pissarro, Toulouse-Lautrec, etc.
1949-1954	Donation Gachet: van Gogh, *Autoportrait (Self-portrait) L'église d'Auvers, (The Church at Auvers)*, etc. Cézanne, Guillaumin, etc.
1956	Gift of M. et Mme Jean-Victor Pellerin: Cézanne, *La femme à la cafetière (Women with Coffee-Pot)*
1961	Donation Mollard: Boudin, Pissarro, Sisley, etc.
1964	Gift of the heirs of Jean-Victor Pellerin: Cézanne, *Achille Emperaire*
1973	Donation Max and Rosy Kaganovitch: Derain, Gauguin, Monet, van Gogh, Vlaminck, etc.
1976	Gift (usufruct) of Mme Ginette Signac: 5 Neo-Impressionist works Paul Signac, Théo van Rysselberghe, Henri-Edmond Cross, *L'air du soir (Evenina Breeze)*
1980	Gift of M. and Mme David Weill: Daumier, *Bustes des parlementaires (Busts of Parliamentarians)* Mackintosh, *Bedroom*
1981	Gift of Mlle Solange Granet, Mme Bernard Granet and her children: Gustave Eiffel archives
	Gift of the Ruprich-Robert family: Victor-Marie-Charles Ruprich-Robert, architectural drawings
1982	Donation Arï and Suzanne Redon: Odilon Redon, 66 paintings, 462 pastels and drawings
1983	Bequest Mlle Henriette Boutaric: Paul Sérusier, 5 paintings
	Gift of Kodak-Pathé Foundation: Collection of approximately 1,200 French and foreign photographs and daguerreotypes
1984	Gift of M. du Pasquier: Jean-Louis Ernest Meissonier, *Le voyageur (The Traveller)*, wax statuette
1985	Gift of M. Daniel Wildenstein: Pierre Bonnard, *La partie de croquet (The Croquet Game)*
	Acquisition, through the generous intervention of M. Philippe Meyer: Paul Sérusier, *The Talisman*
1986, 1987	Gifts of M. Jean Bourgogne: Emile Gallé, furniture, glassware, faience; document collection
1987	Gift of Charles Terrasse's four children: Pierre Bonnard, approximately 250 photographs taken between 1895 and 1912
	Acquisition, thanks to the patronage of the Crédit Lyonnais: Henry van de Velde *Ecritoire et fauteuil (Writing desk and Armchair)*
1988	Gift (usufruct) of M. Clément Rouart: Edgar Degas, *Portrait of Manet*, ink and wash
1989	Gift (usufruct) of M. Charles Cachin: Paul Signac, *Femme à l'ombrelle (Woman with Umbrella)*
1990	Acquisition, through the generous intervention of M. Philippe Meyer: Edgar Degas, *The Ballet* (gouache)
1991	Gift of Mme Jacqueline Georges Besson: Albert André, 4 paintings
	Bequest Mlle Yolande Osbert: Alphonse Osbert, workshop reserve
1992	Gift of M. Paul Mellon through the intervention of the Foundation for French Museums: Edgar Degas, *Etude pour la danse espagnole (Study for the Spanish Dance)*, sculpture

Numerous gifts of the Société des Amis du Musée d'Orsay have enriched the collections of paintings and drawings (Hans Thoma, *Siesta*; Fèvre-Degas Collection; Albert Bartholomé, *Dans la serre — In the Greenhouse*), sculptures (Albert Bartholomé, *Mask of Hayashi Tadamasa*), objets d'art (William Morris, *Panel in Ceramic Tiles*), architectural drawings (Jean-Camille Formigé Collection), photographs (Eugène Atget, *Nu de dos — Nude, Backview*, Edouard Baldus, Man Ray *(Marcel Proust on his Deathbed)*, etc.

"The railway station is superb; it looks exactly like a Palais des Beaux-Arts. Since the Palais des Beaux-Arts happens to resemble a railway station, I suggest that Laloux" (the architect of the Gare d'Orsay) "...should switch their functions while there's still time." So wrote the painter Detaille, just before the inauguration of the two buildings in 1900. One of them had been designed to receive and lodge the visitors to the Universal Exhibition (the station was enveloped, so the speak, by its hotel), and the other to present the masterpieces of the 19th century, then at its triumphant close.

Eighty-six years later, Detaille's ironical suggestion has been in part adopted. The 'palais'-cum-railway station has become a terminus for sixty-six years of prodigious artistic output. The Musée d'Orsay is a showcase for the years 1848 to 1914, with coverage of the beginning and end of this period slightly blurred in terms of chronology. For example, the museum could hardly omit photography prior to 1848, the science having been invented in 1839; likewise the ensemble of Daumier's work is shown, including early canvases from the 1830's. The close of the museum's chronological cycle is roughly 1905, to coincide with the beginning of the period covered by the Musée d'Art Moderne; but again exceptions are made for artists such as Bonnard, Degas, Maillol, Monet, Rodin and Vuillard whose work straddles the epoch. Broadly speaking, these choices have been made using generations, rather than years, as a yardstick. The Musée d'Orsay can be said to contain the work of architects, painters, sculptors, photographers and creators of decorative and industrial art, born between 1820 and 1870.

The museum is planned chronologically in broad sequences, technique by technique. Our goal was to evoke every aspect of creativity properly belonging to the epoch, including music and literature; but we rejected the type of 'atmospheric reconstitution' which (for example) would have placed a Napoleon III canapé, the maquette of a Haussmann façade and a 'history' painting of the kind favoured by the Salons, all in the same room with soft background music composed by Meyerbeer. Nor did we like the idea of a 1900 Charpentier dining room, with articles by Octave Mirbeau on a Thonet pedestal table beside a Gallé vase with a painting by Gaugin hanging above!

Of course not. The works in the Musée d'Orsay are exhibited to the visitor in stylistic families, and wherever possible artist by artist. The main rooms are dedicated to Daumier, Courbet, Degas, Manet, Puvis, Monet, Renoir, Cézanne, van Gogh and Gauguin, Seurat, Bonnard, etc., along with a Carpeaux square, a Rodin terrace and a Guimard tower. The visitor will have no difficulty afterwards in remembering these juxtapositions.

Only in one case did a room impose its own style; this was the ballroom of the former hotel, whose boisterous 1900 rococo décor has been complemented by paintings and sculptures selected for their qualities of technical brio, decorative effect and suitability to the surroundings.

Elements which can help the visitor understand the context of the works exhibited are shown as supplements to the main circuit. Contemporary events, along with changes in ideas, attitudes and means of communication, are dealt with in separate exhibition rooms ("Ouverture sur l'Histoire", the history of the period; "Naissance du Cinématographe", the birth of cinematography) and galleries ("Passage de la Presse", a review of the contemporary newspaper industry). Additional contextual information is provided by temporary exhibitions organised around specific themes, or by films and conferences. The visitor whose time is limited, or who has come to the museum to see a specific part of it, will naturally follow his own itinerary. Lovers of Second Empire art will stay on the ground floor, while amateurs of the Impressionists will turn left immediately after Courbet towards the upper galleries. Those whose main purpose is to rediscover the long-derived 'Pompier' painters of the official Salons will go to the ground floor room devoted to young academics (Bouguereau, Cabanel) then climb via the ballroom to the first intermediate level. Here they will find 'naturalist' works dealing with the type of popular and historical subject matter favoured by the Salons of the Third Republic and the compilers of contemporary illustrated encyclopaedias. Lastly, admirers of the Post-Manet modernist tradition will go straight to the 1st floor display of Cézanne, Seurat, Van Gogh, Gauguin, the Nabis and Rodin; the works of these painters are contained in three rooms to the left and right of the towers, which are devoted to international Art Nouveau. Their tour will be completed by a review of Vuillard and Bonnard, or the early days of cinema.

The bulk of the collection now a the Musée d'Orsay originally came from the museum of living artists of the period, which was moved in 1939 from the Luxembourg to the Musée d'Art Moderne. On the deaths of the artists concerned, their work was gradually absorbed by the Louvre. Until about 1920, the state's acquisition policy tended to be linked to the ideas of the Ecole des Beaux-Arts, which consistently opposed independent art; ie., Courbet, Manet, the Impressionists and their successors. Hence it was by a gradual process of private donation that most of these paintings reached public ownership. The table on page 4 shows how great is the debt owed by the museum to the taste and generosity of such private donors; for a majority of the great masterpieces now at Orsay came from individual collectors.

From 1920 onwards, the paintings which had originally adorned the old Luxembourg museum were gradually placed in reserve or sent to the provinces: The opening of the Jeu de Paume museum in 1947 marked the ultimate victory of the Impressionists, while the Musée d'Art Moderne continued to enlarge its collection of contemporary painters. Nonetheless, there was a hiatus between the two; no single institution existed which did justice to the generation between Monet and Picasso, that of Seurat the neo-impressionists, Gauguin and the School of Pont-Aven and the "Nabis". Unclassifiable personalities like Puvis or Moreau, and others belonging to no particular movement, such as Couture, Cottet, Carolus-Duran, Carrière, Dalou, Bernard, Winslow Homer and Pelizza da Volpedo, were practically never shown at all, and the former lions of the official Salons seemed to have sunk without trace.

The Musée d'Orsay answers this need. A spate of gifts and acquisitions has reinforced the state collection of fin de siècle French and international modernits, with many representative paintings and works of decorative art. All along, however, the curators of the Musée d'Orsay have remained open to all the creative trends of this extraordinarily brilliant half century, which spans the era between the Louvre and the Musée national d'Art Moderne. Without imposing strict premises about what is good and what is bad, we have sought to demonstrate the epoch's most significant developments, its priorities, and its choices, by supplying the visitor with the evidence on which to make his own comparisons and draw his own conclusions.

We hope that this guide by Caroline Mathieu, curator of the Musée d'Orsay, will help you find your bearings, show you the way around the museum's various circuits, and make it easier for you to discover its visual, spiritual and historical wealth. We also hope that it will inspire you to come back again – frequently, and at length.

Françoise Cachin,
Director of the Musée d'Orsay

The Gare d'Orsay was born of a need common to all the great French railway companies; the need for a terminus close to the centre of Paris. The Compagnie des Chemins de Fer d'Orléans was placed at a considerable disadvantage by its lack of such a terminus. In 1897, however, three years before the opening of the 1900 Universal Exhibition, the company purchased a piece of land in the heart of the city, on the Quai d'Orsay. This was the site of the old Palais d'Orsay, or Cour des Comptes, which had been burnt down during the Commune uprising of 1871.

The station had to be planned for the exclusive use of railway passengers, but at the same time was supposed to exhibit a high degree of comfort and luxury, in keeping with the beauty of the site and the elegance of the quarter. A limited competition was organised between three famous architects, Emile Bernard, Lucien Magne and Victor Laloux. Laloux, a professor of architecture at the Ecole des Beaux-Arts and winner of the Grand Prix de Rome in 1878, was awarded the contract. In his design, the industrial nature of the construction was carefully masked on the outside by a pompous, eclectic stone façade, and on the inside by a staff coffered ceiling. The metal gabling over the main hall was hidden by the façade of the station hotel, attached to the station proper, whose 370 rooms faced the rue de Bellechasse and the rue de Lille. In short, the Gare d'Orsay was the ultimate in academic architecture, in which stone and stucco were used to cover steel structures of astonishing strength; the same methods were used for the Petit Palais and the Grand Palais, built at exactly the same time to coincide with the Universal Exhibition.

Every aspect of the station's décor, down to the last detail, was planned by the architect, and it was apparently he who selected the artists, most of whom were officially recognised painters and sculptors. The statues personifying towns outside the station were done by Jean Hugues, Laurent-Honoré Marqueste and Jean-Antoine Injalbert. The paintings in the departure hall are the work of Fernand Cormon and the salons of the hotel were decorated by Pierre Fritel, Adrien Moreau-Neyret, Gabriel Ferrier and Benjamin Constant. The entire building was completed in under two years, and inaugurated on the 14th of July 1900.

The rapid progress of mechanisation soon made the Gare d'Orsay difficult to operate and the mainline railway service finally ceased in 1939. Laloux's monument, having been abandoned by the SNCF, was subsequently used for a wide variety of other purposes. Among other things, it was used as a clearing-house for prisoners of war in 1945 and as a set for Orson Welles' film "The Trial" in 1962.

Victor Laloux
1850-1937

The great clock
in the central aisle

A head of Mercury,
patron of travellers,
crowns the station's
two metal gables

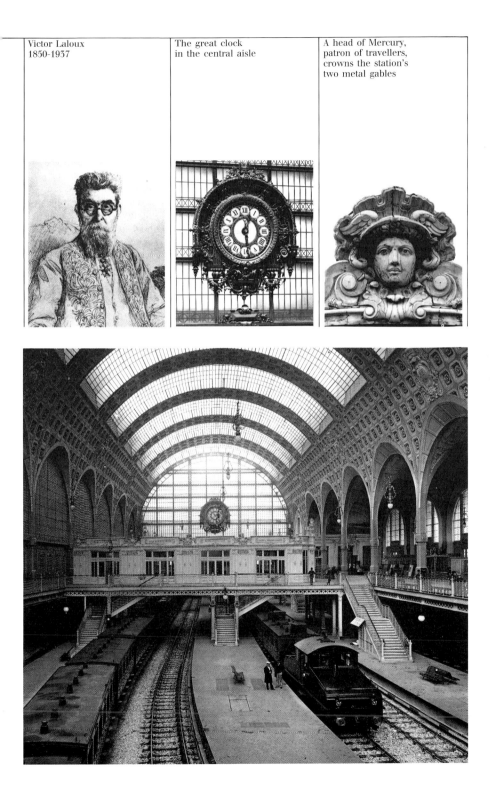

Plans for the conversion of the station into a museum exhibiting all aspects of art in the second half of the 19th century were put forward by the Pompidou government in 1973, in response to the wishes of the Direction des Musées de France. In effect, the Gare d'Orsay benefited from a revival of interest in the 19th century, which unfortunately came too late to save Baltard's Halles. A threat to demolish the station and replace it with a gigantic hotel was fortunately averted, and the museum project was taken in hand and promoted by President Giscard d'Estaing, who set up a public institution to complete the works. This initiative was confirmed by President Mitterrand in 1981.

In 1979, a team set up by ACT Architecture (Renaud Bardon, Pierre Colboc and Jean-Paul Philippon) was selected after an open competition to carry out the necessary structural works. In 1980 a second contest led to the naming of the Italian woman architect Gae Aulenti for the interior design and adaptation of the building to museum purposes. New elements were added to the main hall, opening the main sweep of the arches to the gaze and installing exhibition rooms topped by terraces on either side of a central aisle. These rooms and terraces communicate with other rooms on two levels, in a series of vestibules along the façade facing the Seine. At the top of the building, under the roof of the station and the old hotel, are a number of broad galleries illuminated by natural light. The various hotel reception rooms have also been integrated into the museum, and the hotel restaurant now fills the same function for the museum. Everywhere, Laloux's cast iron pillars and stucco decorations were respected, restored and opened up to the view. The new structures were designed to leave a palpable impression of the old.

The interior architecture is unified by the materials and colours of its surfaces (Burgundy stone, partitions painted in light shades, metals coloured dark brown or blue), and the succession of display rooms is organised around the presentation of works of art, offering a variety of architectural possibilities to that purpose.

1st floor:
view from
the terraces

1st floor:
view from one of the
domed exhibition rooms

View from one of
the ground-floor
exhibition rooms

Conversion of the station into a museum, 1984-1985

Practical Information

The Musée is not only a place of exhibition for works of art; it is also a place for entertainment, contemplation and learning:

- A programme of *concerts* from the repertoire of 1848-1914 is continuously played in the auditorium and the restaurant.
- The auditorium is also used for various *film projections,* notably an annual festival devoted to early cinema.
- Regular *conferences* and *debates* are held on subjects relating to temporary exhibitions. Cultural history courses are also available to museum members.
- A number of *educational activities* have been arranged, for ages 5-15 in particular; these take place in the rooms set aside for use by young people.
- Various documentary devices are available for consultation in the Passage des Dates (dates corridor) and the Salle de Consultation (documentation room).

Measurements of Artworks

Whatever the techniques used in their fabrication (painting, sculpture, objets d'art, furniture) all dimensions are given in centimetres, and the first figure given is always the height.

A - Paintings

Height followed by width; the dimensions are always those of the canvas itself, not counting the frame.

B - Sculpture

The only dimensions of sculptures given here are height and width.

C - Objets d'art

Objets d'art are treated as an exception. The height is always mentioned; in the case of circular objects, the second figure represent diameter. Two parts of the same object may also be dissociated, as in the case of a cup and basin. In this case the height and diameter of each element is given.

D - Furniture

For the purpose of this guide, the volume of a piece of furniture is expressed in terms of its height, width and depth.

Musée d'Orsay
62, rue de Lille
75343 Paris Cedex 07
Tel. 40 49 48 14

Main entrance:
1, rue de Bellechasse
Entrance to temporary exhibitions:
Place Henry-de-Montherlant

Opening hours:
Tuesday, Wednesday, Friday and Saturday
10am to 6pm
Thursday 10am to 9.45pm
Sunday and on working days from 20 June to 20 Sept.
9am to 6pm
Closed on Monday

Last admission 5.15pm (9.15pm on Thursday)

Available to visitors

In the entrance hall:
Telephones
Letterboxes
Exchange bureau
M'O bookshop open 9.30am to 6.30pm, 9.30pm on Thursday
Audioguide rental, museum opening hours, except late night opening

On the middle level:
Restaurant, accessible to museum entrance ticket holders, museum opening hours.

On the upper level:
Rooftop Café, museum opening hours

Access from the outside:
M'O Boutique, open 9.30am to 6.30pm, 9.30pm on Thursday

After the ticket offices and throughout the visit: Lifts reserved for wheelchair users

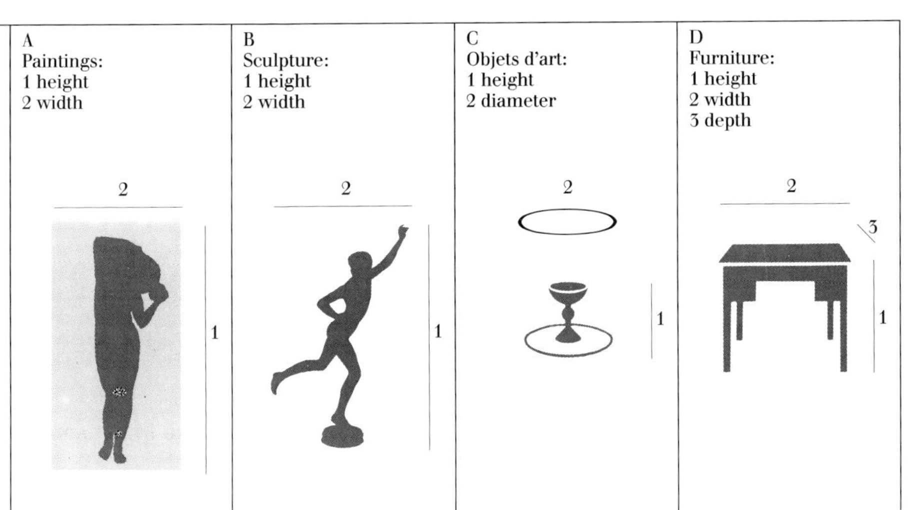

The M'O Dossier-exhibits

One of the original features of the Musée d'Orsay is the integration of small exhibitions in the regular museum circuit, ranging from simple displays to complex presentations that:
– present works of graphic art (drawings, engravings, posters, photography), which due to their fragile nature cannot be shown permanently;
– depict creative and cultural life in the second half of the 19 th century outside of painting and sculpture: the press, publications, theatre, music, dance, etc.;
– deepen the insight into a work or group of works, by building up an actual "dossier" around a new acquisition or recent restoration for example, through explanatory articles, reproductions, short films, etc.;
– organize small satellite exhibitions around a major exhibition or theme.
Access to these exhibitions is included in the museum admission charge.

They may be found at various points on all three floors and are signposted by coloured banners. The dossier-exhibits genuinely provide another approach to the museum, a way of complementing or renewing one's visit.

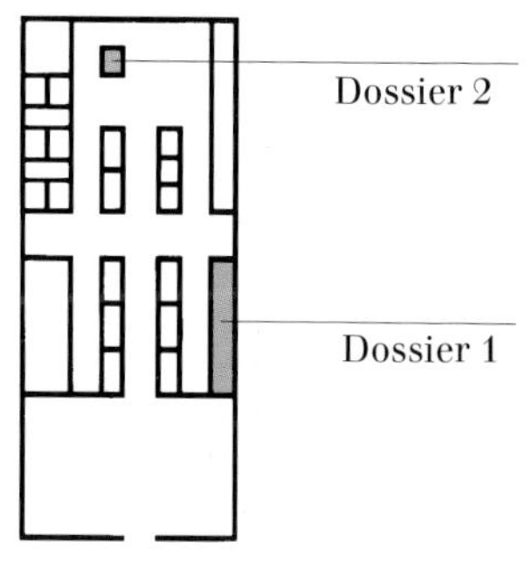

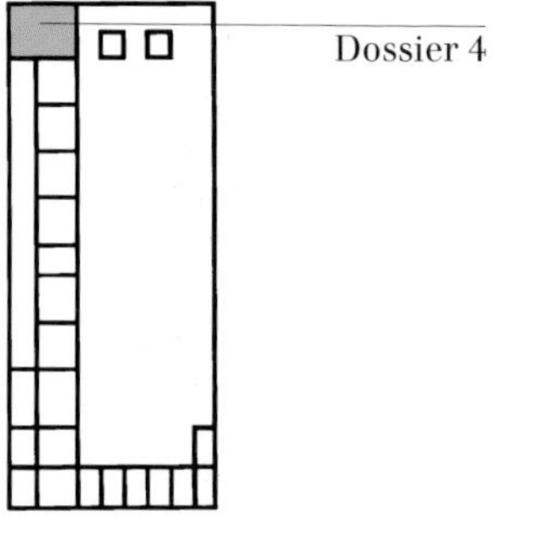

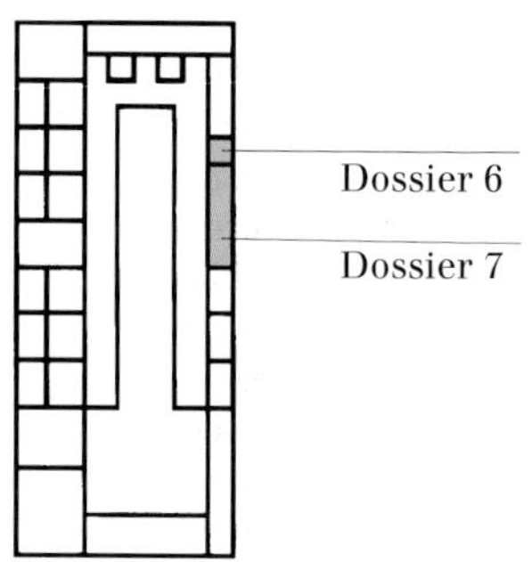

Ground floor first part of the visit	Dossier 1 This spacious area is provided with audiovisual equipment, which is used to mount general exhibitions relating to cultural movements between 1848-1870 (music, literature, etc.).	Dossier 2 This room is located in a sector of the museum whose theme is the Paris Opera, its history and surrounding quarter. Exhibitions here deal with various aspects of this subject.
Upper level second part of the visit	Dossier 4 Three floors of the "pavillon amont" are devoted to architecture, and reserved for exhibitions or the presentation of works from the museum's collections.	
Middle level last part of the visit	Dossier 6 and 7 These spaces may or may not be combined and are provided with audiovisual equipment; like Dossier 1, they are used for multidisciplinary exhibitions, but	cover the following 1870-1914 period. Dossier 6 may also be used to display the museum's new acquisitions.

Photography and the Graphic Arts

Photography and the graphic arts (drawings, pastels, engravings, etc.) are presented in rotation in the museum's dossier-exhibition rooms 3 and 5.
Photography was a major 19th century art form, practised even by such painters as Degas and writers like Zola and Lewis Carroll. A collection of about 10,000 works reveal the wealth and variety of photographic creation, both in France and abroad, between the invention of the daguerreotype (1839) and the end of the First World War, when the main secessionist trends disappeared to make way for experimental photography. The creation of this new sector has prompted the interest of many generous donators (Kodak-Pathé Foundation, ASDA, Mme de Robien, M. de Bry, Mme Marie-Thérèse and M. André Jammes, Mme Andrée Gaveau, M. le Prévost d'Iray, M. Roger Thérond, Galerie Texbraun).

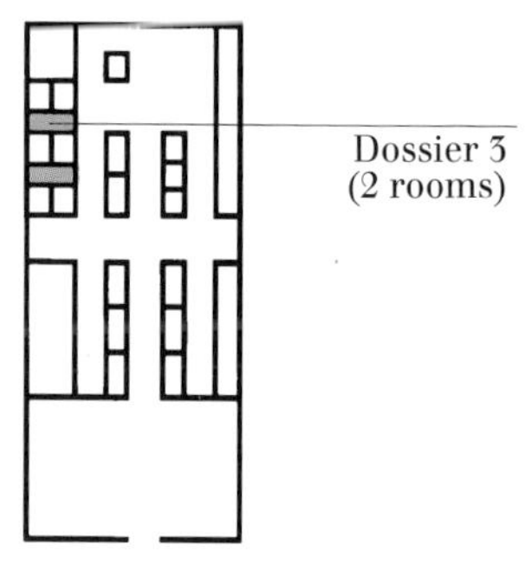

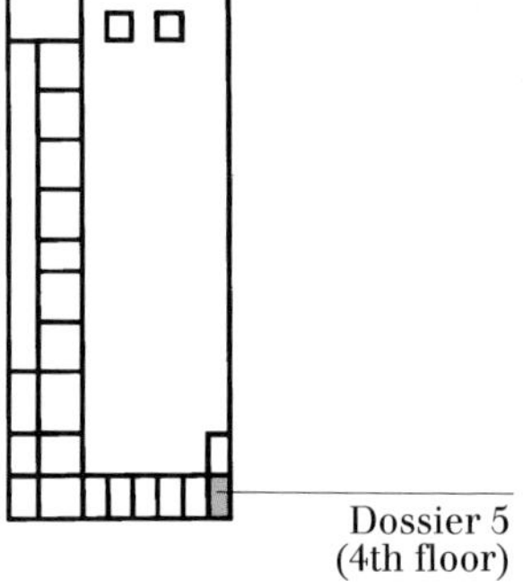

Clarence White
1871-1925
The Kiss
1904
Print
24/12 cm
Gift of
CDF Chimie-Terpolymères, 1985

Ground floor, first part of the visit	Dossier 3 The 1850's: The "Golden Age" of photography in France (Felix Nadar, Gustave Legray, Edouard Baldus), and abroad (Lewis Carroll, Julia Margaret Cameron);	the Daguerreotype, one of the earliest photographic techniques. Alternating with photographs are drawings and pastels from the	period between 1848 and 1870, and exhibitions of engravings mounted with the assistance of the Bibliothèque Nationale (National Library).
Upper level, second part of the visit	Dossier 5 Photography at the turn of the century: pictorialists (P.H. Emerson, Alfred Stieglitz, Edward Steichen, Clarence White, Eugène Atget, Pierre Bonnard, Edgar Degas).	Late 19th c. and early 20th c. engravings and drawings.	

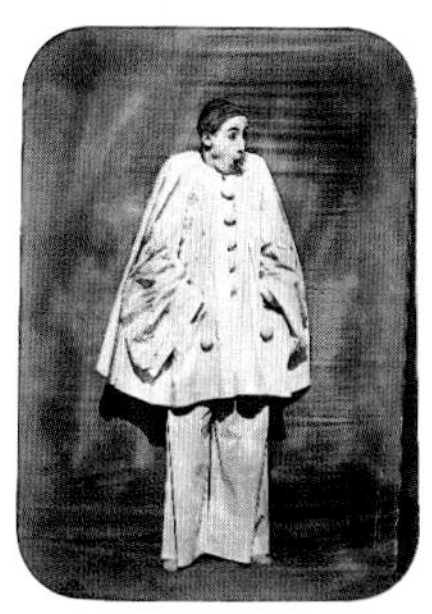

Félix Tournachon, known as Nadar
1820-1910
and Adrien Tournachon
1825-1903
Le mime Debureau en Pierrot
(The Mime Debureau in Pierrot costume)
1855
Print from collodion glass negative.
30 / 24 cm

Georges Seurat
1859-1891
La voilette
(The Lady's Veil)
circa 1883
Crayon on Ingres paper
30 / 23 cm

Ground floor, first part of the visit

1
Sculpture 1850-1870
Carpeaux

2
Ingres
and his school,
Delacroix,
Chassériau,
History Painting
and Portraiture
1850-1880

3
Daumier,
Chauchard
Collection 1 and 2,
Millet, Rousseau,
Corot,
Realism, Courbet

4
Puvis de Chavannes,
Gustave Moreau,
Degas pre-1870

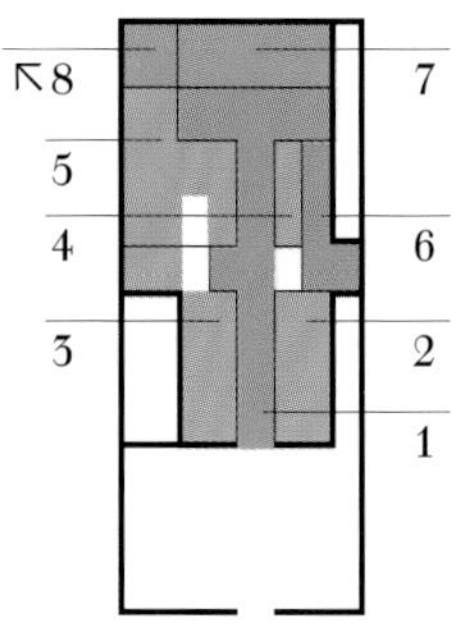

5
Manet pre-1870,
Monet, Bazille,
Renoir pre-1870,
Fantin-Latour,
Landscape painting,
Personnaz
Collection,
Eduardo Mollard
Collection,
Realism,
Orientalism

6
Decorative Arts
1850-1880

7
The Opera

8
'Pavillon amont':
Architecture
1850-1900,
Viollet-le-Duc,
Pugin, Morris,
Webb, Mackmurdo,
Jeckyll,
Godwin, Dresser,
Sullivan

Upper level, second part of the visit

9
Impressionism:
Moreau-Nélaton Collection,
Whistler, Morisot, Caillebotte; Degas, Manet post-1870
Monet, Renoir, Pissarro and Sisley pre-1880
Pissarro post-1880
Cézanne

10
Pastels: Degas
Rooftop Café
Documentation Room (Salle de Consultation)

11
Van Gogh
Gachet Collection
Redon, Pastels
Douanier Rousseau
Pont-Aven School: Gauguin, Bernard, Sérusier
Neo-Impressionism: Seurat, Signac, Cross, Luce
Toulouse-Lautrec
Small paintings: Bonnard, Denis, Vuillard, Vallotton

12
Press Passage

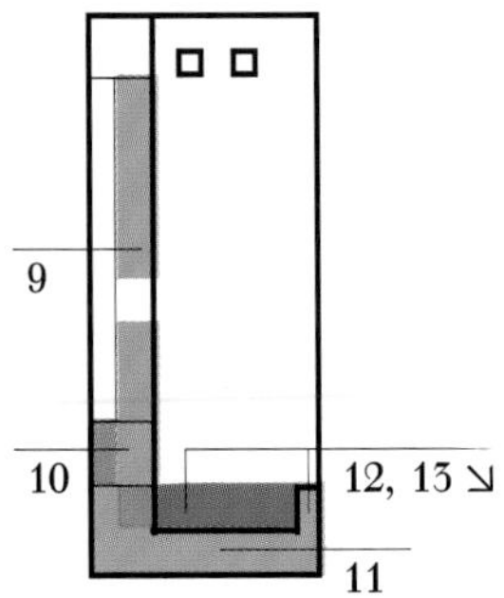

13
Max and Rosy Kaganovitch
Collection
(4th floor)

Middle level, last part of the visit

14
Arts and Decors under the Third Republic, Public Monuments

15
Sculpture: Fremiet, Gérôme, Rodin, Rosso, Bartholomé, Bourdelle, Maillol, Joseph Bernard

16
Salon Paintings 1880-1900, Foreign schools Symbolism

17
Art Nouveau: France, Belgium, Holland, Germany, Scandinavia, Odilon Redon, Nancy School, Gallé, Carabin, Charpentier, Dampt

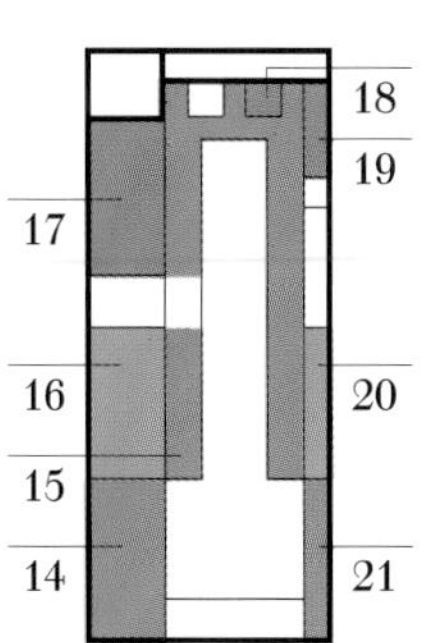

III

18
International
Art Nouveau,
architects'
furniture
industrial
furniture

19
Vienna, Glasgow,
Chicago

20
The Nabis:
Bonnard, Denis,
Vallotton, Vuillard,
Roussel

21
Birth of
cinematography and
the phonograph

Several areas within the Musée d'Orsay have been assigned to the evocation of history, on the premise that visitors should be aware of the major chronological references of the period covered by the museum's collections. These references are also intended to satisfy the curiosity of anyone who may wish to know what was going on in the political and cultural worlds at the time when Baudelaire was writing his *Fleurs du Mal (Flowers of Evil)*, when Manet was painting *Le déjeuner sur l'herbe (Lunch on the Grass)*, when Charpentier's *Louise* was having its triumphant success, or when Maillol was sculpting *Méditerranée (The Mediterranean)*. Moreover, the connections and juxtapositions of history, which may be obscured by the museum's stylistic presentation, can also help us understand the material conditions governing artistic production, the artist's status within society, and the status of art in general in a given social context.

The main preoccupation of those responsible for presenting the museum's historical framework has been to inform and suggest, without pontificating, and their priority has been to place history in perspective. The area chosen for this purpose is beside the museum entrance; its function is to show historical films around the clock, and it is surrounded by a circular window display. This display covers French history between 1848 and 1914, with the aid of historical objects (flag of the National Guard in 1848, worker's handbook); technical objects (sewing machines, telephones, typewriters); images and photographs (portraits of great men of the period); posters (1848 posters, the battle of Sedan, posters from the Commune, general mobilisation orders); newspapers (the Dreyfus affair in the press); paintings (Clairin *The Fire at the Tuileries)*; and sculptures (Dubois *L'Alsace et la Lorraine – Alsace and Lorraine*, busts of Presidents of the Republic). In short, the perspective offered is a French one, and entirely chronological. This area of reference, which may at first sight appear too cursory, should be viewed as a double introduction: first to the museum, and second, to the Passage of Dates further along the circuit.

1848
1914

Ground floor, first part of the visit

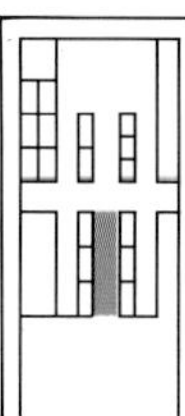

Along the central aisle devoted to the sculpture of the 1850-1870's, one attempts to grasp and appreciate the many currents that run through the period; romanticism, strict classicism, respect for the vigour and elegance of the Renaissance, or even eclecticism, with its many influences and materials. But above all, we realise that the sculpture of these twenty years was dominated by the dynamic talent of Carpeaux.

Romanticism in sculpture first made its appearance in the 1830's. Its ultimate goal was expression, not purity of form. For purposes of expression, the sculptor did not hesitate to distort proportion and relief, or to use highly animated compositions containing powerful contrasts. Perhaps the best example of this is François Rude, whose *Le Génie de la Patrie (Spirit of the Fatherland)* stands at the Museum entrance. (This is a cast taken from the 1836 relief on the Arc de Triomphe.) But the premier romantic hero of the age was undoubtedly Napoleon, whose legend and destiny were an important source of inspiration for painters and sculptors. *Napoléon s'éveillant à l'immortalité (Napoleon Awakening to Immortality)* was originally commissioned by a fervent Bonapartist, Noisot, the former commandant of the Grenadier regiment on the island of Elba. It depicts the emperor rising from his shroud, awakening to perpetual glory.
(The original bronze is now at Fixin-lès-Dijon).

The wild expression and exaggerated features of Rude's *Génie de la Patrie (Spirit of the Fatherland)* embody the spirit of Romanticism; like Victor Hugo's famous character Hermani, this relief seems to personify "... une force qui va" (a moving force).

Even James Pradier, whose work is essentially classical, has slight romantic overtones; while the clothing and face of his *Sapho* conform to accepted traditions, the subject matter and melancholy pose imply a very different spirit.

At the same time, there was a return to an almost archeological severity in sculpture, which had its roots in classicism. This movement is exemplified by Pierre-Jules Cavelier, with his group entitled *Cornélie, Mère des Gracques (Cornelia, Mother of the Gracchi)* and by Eugène Guillaume, who remained faithful to the cult of antiquity throughout his life. *Le cénotaphe des Gracques (The Cenotaph of the Gracchi)* is a faithful rendering of a certain type of funerary monument, much favoured during the closing years of the Roman Republic and in the early Empire, when the myth of the pure, virile Roman was current. *Le faucheur (The Reaper)*, an 1855 bronze, has a similar formal perfection, though cold and lifeless in effect.

Eugène Guillaume
1822-1905
Cénotaphe des Gracques (Cenotaph of the Gracchi)
1848-1853
Bronze
85 / 90 cm

Pierre-Jules Cavelier
1814-1894
Cornélie mère des Gracques (Cornelia, mother of the Gracchi)
1861
Marble
171 / 121 cm

James Pradier
1790-1852
Sapho
1852
Marble
118 / 70 cm

François Rude
1784-1855
Napoléon s'éveillant à l'immortalité (Napoleon Awakening to Immortality)
1846
Plaster
225 / 195 cm

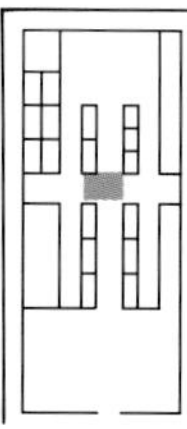

Carpeaux

"When I had recognised my own features in the four faces, I gnawed my hands with grief, and my children, thinking that I did this out of hunger, rose up crying "Oh father! Our pain would be less if you ate of our flesh instead...".

The tragic theme of Ugolin, one of the damned heroes of Dante's *Divine Comedy* (Canto XXXIII of *Hell*) has often inspired romantic and symbolist painters, including Delacroix and Rodin. The subject is a very terrible one, that of Count Ugolin della Gherardesca, a 13th century tyrant of Pisa who was imprisoned with his children and grandchildren by his enemy, archbishop Ubaldini, and condemned to die of starvation – which he eventually did, having first eaten the bodies of his offspring.

This group was executed by Jean-Baptiste Carpeaux while he was studying at the Villa Medicis, the seat of the French Academy in Rome. *Ugolin* did not correspond to the Academy's norms; the subject was neither mythological nor biblical, the work included several figures, and it could not be completed within the space of one year. Nonetheless, the subject provoked considerable interest, and the sculptor's first studies, executed in 1853, resulted in the rules being waived. Carpeaux' original intention was to construct a bas-relief around the theme; his researches show that he was heavily influenced by Michelangelo, whose *Last Judgement* he revered and studied. Dante and Michelangelo had always been linked in the mind of Carpeaux. "A statue conceived by the poet of the *Divine Comedy* and created by the originator of Moses would surely be a masterpiece of the human spirit", he wrote in 1854, when he won the Prix de Rome after ten years of study at the Ecole des Beaux-Arts under Rude and Duret.

In 1860, during a visit to Paris, Carpeaux fashioned a terra cotta model of *Ugolin* (exhibited behind glass) in which a fourth child was featured. In November 1861, he completed the plaster cast (now at the Musée du Petit Palais in Paris) which was triumphantly exhibited in Rome. In Paris, the group was not so well-received by the Institute. Nonetheless, the bronze exhibited here was commissioned in 1862 and placed in the Tuileries gardens.

Jean-Baptiste
Carpeaux
1827-1875
Ugolin
1860
Terra cotta
56 / 41,5 cm

Jean-Baptiste
Carpeaux
1827-1875

Ugolin
1862
Bronze
194 / 148 cm

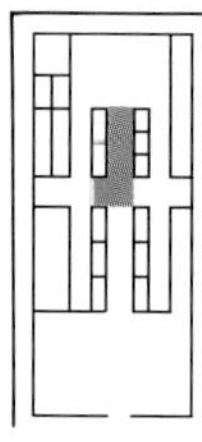

In its search for legitimacy and roots, the Second Empire attempted to create a distinctive décor by resorting to earlier styles and to history. Among the different tendencies embodied in this eclecticism were Falguière, Dubois, Mercié and Moulin, who were nicknamed the 'Florentins' because of their fascination with the art of the Renaissance. To this group we may add Ernest Christophe, whose *Comédie Humaine (The Human Comedy)*, "...an allegorical statue in the manner of the Renaissance", inspired the XXth canto of *Baudelaire's Fleurs du Mal: Le Masque (Flowers of Evil: the Mask)*. (This statue is exhibited on the left, just before the second stage of the central aisle). Carrier-Belleuse, another artist who was greatly impressed by the Renaissance and the 18th century, sometimes turned to antiquity for inspiration, as evidenced by his marble group *Hebe* (1869). Falguière's *Vainqueur au combat de coqs (Winner of the Cockfight)* and Moulin's *Trouvaille à Pompéii (A Find at Pompei)* show similar influences; their precise and harmonius treatment reflect the hellenistic bronzes recently discovered at Pompeii, as well as the importance of the *Mercury* sculpted by John of Bologna (1529-1608) as a pioneering work of physical rhythm and balance. Mercié, for his part, was heavily influenced by the cult of Tuscan sculpture (See his *David*, a bronze done in 1872, in the first section of the central aisle).

The Second Empire discovered polychrome sculpture from reports of ancien Greek and Roman figures, still bearing traces of paint, which were sent back to France by the architects and sculptors studying at the Académie de France in Rome. These reports were propagated through publications like that of the architect Hittorf. One of the leading lights in the revival of polychrome sculpture was Charles Cordier, who was attracted by ethnography, excited by the possibilies of the Algerian onyx quarries, and generally won over by the Oriental vogue then spreading across Europe. His *Nègre du Soudan (Negro of the Sudan)* represents a highly individual type, wearing an authentic costume. This penchant for ostentation corresponded exactly with the general outlook of Second Empire society, and was later enshrined in Charles Garnier's Opera House, a triumph of polychrome architecture and sculpture.

Alexandre Falguière
1831-1900
Vainqueur au combat de coqs
(Winner of the Cockfight)
1864
Bronze
174 / 100 cm

Hippolyte Moulin
1832-1884
Trouvaille à Pompéi
(A Find at Pompeii)
1863
Bronze
187 / 64 cm

Ernest Christophe
1827-1892
La Comédie humaine
ou *le Masque*
(The Human Comedy
or *the Mask)*
1859-1876
Marble
245 / 67 cm

Antonin Mercié
1845-1916
David
1872
Bronze
184 / 76 cm

Charles Cordier
1827-1905
Nègre du Soudan
(Negro of the Sudan)
1857
Bronze and onyx
96 / 66 cm

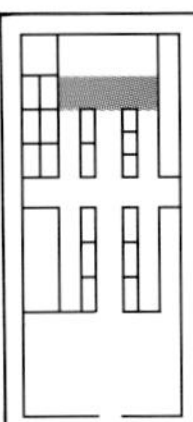

Carpeaux

Carpeaux' brief and meteoric career, which lasted for only fifteen years after his winning of the Prix de Rome, was closely involved not only with the imperial family, but also with the decoration of some of the most important public monuments of the Second Empire.

To the left of the central aisle are a number of his plaster and terra cotta studies, busts, and marble groups, protraying Napoleon III and his family with considerable liveliness and psychological insight. Also shown here is a lesser-known side of Carpeaux: his work as a painter. He was brought to the Tuileries by Princess Mathilde, the Emperor's cousin, became prince Napoleon's drawing master, and received a commission for a sculpture of the prince and his dog. *Le Prince Imperial et son chien Néro (The Prince Imperial and his dog Nero)*, a marble executed in 1865, was preceded by a number of studies which testify to Carpeaux' manifold gifts, among them an acute sense of observation and a taut, vigorous knack for rendering life.
The group was an immense success and was reproduced in countless editions and materials. Carpeaux' psychological insight and finesse in expressing personality may still be seen in his busts of friends and contemporaries (at right, central aisle). Among these, *Eugénie Fiocre*, a plastercast from 1869, highlights the gracefulness of the subject (who was 'première danseuse' at the Opera) and echoes the XVIIIth century in its concern for presence and overall decorative effect.

During the Second Empire, Paris became an enormous building site. "Paris gashed by sabres, with her veins opened, nourishing 100,000 navvies and masons", wrote Zola. Orders for statuary came thick and fast. Carpeaux was commissioned to decorate the façade of the Pavillon de Flore (1863-1866) overlooking the Seine, as part of Lefuel's reconstruction of the Louvre. The pavillon is crowned with an allegorical group, *France impériale protégeant l'agriculture et les sciences (Imperial France protecting Agriculture and Science)*, which resembles the compositions of Michelangelo in the Medici Chapel at Florence. Beneath it is a lively group of dancing children depicting the *Triomphe de Flore (Triumph of Flora)* and testifying to Carpeaux' rediscovery of Rubens and the Flemish school. This group is the first indication of Carpeaux' special quest for movement in sculpture. He was not to acquire real fame until the scandal provoked by *La Danse (The Dance)*, which was originally commissioned in 1863 by the architect Charles Garnier, for his new Opera house.
It took Carpeaux three years of research before he found his theme of five figures dancing round a leaping male spirit, which

Les quatre parties du monde soutenant la sphère céleste (The four quarters of the World bearing the celestial sphere) 1867-1872 Plaster 280 / 177 cm	*Alexandre Dumas fils* 1824-1895 1873 Plaster 81 / 60.3 cm	*Eugénie Fiocre* 1869 Plaster 83 / 51 cm	*Le prince impérial et son chien Nero (The Imperial Prince and his dog Nero)* 1865 Plâtre 43.8 / 16.1 cm

Jean-Baptiste Carpeaux
1827-1875
La France impériale protégeant l'agriculture et les sciences (Imperial France protecting Agriculture and Science)
1866
Plaster
260 / 423 cm

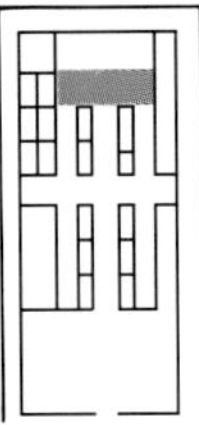

'detaches' the relief from its background. The work was unveiled in 1869 and caused an immediate furore; it was qualified as an 'ignoble saturnalia' and 'an offense to public morals'. Another group was commissioned from the sculptor Gumery (which is now in the Musée d'Angers). Carpeaux' dancers, much eroded by Paris pollution, were brought to the Louvre in 1964; a copy by Belmondo replaced them at the Opera. The same circular format was used in one of Carpeaux' last great creations, the fountain representing the *Quatre Parties du Monde (Four Quarters of the World)* in the Observatoire Gardens. The subject was to be the four cardinal points of the globe (the horses emerging from the pool below were executed by Fremiet); Carpeaux, rejecting the immobile stance usually adopted for this kind of sculpture, chose to portray "...the four cardinal points moving round and round, as if following the rotation of the globe. Hence I have one full face, one three quarters profile, one half profile, and a back". He even considered patinating the figures in tones corresponding to the skin colours of the various races, but never succeeded in doing so.

Jean-Baptiste Carpeaux
1827-1875
La Danse
(The Dance)
1869
Stone
420 / 298 cm

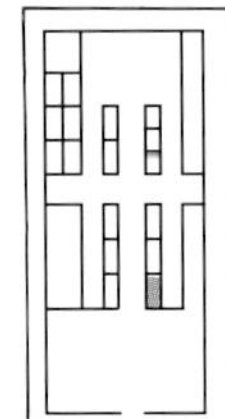

Ingres and his school

Ingres and Delacroix, who personify the conflict of classic and romantic, remained as dominant personalities in painting throughout the 1850's. These two painters, both of whom were born at the end of the 18th century, are represented at the Musée d'Orsay by a few later works, and by the canvases of artists whom they influenced directly in terms of subject matter, style, form and colour. Most of the paintings of Ingres and Delacroix belong to the first half of the 19th century and are therefore exhibited at the Louvre.

Ingres perfected the art of arabesque and contour, the taste for undulating line and warp. All these features characterise *Venus at Paphos* (1852-1853), in which the subtle line of the back and the junction of neck and breast form so many interconnecting curves. The landscape in this painting was painted by Alexandre Desgoffe, a pupil and assistant of Ingres. *La Source (The Spring)*, begun in 1820 in Florence and completed in Paris in 1856, represents a harmonious female body with gentle curves accentuated by a dislocation of the hip; this is a feature common to all of Ingres' nudes.

Ingres had a particularly strong influence on his pupils Amaury Duval and Hippolyte Flandrin. Duval was a talented portrait painter, who had a stange and rather elegant gift for colour *(Mme de Loynes*, 1862), whilst Flandrin's portraits *(Prince Napoléon*, 1860) have the qualities of sobriety, rigour and careful equilibrium.

Another group, the 'Neo-Greek', was much attracted by antiquity in general and the art of Ingres in particular. Jean-Léon Gérôme belonged to this school: his *Un combat de coqs (Cockfight)* (1846) shows a taste for scrupulously finished work, limpid colouring and smooth paint surfaces.

Ingres has remained a solitary genius of form, line and draughtsmanship. Nonetheless, other great painters, notably Gustave Moreau, Puvis de Chavannes and Degas, openly acknowledged their debt to him. For this reason their works are exhibited alongside his, on the right hand side of the central aisle.

Jean-Auguste-Dominique Ingres
1780-1867
La source
(The Spring)
1820-1856
Oil on canvas
163 / 80 cm

This painting was completed with the assistence of Paul Balze and Alexandre Desgoffe.

Its first showing was to a select group of amateurs in the artist's studio; later it was enthusiastically received by the public, and inspired many contemporary writers and poets. *La Source (The Spring)* has remained popular ever since and has been copied and reinterpreted unremittingly (by Suerat, Picasso and Magritte).

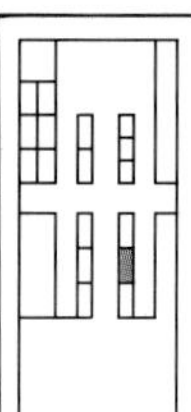

"Never have lovelier, more intense colours penetrated to the human soul by way of human eyes", wrote Baudelaire in his *Salon of 1855*. This comment referred to *La Chasse aux Lions (The Lion Hunt)* now at the Musée de Bordeaux, the upper part of which was destroyed by fire in 1870; but it could equally well apply to the huge sketch now at the Musée d'Orsay, which, with one or two differences, reflects the exact composition of the Bordeaux painting. Here, the feverish, rapid brushwork, the harmonius blend of yellows, oranges, browns and reds, emphasised by occasional scarlets and greens, make *La Chasse aux Lions* a powerful and innovative painting. This uninhibited brushwork and primal colouring are also to be found in the two other Delacroix paintings at the Musée d'Orsay; *Chevaux arabes se battant dans une écurie (Arab stallions fighting in a stable)*, 1860; *Passage d'un gué au Maroc (Crossing a Ford in Morocco)*, 1858.

Paul Huet, an intimate friend of Delacroix, preserved the master's romantic landscape style well after his death — with considerable brio, as *Le Gouffre (The Abyss)* (1861) testifies.

Théodore Chassériau, a pupil of Ingres and a great admirer of Delacroix, created an original manner of his own by reconciling "the two rival schools of draughtsmanship and colour". Chassériau's *Tepidarium*, the subject of which was suggested to the painter by the thermal baths excavated at Pompeii, is a marriage of line and colour which celebrates the oriental languor beloved of both Delacroix and Ingres.

In the world of sculpture, Augustin Préault established himself a romantic par excellence, with his superb pronouncement "Je ne suis pas pour le fini, je suis pour l'infini." ("I am for what is infinite, not for what is finished.") Préault's *Ophélie* is almost more literary than sculptural; its main concerns are emotion, death and the ephemeral nature of existence, and its principal characteristic is a refusal to define forms. Another romantic, Barye (whose proud lion overlooks the museum entrance), used a powerful classical style in his portrayal of male allegories for the new Louvre: *Force (Strength), Guerre (War), Ordre (Order)* and *Paix (Peace)*, plaster, 1854.

Eugène Delacroix
1798-1863
La chasse aux lions
(The Lion Hunt)
Sketch 1854
Oil on canvas
86 / 115 cm

Théodore Chassériau
1819-1856
Le tépidarium
(The Tepidarium)
1853
Oil on Canvas
171 / 258 cm

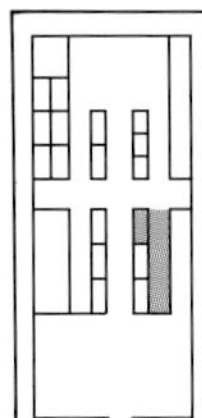

The Prix de Rome was the crowning accolade of the Ecole des Beaux-Arts; it was awarded to an artist after he had studied at the Villa Médicis in Rome, entered the Académie des Beaux-Arts and been appointed as a professor at the Ecole itself. The recipients of the prize were assured of a brilliant career, studded with official commissions, state portraits and Salon exhibitions; they were afforded every privilege as a reward for scholarly and idealised output. This was the case of painters such as Cabanel, Bouguereau, Delaunay, Baudry and Henner.

Alexandre Cabanel won great fame for his carefully-composed history paintings, with their precise treatment and exact detail *(Mort de Francesca de Rimini et Paolo Malatesta*, 1870). He was even more successful with his idealised mythological nudes. *La Naissance de Vénus (Birth of Venus)*, which was shown at the 1863 Salon, was an immediate success: it was purchased by Napoelon III himself. Meanwhile, Manet's *Déjeuner sur l'herbe (Lunch on the Grass)* was excluded from the Salon altogether, having been judged obscene. The tilted hip an sinuous lines of Cabanel's 'Venus' clearly show the influence of Ingres. Notwithstanding, Zola described the painting in the following terms: "The goddess, drowned in a river of milk, looks like a delicious harlot; she is not a woman of flesh and blood — that would be indecent — but made from a kind of pink-white marzipan". Cabanel was also a talented portraitist; see his biting character portrayal of *La Comtesse Keller (Countesse Keller)*, 1873.

The Second Empire placed great store by talented society portrait painters such as the German artist Franz-Xaver Wintherhalter, who became official portraitist to the court of Napoleon III. *Mme Rimsky-Korsakov* attests to Winterhalter's virtuosity and ability to convey his subject's special quality of sensuality.

Paul Baudry's Titian-inspired *La Fortune et le jeune enfant (Fortune and the Young Child)* was shown at the 1857 Salon. This painter's masterwork was the décor of the main hall of the Opéra, which he painted for his friend Charles Garnier. Baudry's vibrant portrait of Garnier may be seen nearby.

The Italian Renaissance is a major influence in Jean-Jacques Henner's *La chaste Suzanne (The Chaste Suzanne)*, 1864, with its vigorous flesh tones and rich paint base.

Henri Regnault, by contrast, rejected the Italian masters in favour of Goya and Velasquez. The work of this gifted young painter, who was killed in action during the war of 1870, is concerned with romantic ardour *(Le Genéral Prim*, 1869*)* or with sumptuous Oriental cruelties *(Execution sans jugement sous les rois maures de Grenade — Arbitrary execution under the Moorish Kings of Granada*, 1870).

Jean-Baptiste Clésinger, known as Auguste
1814-1883

Femme piquée par un serpent (Women bitten by a snake)
1847
Marble
56.5 / 180 cm

Franz-Xaver Winterhalter
1806-1873
Mme Rimsky-Korsakov
1864
Oil on canvas
117 / 90 cm

I

Alexandre Cabanel
1823-1889

La naissance de Vénus (The Birth of Venus)
1863
Oil on canvas
130 / 225 cm

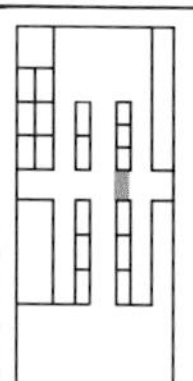

Thomas Couture
1815-1879
Les Romains de la décadence (Romans in the Period of Decadence)
1847
Oil on canvas
466 / 775 cm

"Vice, a scourge more cruel than war, swooped down on Rome to avenge the conquered universe." (Juvénal, 6th Satire)

Couture was a pioneer of eclecticism, whose paintings are ambitious, vigorous and full of technical virtuosity. Manet, among many others, was a frequent visitor to his studio. *Les Romains de la décadence (Romans in the Period of Decadence)* which was shown at the 1847 Salon, reflects the influence of Veronese and Tiepolo.

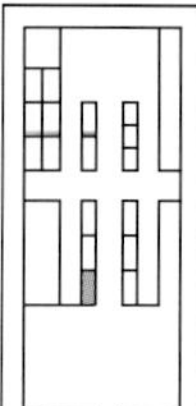

Daumier

Honoré Daumier represents the link between romanticism and realism. His was a genius of many facets; he was not only a great painter, but a shrewd and expressive sculptor, a draughtsman and a lithographer. He occupies a unique place in the art of his generation.

Daumier's sculptures often served as a point of departure of his paintings and drawings, as in the case of his *Parlementaires (Parliamentarians)*, a series of 26 clay busts painted with oils. These busts were executed from 1831 onwards, and later used by Daumier as models for his cartoon-portraits in *La Caricature*. By a process of distortion and plastic synthesis, these busts reveal the inner truth of their subjects, who are thus transformed into universal types; in addition, their features are emphasised by colour, which has the effect of ruthlessly exposing physical peculiarities and blemishes. Bronze editions of these busts were manufactured between 1927 and 1953, in more or less limited series according to choice; a complete collection now exists at the Musée des Beaux-Arts, Marseille. *Les Emigrants (The Emigrants)*, and 1848 plaster relief, shows Daumier's powerful, expansive style and his method of working from mass and form; the strength and movement implicit in this group lend a timeless quality to the subject, which was a favourite of the artist's. Lastly, *Le Ratapoil (The Old Campaigner)*, a bronze dating from 1850, has become the symbol of the soldier on half-pay. This 'revanchard' veteran of Napoleon's army, forced into retirement by the monarchy but actively plotting to bring Napoleon III to power, is a monument to Daumier's baroque, expressionist talent.

Daumier's career as a painter began later, when he was about forty. He entered a competition organized by the short-lived Second Republic, in 1848*.

The artist's baroque power was again evident in his painting, as may be seen in *Les voleurs et l'âne (The Thieves and the Donkey)* of 1858, with its convulsive, tangled forms, fiery rhythm and vivid colours; *Crispin et Scapin* demonstrates a theatrical taste for strong light contrasts that allows Daumier to lay extra stress on the distorted features of his figures and enhances their individuality. Both subject and treatment were completely new; other painters, notably Degas and Toulouse-Lautrec, were quick to notice this and profit from it.

* This first painting, *La République nourrit ses enfants et les instruit (The Republic nourishing and teaching her children)*, belongs to the Moreau-Nélaton Collection, presented in the first room of the Impressionist gallery; see relevant passage on this collection.

Honoré Daumier - 1808-1879 - *Les célébrités du Juste-Milieu* ou *Les Parlementaires* - 1831
Oil-glazed potter's clay

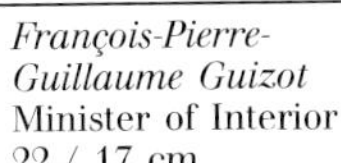

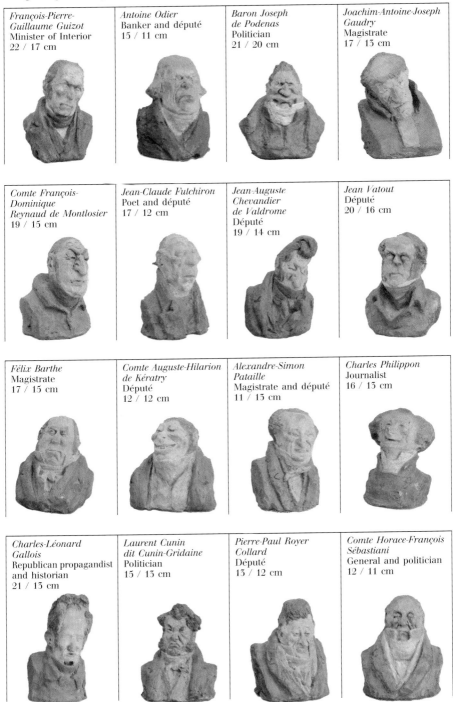

François-Pierre-Guillaume Guizot
Minister of Interior
22 / 17 cm

Antoine Odier
Banker and député
15 / 11 cm

Baron Joseph de Podenas
Politician
21 / 20 cm

Joachim-Antoine-Joseph Gaudry
Magistrate
17 / 13 cm

Comte François-Dominique Reynaud de Montlosier
19 / 15 cm

Jean-Claude Fulchiron
Poet and député
17 / 12 cm

Jean-Auguste Chevandier de Valdrome
Député
19 / 14 cm

Jean Vatout
Député
20 / 16 cm

Félix Barthe
Magistrate
17 / 15 cm

Comte Auguste-Hilarion de Kératry
Député
12 / 12 cm

Alexandre-Simon Pataille
Magistrate and député
11 / 13 cm

Charles Philippon
Journalist
16 / 13 cm

Charles-Léonard Gallois
Republican propagandist and historian
21 / 13 cm

Laurent Cunin dit Cunin-Gridaine
Politician
15 / 13 cm

Pierre-Paul Royer Collard
Député
13 / 12 cm

Comte Horace-François Sébastiani
General and politician
12 / 11 cm

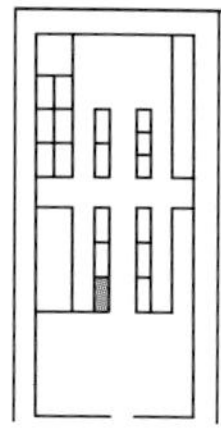

La blanchisseuse (The Laundress) is one of the last of a series done by Daumier on this theme, which was a favourite with him. The painter's desire to convey both movement and a third dimension to his work are here perfectly expressed; the figure, which is rendered with subtle, muted colours, stands enveloped in a light mist against an almost obliterated background. Here observation and dream are intricately blended. *Don Quichotte et la mule morte (Don Quichotte and the Dead Mule)* is also part of a series; this painting, with its extremely simplified forms, was originally commissioned for Charles Daubigny's house at Auvers.

At the end of his life, Daumier was blind and destitute, misunderstood by his contemporaries but admired by every artist of the epoch; including Delacroix, who wrote to him in 1846 that: "...There is no man alive whom I admire and revere more than yourself..."

Honoré Daumier
1808-1879
Crispin and Scapin
Circa 1864
Oil on canvas
60.5 / 82 cm

Honoré Daumier
1804-1879
La blanchisseuse
(The Laundress)
Circa 1863
Oil on wood
49 / 33.5 cm

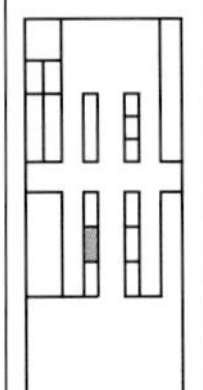

Chauchard Collection 1

Corot, Diaz, Dupré, Millet, Rousseau

Alfred Chauchard (1822-1909) was the founder of one of the great department stores adjoining the Louvre; from 1885 onwards, he began collecting works of art, notably French, by 19th century painters such as Rousseau, Dupré, Diaz, Corot and Daubigny of the Barbizon school, along with Millet and many others. Chauchard bequeathed his collection to the Louvre, where it arrived in 1909.

The prominent role of the peasant figure in 19th century arts stems from the departure of much of the rural populace to the new industrial centres, and from their resultant nostalgia. It is significant that Alfred Chauchard's first great purchase, made in 1890, was that of Millet's *Angelus (The Angelus)*; he was forced to outbid several rich American collectors to acquire the painting. Millet's paintings show country people in their natural surroundings; in *Angelus*, the two static figures are rendered monumental by the artist's simple presentation and vigorous, synthetic draughtsmanship. They stand foursquare amid countryside which seems to stretch to the horizon like an ocean. The brushwork is dense and the tones muted. The image is a very strong one; it is also extraordinarily popular, which has if anything worked to the painting's disadvantage.

Alfred Chauchard
1822-1909

In 1849, Millet joined a group of painters based at Barbizon, a small village on the edge of the forest of Fontainebleau. This group established the natural landscape, taken from life, as a major theme for the painter's art; what had formerly been mere background became the principal focus of interest for these artists, drawn as they were to woodlands, ponds, undergrowth, trees and clearings. Theodore Rousseau, perhaps the most important figure in the group, was fascinated by the study of fleeting light effects. In his *Une avenue, forêt de l'Isle-Adam (An Avenue in the Forest of l'Isle-Adam)*, he succeeded in conveying the noon heaviness of summer sunshine; likewise, the 'dim clarity' just before a storm is subtly rendered in *La mare, ciel orageux (Pond and Stormy Sky)*, circa 1860-1865. Jules Dupré was more sombre and romantic in manner, whilst Narcisse Diaz de la Peña, a close friend of Rousseau from 1837 onwards, was a master at rendering the play of light in foliage *(Les Hauteurs du Jean de Paris — The Heights of Le Jean de Paris*, 1862).

The work of Corot and the Barbizon painters, which properly belongs to romanticism and the first half of the 19th century, is exhibited not at the Musée d'Orsay, but at the Louvre.

Narcisse Diaz
de la Peña
1807-1876
*Les hauteurs
du Jean de Paris*

*(The Heights of
Le Jean de Paris)*
1867
Oil on Canvas
84 / 106 cm

Théodore Rousseau
1812-1867
*Une avenue,
forêt de l'Isle-Adam*

*(An Avenue in the
Forest of l'Isle Adam)*
1849
Oil on canvas
101 / 82 cm

Jean-François Millet
1814-1875
L'Angélus

(The Angelus)
1858-1859
Oil on canvas
55 / 66 cm

L'Angelus quickly became well-known in the remotest regions of France, through a profusion of copies, caricatures and reproductions.

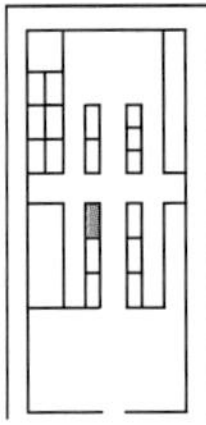

Millet, who was born at Gruchy, near Cherbourg, began his career doing portraits of the Norman bourgeoisie. He favoured a vigorous structure underpinned by full, powerful colours *(Mme Lecourtois*, circa 1841; *Mme Canoville*, 1845). The Musée Thomas-Henry at Cherbourg possesses a complete and very beautiful series of these portraits. *Les Baigneuses (Women Bathing)*, 1848, is a more ambitious work from Millet's youth, which shows the mastery of human anatomy, powerfully outlined, which gave his peasant figures their weight and density. The same is true of *Des glaneuses (Gleaners)*, 1857, in which the deliberate sculptural heaviness of the women is conveyed through a simplified synthesis of their forms. The figures seem to stand out, as in a bas-relief; their ritualised gestures are slow and essentially noble. The worn, heavy fabrics of the clothes are rendered in muted coulours with bright undertones of pink and blue.

After 1860, Millet's attention was more and more concentrated on landscape work, and on the villages and hills of his native Cotentin. *L'église de Gréville (The Church of Gréville)*, 1871-1874, with its impressive perspective and spirituality, had a strong influence on Van Gogh. In his last years, the painter's landscapes became powerfully lyrical; *Le Printemps (Spring)*, one of his unfinished four seasons series, shows the influence of Ruysdaël and Constable in its variety of tender green, its rainbow, and its enthusiasm for sudden light and shade in nature. At the same time, Millet was producing many large pastels, which gave evidence of his exceptional gifts as a draughtsman.

The Barbizon group is again represented here by Rousseau *(Le vieux dormoir du Bas-Bréau* was begun in the winter of 1836-1837; Rousseau was to work on it intermittently for the rest of his life), as well as Charles Daubigny and Camille Corot. Daubigny was attracted by the open air and was a frequent visitor to Barbizon from 1843 onwards. He had converted a boat into a floating studio, in which he roamed the various reaches of the Seine and Oise; with his love of rivers, Daubigny was one of the first to attempt the 'ephemeral' in painting, using light tones and rapid brushwork *(Château-Gaillard*, 1877).

Jean-François
Millet
1814-1875
Le printemps (Spring)
1868-1873
Oil on canvas
86 / 111 cm

Jean-Baptiste-Camille
Corot
1796-1875
La danse des nymphes
(Nymphs Dancing)
1850
Oil on canvas
98 / 131 cm

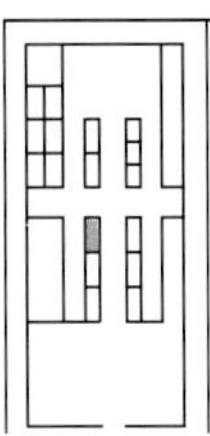

Executed during the winter of 1872-1873, the striking canvas *La Neige (Snow),* with its spareness, its vigorous treatment, its play on black and white and its great, low, reddening sky, reveals the artist's links with the Impressionists.

Corot, who was born at the close of the eighteenth century, developed a lyrical, misty painting technique in the 1850's. He was greatly influenced by the special light of the Ile-de-France area around Paris, which tends to be soft, diffuse and nacreous, and his landscapes from this period are peopled with nymphs, as in *La danse des nymphes (Nymphs Dancing)*, 1850. Corot also favoured isolated figures, often in fantasy costume, shrouded in melancholy or mystery *(L'atelier de Corot. Jeune femme à la mandoline – Corot's Studio. Young Woman with Mandolin,* circa 1865-1870; *Homme en armure assis – Seated Man in Armour*, circa 1868-1870).

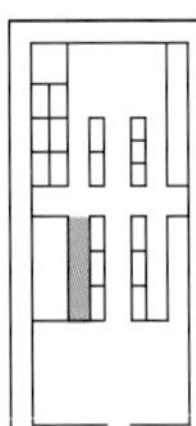

Chauchard Collection 2

Decamps, Meissonier, Ziem, Corot, Daubigny

Delacroix' violent *Chasse au tigre (Tiger Hunt)* (1854) is a reminder of Second Empire romanticism. By contrast, Meissonier, a very popular artist whose works were much discussed and very expensive, looked to the 17th century Dutch masters for inspiration. Careful, skilfully-executed paintings like his *Amateurs de peinture (Art Lovers)*, 1860, or *Liseur blanc (Man in White, Reading)*, 1857, convey an extraordinary calmness and delicacy. In other genres, *Antibes, la promenade à cheval (Riding at Antibes)*, 1869, shows Meissonier's precision in translating the effect of strong sunlight in oils, and *Campagne de France, 1814 (The Campaign of France, 1814)* demonstrates his ability to record a dramatic episode from history. His realistic representation of *Le Voyageur (The Traveller)* is highly convincing. In this surprising polychrome wax statuette, he even goes as far as to use fabric to clothe the rider and a metal bit and leather reins for the horse, whose framework resembles a miniature skeleton. Félix Ziem, a specialist in views of Venice, uses a heavily impasto technique with scintillating, theatrical colours *(Venise, vue du Palais des Doges – Venice from the Doges'Palace,* circa 1880-1890).

Charles-François Daubigny
1817-1878
La neige (Snow)
1873
Oil on wood
90 / 120 cm

Ernest Meissonier
1815-1891
Campagne de France, 1814 (The Campaign of France, 1814)
1864
Oil on wood
57.5 / 76.5 cm

Ernest Meissonier
1815-1891
Voyageur dans le vent (Traveller in the Wind)
Grey and red wax, fabric and leather
47 / 60 / 39.5 cm

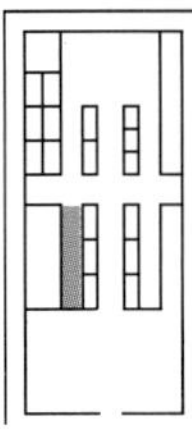

Painters like Antigna, Tassaert, Pils or Jules Breton were observers of daily life, regional custom, change, and above all the difficulties brought about by the evolution of industrial society. Like Daumier, Millet and Courbet, they testify to the emergence of realism as an approach to the painter's art. Pils, Breton and Antigna did not hesitate to attempt contemporary, popular themes using huge canvases and life-size figures, in the hope that a frankly modern approach would gain them equal rank with the history painters.

Alexandre Antigna's *L'éclair (Flash of Lightning)*, 1848, was executed right at the start of the realist movement. This painting, despite the overtones of romantic drama evident in its terrified figures, nonetheless shows a thoroughly modern sense of observation. The protagonists are lifesize and the scene is a 'popular' one. A similar dramatic atmosphere prevails in Octave Tassaert's *Une famille malheureuse (An Unlucky Family)*, 1849, which was commissioned by the state; melodrama apart, this canvas deals writh a bitter reality of the time, the abject poverty of the lowest classes in society. The same theme of destitution is more superficially expressed by Merle, with his *Jeune mendiante (Young woman begging)*, 1861, while Evariste Luminais handles the poverty of his *Famille de pêcheurs (Family of Fisherfolk)*, 1865, with studied understatement.

Isidore Pils' *La mort d'une sœur de Charité (Deathbed of a Sister of Charity)*, 1850, marks a new departure in realism: the religious genre scene. Critics and amateurs alike have praised the dignity and nobility of this work, along with the artist's brilliant rendering of the various facial expressions of emotion. The colouring is deliberately sober, and the restrained atmosphere conveyed by the ensemble is reminiscent of the work of Philippe de Champaigne.

Jules Breton, having begun in much the same thematic vein as Antigna, soon turned to landscape work. From 1853 onwards, he painted scenes of life in the fields which brought him immediate fame. *Le rappel des glaneuses (Calling the Gleaners Home)*, 1859, brought him a 'Medaille 1re Classe' at the 1859 Salon and was immediately acquired for the national collection; this canvas is perhaps the best-known of Breton's harvest series. The nobility of the figures was much admired by the contemporary writer and critic, Maxime du Camp, who referred to Breton's gleaners as "beautiful rustic caryatids".

Isidore Pils
1823-1875
La mort d'une sœur de charité
(Deathbed of a Sister of Charity)
1850
Oil on canvas
241 / 305 cm

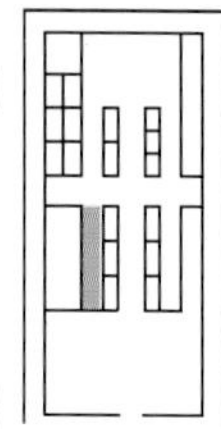

Constant Troyon was at first attracted by the Barbizon group, but became interested in animal painting after a journey to Holland in 1847, during which he was impressed by the work of Paulus Potter. Henceforward, Troyon mainly devoted himself to painting domestic animals, from time to time renewing his inspiration. This kind of painting was hugely successful, like the work of Rosa Bonheur, whose *Labourage nivernais, le sombrage (Ploughing in the Nivernais Region)*, commissioned by the state in 1848, is still considered a masterpiece of realism, comparable to a page from George Sand. Rosa Bonheur was a sculptor as well as a painter; appointed director of the Imperial drawing school, she became a darling of the court of Napoleon III and quickly acquired an international reputation.

The career of Ernest Hébert was somewhat different. Having won the Prix de Rome in 1839, he spent much of his time in Italy, where he soon forsook history painting in favour of scenes taken from everyday life. Hébert's first great success was *La Mal'aria (Malaria)*, 1851, which portrayed the malaria-stricken peasants of the Pontine marshes in vivid realist terms. Meanwhile, Daubigny's *La Moisson (Harvesting)*, 1851, with its broad, open horizon and clear sky rendered in pure, simply-juxtaposed colours, offers a foretaste of impressionist spontaneity.

Jules Breton
1827-1906

Le rappel des glaneuses
(Calling
the Gleaners Home)
1859
Oil on canvas
90 / 176 cm

Rosa Bonheur
1822-1899

Labourage nivernais :
le sombrage
(Ploughing in the
Nivernais Region)
1849
Oil on canvas
134 / 260 cm

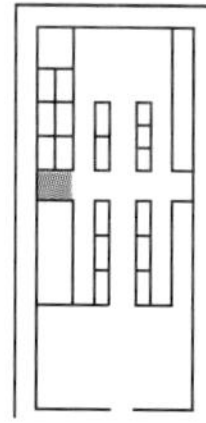

"How can it be possible to paint such hideous people?... "Enough to thoroughly put one off the idea of being buried at Ornans"... Such were the terms used by the critics to describe Courbet's *Un enterrement à Ornans (Burial at Ornans)*, a kind of realist manifesto which caused a scandal at the 1850 Salon. Courbet, like Millet, was roundly abused as a representative of the hated school for which realism meant representative truth: in *Un enterrement à Ornans*, the people are all identified and displayed exactly as they are, in a real place; hence many of them are ugly and coarse. The novelty of Courbet's canvas lies in its format which raises a commonplace episode to the stature of a history painting; deaths, funerals and cemeteries being already firmly established as romantic subject-matter. The work is monumental and sculptural; the massive outlines of the weeping women resemble the figures on great Burgundian tombs of the Middle Ages. *L'Enterrement* is a hymn to austerity and silence, which especially demonstrates Courbet's magnificent gifts as a colourist: every shade of black in the painting is distinct from the rest, and all are heightened by the gleams of white, the red costumes and the teal-blue stockings. Delacroix himself, while he deplored the vulgarity of the characters in the painting, acknowledged that it contained "...superb details; the priests, the choirboys, the jug of holy water and the weeping women".

L'Atelier (The Studio) was conceived with an eye to the Universal Exhibition of 1855. In this painting, Courbet sought to represent his likes and dislikes, ideals and rejections through portraits of real people, thereby expressing his sentiments as a man and as a painter. The picture was refused by the jury of the Salon, as was the 'Enterrement', which Courbet also wished to exhibit. Courbet responded by erecting a pavilion of his own, the Pavillon du Réalisme, in which he exhibited about forty works. *L'Atelier* brings out Courbet's best qualities as a portraitist, animal draughtsman and still-life painter, along with his sensitivity in rendering the female body; qualities which were to serve him throughout his life. Poetry and mystery are aspects which are shared to some extent by all of Courbet's paintings, but their presence is almost palpable in *L'Atelier*, with its strange light that seems to have no definable brightness, whilst others are made artificially dark, which contributes to the dreamlike effect of the ensemble.

Gustave Courbet
1819-1877

La falaise d'Etretat après l'orage (The Cliffs at Etretat after a Storm)
1869
Oil on canvas
133 / 162 cm

Gustave Courbet
1819-1877
La remise de chevreuils au ruisseau de Plaisir-Fontaine (Stags by the Stream at Plaisir-Fontaine)
1866
Oil on canvas
174 / 209 cm

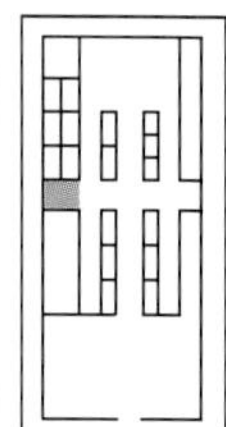

In addition to these major works, Courbet painted a number of landscapes and portraits which won him a following. The success of such canvases as *La remise de chevreuils au ruisseau de Plaisir-Fontaine (Stags by the Stream at Plaisir-Fontaine)* (1866) and *Le combat de cerfs (Stags fighting)* (1861), led him to return often to subjects of this type. *La Falaise d'Etretat après l'orage (The Cliffs at Etretat after the Storm)*, a pure, limpid landscape unencumbered by anecdote or human presence, makes it easy for us to understand the Impressionnists' deep admiration for Courbet's frank approach and treatment of light. The disturbing *La Mer Orageuse (Stormy Sea)*, was also painted at Etretat, where Courbet went to live in 1869. Recalling a visit to the painter, Guy de Maupassant wrote: "In a large, bare room, a fat man, greasy and soiled, was using a kitchen knife to smear plaques of white paint over a fresh canvas. From time to time he pressed his face to the glass and gazed out into the storm. The sea was so close it seemed to lash the house, enveloping it in noise and flying spray. The salt water struck the window panes like hail and ran down the walls. On the chimney piece stood a bottle of cider beside a half-filled glass. Occasionally, Courbet would go to drink a few drops, then return to his work. This painting was to become *La Vague (The Wave)*, which later caused somthing of a stir in the world." Finally, *La Source (The Spring)*, with its luminous, extraordinarily vivid feminine flesh, has both the immediacy of a scene from real life, and the mystery of legend.

Gustave Courbet
1819-1877
La source
(The Spring)
1868
Oil on canvas
128 / 97 cm

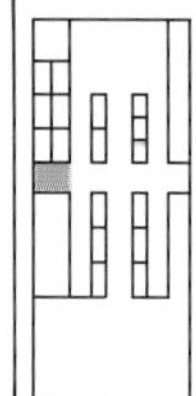

Gustave Courbet
1819-1877

Un enterrement à Ornans
(Burial at Ornans)
1849-1850

Oil on canvas
315 / 668 cm

The people of Ornans, much flattered to pose for Courbet, came to his studio one by one for sittings. The studio was very cramped, being the attic of a house inherited by the painter from his grand-father Jean-Antoine Oudet. This house may be seen on the far left hand corner of the painting.

I

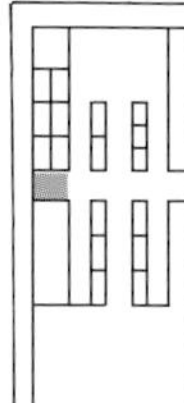

Gustave Courbet
1819-1877
L'atelier du peintre.
Allégorie réelle
déterminant une phase
de sept années
de ma vie artistique
et morale

(The Painter's Studio:
Allegory of Seven Years
of my Artistic and
Moral Life)

1855
Oil on canvas
359 / 598 cm

Gustave Courbet

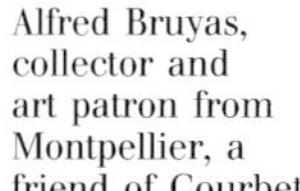

Alfred Bruyas, collector and art patron from Montpellier, a friend of Courbet

Pierre Joseph Proudhon, socialist philosopher

Champfleury writer, art historian and journalist

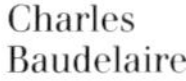

Charles Baudelaire

I

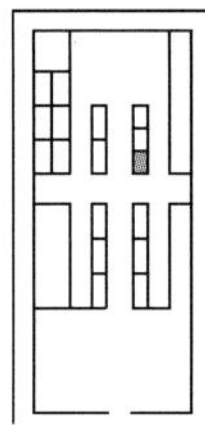

Puvis de Chavannes

Ever since it was painted in 1881, Puvis de Chavannes' *Le pauvre pêcheur (The Poor Fisherman)* has exercised a strange fascination. However much critics, poets and men of letters have disagreed on this painting, they have never been able to resist the temptation to write about it. For some, *Le pauvre pêcheur* is a symbolist work, for others it is classical; nonetheless, it intrigued a succession of later painters from Gauguin, Seurat, Signac, Redon, Carrière, Maillol and Maurice Denis down to Picasso.

The repressed emotion inherent in this painting is derived from a composition dominated by empty spaces, subdued colours, stillness, shade and relief, within a timeless landscape. The same feel for monumentality coupled with spareness of composition can be seen in *Jeunes filles au bord de la mer (Young Girls at the Seaside)*, 1879, in which the modulated colours and tranquil linear harmony suggests an atmosphere of peace, a blend of inner melancholy and joy, which leaves plenty of room for symbolist interpretation. Even when he is dealing with a familiar theme, as in *La toilette (A Woman at her Toilette)*, 1883, Puvis de Chavannes leaves an impression of dreaminess and eternity. Here he favours the same clear, mat tones, an in his mural decorations (at the museums of Amiens, Marseille, Lyon and Rouen; at the hôtels de ville of Poitiers and Paris; and at the Sorbonne and the Panthéon). *Le Ballon (The Balloon)*, 1870, and *Le Pigeon (The Pigeon)*, 1871, both executed in brown monochrome, with large female figures in mourning, are movingly symbolic of Parisian resistance. Moreover, Puvis had the idea of painting *Le Ballon* while on guard duty on the ramparts, during the siege of Paris; he later added its companion picture which features a carrier-pigeon escaping from an attack by a falcon hovering over the snowbound Ile de la Cité.

One of Puvis' largest canvases, *L'été (Summer),* 1873, is displayed at the entrance to the Musée d'Orsay. This subject was one of the artist's favourites, which he repeated in his decoration of the Paris Hôtel de Ville. The painting has the same calm, poetic atmosphere, and the same monumental breadth and decorative quality, that characterize the rest of his work.

Pierre Puvis
de Chavannes
1824-1898
Le pauvre pêcheur
(The Poor Fisherman)
1881
Oil on canvas
155 / 192.5 cm

Pierre Puvis
de Chavannes
1824-1898
Jeunes filles
au bord de la mer
(Young Girls
at the Seaside)
1879
Oil on canvas
205 / 154 cm

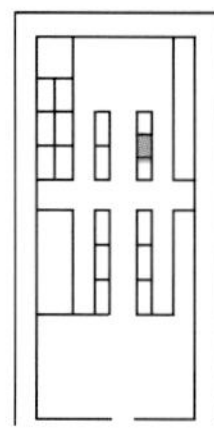

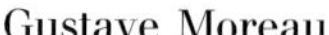

Gustave Moreau

Gustave Moreau was a romantic born too late, whose main formative influences were Delacroix and Chassériau, and a taste for the rare and strange. He first came to the public eye at the 1865 Salon, with his *Jason et Médée (Jason and Medea);* the even more famous *Jeune fille Thrace portant la tête d'Orphée (Thracian Girl carrying the Head of Orpheus)* was presented at the 1866 Salon and was immediately purchased by the state. These two canvases show Moreau's refined wealth of colour and the languid grace of his protagonists, as well as his great gifts as a miniaturist and the oddity of his accessories; see the column in *Jason*, which is encrusted with pearls and gemstones, and the multicoloured humming-birds in the background.

The myth of Orpheus was a favourite symbolist theme, because it illustrates the immortality of the artist as ensured by his creations or his thought. *Orphée* gives the story one of its earliest — and most original — interpretations.

When he was teaching at the Ecole des Beaux-Arts, Moreau attracted young *Fauves* like Matisse and Marquet with the freedom of his methods, along with Georges Rouault, a highly independent personality who became one of his most loyal pupils. At his death in 1898, Moreau bequeathed his studio at 14, rue de La Rochefoucauld to the state, along with all the works it contained. This museum, which has held to the artist's original scheme for the hanging of his paintings, exhibits thousands of works of every possible size and description. Some of these are lent to the Musée d'Orsay on a rotational basis.

Gustave Moreau
1826-1898
Orphée (Orpheus)
1866
Oil on wood
154 / 99.5 cm

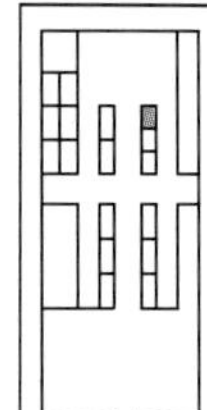

Degas, pre-1870

From the beginning, Degas showed himself to be totally original, a painter for whom the influence of the Italian Renaissance and such modern masters as Ingres was no more than a point of departure for his own art. After studying under Lamothe, a disciple of Flandrin, Degas went to live with relatives in Italy between 1856 and 1859. He made friends during this period with other French artists, like Gustave Moreau, who had made the same pilgrimage across the Alps. Degas' work as a young man consisted mainly of portraits, such as that of his 87-year-old grandfather *Hilaire De Gas* (1857), who was living in Naples at the time. In this painting, Degas' rigorous construction, perfect draughtsmanship, psychological mastery of his subject and controlled awareness of light as a vehicle to bring out the model's essential nature, are all precociously present. In a later portrait of *Thérèse De Gas* (1863), his much-lover sister, Degas uses a timid, serious subject as an excuse for a magnificent tour de force, juxtaposing the grey dress with the broad black shawl and the pink knot that holds the hat in place.

La famille Bellelli (The Bellelli Family), 1858-1860, was begun by Degas while staying with his aunt, Baroness Bellelli, in Florence. The monumental format of portraits in an interior is a highly original one, and the finished painting was preceded by a number of sketches. The composition is basically simple, enriched by the open perspectives of a door and mirror; the colours are muted but refined (whites offsetting blacks). In general, *La famille Bellelli* encapsulates a family drama being played out between Laure Bellelli and her husband, an early example of Degas' taste for psychological studies. Despite all the influences that have been attributed to this work (such as Holbein or Van Dyck), *La famille Bellelli* cannot be compared to any other previous or existing painting.

The unfinished and mysterious *Sémiramis construisant Babylone (Semiramis overseeing the construction of Babylon)*, 1861, testifies to Degas' originality as a history painter. This canvas reflects his admiration for Italian Quattrocento painting; it has been compared to the mural paintings of Piero della Francesca at Arezzo. The hieratic figures, the frieze-like composition, the serene, heroic atmosphere and the legendary architecture of this painting combine to lend it an imaginary, poetic quality of time suspended.

The end of the 1860s saw the earliest manifestations of the Opera and racing themes in Degas' work *(Le défilé – The Parade*, also known as *Chevaux de course devant les tribunes – Racehorses in front of the Grandstand*, circa 1866-1868). *L'orchestre de l'Opéra (The Orchestra at the Opera)*, 1868-1869, with its forthright presentation and contrasts of penumbra and bright light, is one of the first manifestations of the Opera theme in the work of Degas. *Course de gentlemen avant le départ (Before the Start of the Gentlemen's Race)*, which was begun in 1862 and completed in 1880, marks the earliest example of another favourite subject, with its attempt to capture movement and its wide range of colours.

Edgar Degas
1834-1917

Sémiramis construisant Babylone (Semiramis overseeing the construction of Babylon)
1861
Oil on canvas
151 / 258 cm

Edgar Degas
1834-1917
La famille Bellelli (The Bellelli Family)
Circa 1858-1860
Oil on canvas
200 / 250 cm

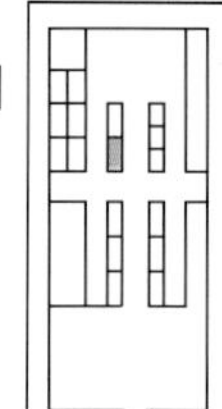

Manet, pre-1870

"This will be the painter, the true painter, who will show us how great and poetic we are, in our cravates and shiny boots", wrote Baudelaire, who dreamed that painting would one day express what was 'marvellous' in the modern world. And indeed, Manet's work embodies and reveals the contrasts, the humour, the poetry and beauty of his time.

Portrait de M. et Mme Manet (1860), which was considered vulgar by contemporary critics, perfectly describes the austere 'grande bourgeoisie' of the Second Empire. It also represents a striking psychological portrait of the artist's parents, beneath the realism of their expressions. This work owes much to Courbet; some of Manet's unique characteristics are already apparent, such as his firm execution, broad, honest brushstrokes and original way of treating space by simplifying perspective. The first scandal of Manet's career was prompted by *Le déjeuner sur l'herbe**, but when *Olympia* was exhibited at the 1865 Salon it caused a veritable storm. This nude was condemned as 'immoral' and ugly; in effect, Manet had taken an ideal model, inspired by Titian's *Venus of Urbino*, and worked back to reality and an individualised image. *Olympia* is no Venus or odalisque, but a richly-paid prostitute. The influence of Goya is palpable in this ruthlessly-executed nude, with its strong light and colour contrasts, which has been described as the vital hinge connecting the classical tradition and modern art. Emile Zola championed *Olympia* and the rest of Manet's work in the press; by way of thanks, the artist painted Zola's portrait against a background expressing some of his tastes and activities, namely Japanese prints, 'Olympia' and the booklet he had written about Manet.

Spanish painting was rich in lessons for Manet. We can recognise the influence of Velasquez in *Le fifre (The Fife-Player)* refused by the 1866 Salon, which shows a figure standing out against a unified background, in a rejection of traditional ideas of perspective. *Le balcon (The Balcony)*, which was shown at the 1869 Salon, echoes a favourite theme of Goya's; in the foreground is Berthe Morisot, also a painter, who later married Manet's brother and took part in the Impressionnist exhibitions. The faces in this painting, like many of Manet's figures, have a curious fixity of expression which suggests a kind of inaccessible, inward dreaminess. This atmosphere, coupled with the aggressive green of the balcony against the refined white lace of the women's dresses, completely baffled contemporary critics.

* This painting properly belongs to the Moreau-Nélaton collection. See page 86 for commentary.

Edouard Manet
1832-1883
Emile Zola
1868
Oil on canvas
146.3 / 114 cm

Edouard Manet
1832-1883
Le balcon
(The Balcony)
Circa 1868-1869
Oil on canvas
170 / 124.5 cm

Edouard Manet
1832-1883
Olympia
1863
Oil on canvas
130.5 / 190 cm

Olympia was acquired for the national collection in 1890, on the initiative of Monet, who raised the money to buy the painting by public subscription.

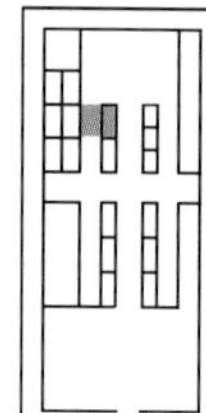

Renoir, Monet, Bazille, pre-1870

In the early 1860's, the private Paris studio of the academic painter Gleyre became a meeting place for young artists wishing to perfect their knowledge of painting and draughtsmanship. First Renoir, in 1861, then Frederic Bazille, Claude Monet and Alfred Sisley joined the group; their common fascination with realism soon led to firm friendships.

On the face of it, the group's earliest works belong to a 'modern' realist school, influenced by Courbet, Daubigny, Corot and even Delacroix, whose energy and sense of colour they admired. From 1863, the example of Manet was a powerful incitement; at the same time Bazille made friends with Cézanne, who in turn introduced him to Pissarro and Guillaumin. Before long, the shared direction of their search for new techniques in art led these painters to form a new school of their own.

Displayed in the gallery are some of Monet's youthful realist works, painted in sombre harmonies *(Trophée de chasse – Hunting Trophy*, 1862), and one his most brilliant figures, *Mme Gaudibert*, 1868, that is an ambitious full-length portrait of the wife of one of the artist's first patrons.

Renoir's *Frédéric Bazille peignant à son chevalet (Frédéric Bazille painting at his Easel)*, 1867, symbolises the friendship of the two painters. With its harmonies of grey and beige, this portrait of Bazille has strong overtones of Manet. The same warm feelings are evoked in Bazille's *Portrait de Renoir*, also painted in 1867, which Renoir kept for the rest of his life.

In 1863, Monet and Bazille worked together at Chailly, a small village on the edge of the forest of Fontainebleau, doing paintings in the Barbizon tradition. It happened that Monet had an accident during this time; Bazille painted a small fine-toned picture of his immobilised friend. *L'ambulance improvisée (The Improvised Ambulance)*, 1865, which again betrays Monet's influence. One of Bazille's lines of research was that of placing figures in direct light; he had been much impressed by this aspect of Courbet's magnificent *La rencontre (The Meeting)*, which belonged to his fellow Montpellierain, Bruyas. *La réunion de famille (Family Reunion)*, accepted for the 1868 Salon, shows how sensitive Bazille was to the hard southern sunlight, which cuts through perspectives, heightens contrasts and accentuates the solidity of forms. The originality of the setting and colours owe much to Manet, but the treatment of light passing through leaves and transforming the tints of clothing and ground are pure Monet. Sadly, Bazille was killed in action at the battle of Beaune-la-Rolande in 1870, aged only 29.

Monet, who had benefitted greatly from the advice of Boudin and Jongkind, emerged early as the group's most developed artistic personality. His début at the 1865 Salon had

Pierre-Auguste Renoir
1841-1919
Frédéric Bazille
1867
Oil on canvas
105 / 73.5 cm

Claude Monet
1840-1926
La Pie
(The Magpie)
1869
Oil on canvas
89 / 130 cm

Frédéric Bazille
1841-1870

Réunion de famille
(Family Reunion)
1867
Oil on canvas
152 / 230 cm

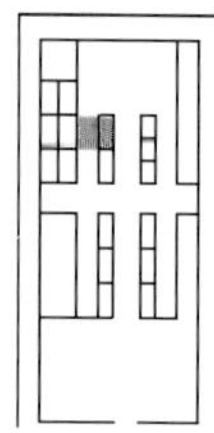

been favourably received by the critics; now he began his own version of the *Déjeuner sur l'herbe.* This large composition (approximately 4.6 m by more than 6 m) was conceived as both a homage and a challenge to Edouard Manet, and was intended for the 1866 Salon. The complete work is only known to us thanks to a study kept at the Pushkin Museum in Moscow, for Monet never finished *Le Déjeuner*, which he later pledged with an Argenteuil creditor; when he redeemed it in 1884, the canvas had deteriorated through being stored in a damp cellar. Monet then cut out three fragments, two of which have survived. The left-hand fragment has belonged to the French national collections since 1957, when it was generously donated by M. Georges Wildenstein, while the central fragment entered the Musée d'Orsay in March 1987. In this youthful work, which shows Monet's art moving towards portrayal of contemporary life, his authority, firm touch and mastery of figurative technique are already apparent, as is his taste for contrasting effects of light, while the overall atmosphere remains refined. Monet had Bazille pose for him in the forest at Fontainebleau, working from small-scale studies painted in the open air. Courbet was also included, as a mark of admiration for the artist's honest approach and treatment of light. Another landmark canvas in the development of Monet is 'Femmes au Jardin' (1867). In this finished work, painted in the open air, Monet attempted to preserve the spontaneity and freedom of a sketch, with strongly-outlined figures in bold light and shade, smoothly integrated into garden surroundings which are treated almost as décor. *Femmes au jardin (Women in a Garden)* was refused by the jury of the 1867 Salon. Zola alone defended it. "...They have rejected his figures of women in bright summer dresses, picking flowers on a garden walk", he wrote. "The sunshine falls straight on their dazzling white skirts; the warm shadow of a tree lies across the path and the sunlit garments like a broad grey cloth. Nothing could be more strange than this effect. A man must be greatly in love with his own time to attempt so spectacular a tour de force, with fabrics cut in two by sunshine and shade, and ladies placed foursquare on a lawn which the gardener's rake has carefully scoured..."

Monet had no better luck with the 1869 Salon, for which the jury refused one of his most important paintings, *La Pie (The Magpie).* This ambitious landscape positively glistens with light, while the refinement and variety of its range of whites confer a strange, unique quality. In the absence of any human figure, the central feature of the painting is the black bird perched on the gate, which is filled with an almost magical significance. In 1858, Monet had discovered painting in the open air with Boudin at Honfleur: *L'hôtel des Roches-Noires à Trouville (The Hotel des Roches-Noires at Trouville),* reflects the atmosphere of a smart

Claude Monet
1840-1926
Le déjeuner sur l'herbe

Left-hand
fragment
of composition
1865-1866
Oil on canvas
418 / 150 cm

Central fragment
of composition
1865-1866
Oil on canvas
248 / 217 cm

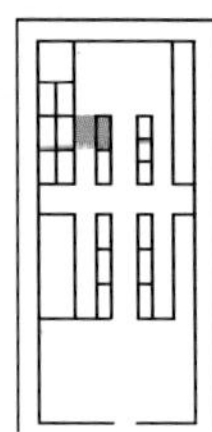

bourgeois seaside resort under the Second Empire, on the brink of the 1870 war. Monet's originality is already apparent in this painting, as flags seem to flutter under his rapid, allusive brushwork and the clouds fly across the sky.

Meanwhile, Paul Guigou, who settled in Marseilles in 1854, and then in Paris from 1862 onwards, remained loyal to the strong provençal light that endowed his figures *(La lavandière – The Washerwoman)* and his landscapes *(Route de la Gineste – Road to la Gineste*, 1859), with stability and permanence.

Claude Monet
1840-1926
Hôtel des Roches-Noires à Trouville
(The Hotel des Roches-Noires at Trouville)
1870
Oil on canvas
81.1 / 58.3 cm

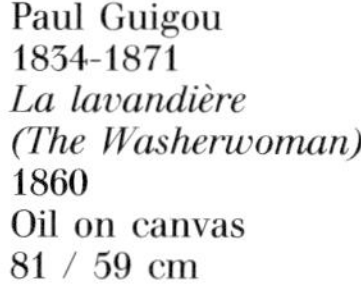

Paul Guigou
1834-1871
La lavandière
(The Washerwoman)
1860
Oil on canvas
81 / 59 cm

Claude Monet
1840-1926
Femmes au jardin
(Women in a Garden)
1867
Oil on canvas
255 / 205 cm

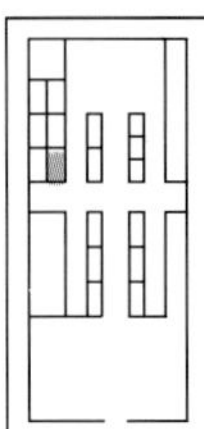

Fantin-Latour

Henri Fantin-Latour was a fervent admirer and friend of the Impressionists, and like them was rejected by the official art establishment. Nonetheless, he remains an isolated personality. His first great paintings, *Hommage à Delacroix** reveals an early taste for psychological insight, exact draughtsmanship and sombre harmonies. Fantin's friendship with Manet and the future impressionnists was confirmed in *Un atelier aux Batignolles (A Studio in les Batignolles)*, 1870, which in fact is a homage to Manet. The painter is portrayed in his studio, surrounded by his friends: the critic Zacharie Astruc, Renoir, Zola, the tall Bazille, and Monet. The subject of the painting was accepted almost without contest and Fantin's talent was rewarded by a medal at the Salon. As in his *Un coin de table (Table Corner)*, 1872, *Un atelier* shows the artist's desire to capture the spiritual affinities between human beings. *Un coin de table* displays an original construction which rejects traditional perspective; the work is entirely centred on Verlaine and Rimbaud, who are intentionally isolated from a group of honorable but mediocre writers, all of whom are utterly forgotten today. Fantin's portraits of relatives such as his sister-in-law Charlotte Dubourg (1882), show brooding individuals who seem to be wrapped in a kind of silent music. His still lifes, like his portraits, display a precise observation of reality, in which flowers, fruits and objects are surrounded by a clear, subtle light *(Fleurs et fruits – Flowers and Fruits*, 1865). By way of contrast, the poetic *La Nuit (Night)*, 1865, depicts the dreamy, unreal world suggested by Fantin's passion for the music of Schumann, Wagner and Berlioz, which he later developed in a series of lithographs. Parallel with the novelty of these artists linked to realism, an official bourgeois realism was developed by Alfred Stevens, James Tissot and Carolus-Duran. Alfred Stevens, who was born in Brussels, became the painter of Parisian life under the Second Empire, a role he shared with high society portraitist James Tissot *(Jeune femme en veste rouge – Young Woman in a Red Jacket*, 1864). The influence of Courbet may be seen in Carolus-Duran's *Le convalescent (The Convalescent)*, 1860, while *La dame au gant (Lady with Glove)*, 1869, testifies to the artist's admiration for the colours and techniques of Velasquez and Van Dyck. The latter painting was such a spectacular success that Carolus-Duran was inundated with commissions and fell back into facile mediocrity.

* This work belongs to the Moreau-Nélaton Collection, presented in the first room of the Impressionist gallery; see relevant passage on this collection.

Henri Fantin-Latour
1836-1904
Un atelier aux Batignolles
1870
Oil on canvas
204 / 273.5 cm

Exhibited at the entrance of the Fantin-Latour Room

Otto Scholderer
Painter

Renoir

Emile Zola

Bazille

Monet

Manet

Zacharie Astruc
Writer, painter and sculptor

Edmond Maître
Art lover

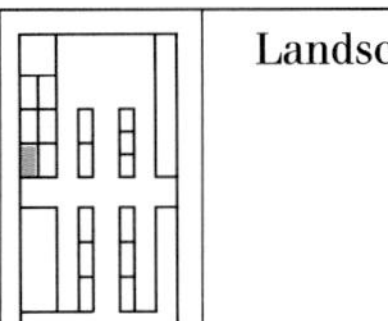

Landscapes

Boudin, Jongkind, Lépine, Maris

Between 1850 and 1860, two painters, Boudin and Jongkind, began to concentrate on direct observation of nature. They followed the example of the English painters (Constable, Bonington and Turner), as well as that of Corot and the Barbizon painters who had already established the need to render fleeting atmospheric changes direct from life.

The Normandy coast, with its murky, changeable skies and constantly shifting light, exerted a strong attraction on Boudin and Jongkind, who have been called "Pre-Impressionists". Boudin, a native of Honfleur, was fascinated by skies and clouds; in 1859, he met Monet, Baudelaire and Courbet, the last of whom strongly advised him to do sea-paintings. "You are the only one of us", Courbet told Boudin, "...who knows the sky". Such paintings as *Le port de Camaret (The Harbour at Camaret)*, 1872, or *Les Voiliers (The Sailing Boats)*, give pride of place to "...great, beautiful, cloud-filled skies, wrinkled with colours, moving and profound", as the painter tenderly described them. In about 1862, Boudin took up a new theme, that of the beaches at Deauville and Trouville, which had lately become fashionable *(La plage de Trouville – The Beach at Trouville*, 1865; *Baigneurs sur la plage de Trouville – Bathers on the Beach at Trouville*, 1869). This subject gave him free rein to paint with clear colours and convey his awareness of luminous, vibrant light.

Stanislas Lépine, born at Caen, tended to work alone and apart from the mainstream of art. Using subtle, delicate tones of grey, Lépine depicted the light and atmosphere of his native landscapes in a series of small paintings containing no human figures whatsoever *(Le port de Caen – The Harbour at Caen*, 1859; *Le marché aux pommes – Apple Market*, 1889).

By contrast, Jongkind was a Dutchman, reared in the tradition of the great 17th century Dutch landscape painters *(En Hollande, les barques près du moulin – Boats by a Mill in Holland*, 1868). For a period, he worked with Boudin, Bazille and Monet in the Honfleur area.

Subsequently, a group of Dutch artists revived the concept of Dutch landscape painting and formed the Hague School; among them were Jacob Maris (whose compositions tend to be dominated by very high skies) *(Ville hollandaise au bord de la mer – Seaside Town in Holland*, 1883), and Anton Mauve, with his pale grey atmospheres and choppy, gale-lashed seas. Mesdag, another devoted marine artist and member of the group, painted stormy seas from life or attempted to convey the fleeting atmosphere of a moment *(Soleil couchant – Setting Sun)*.

Hendrik Willem
Mesdag
1831-1915

Soleil couchant
(Setting Sun)
Oil on canvas
140 / 180 cm

Eugène Boudin
1824-1898

Voiliers
(Sailing Boats)
Circa 1885-1890
Oil on wood
24.5 / 33.5 cm

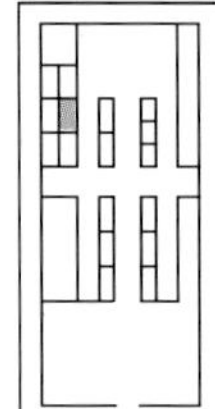

Personnaz Collection

Guillaumin, Monet, Pissarro, Sisley

Antonin Personnaz (1854-1936) was a native of Bayonne like the painter Léon Bonnat, who introduced him into Paris art circles. He became friends with Pissarro, Degas and Guillaumin, and from 1880 onwards began to assemble a rich collection of Impressionist works. After the 1914-1918 war, Personnaz retired to Bayonne, where he supervised the administration of the Musée Bonnat and looked after the works of art bequeathed to the town by his friend. On his own death, Personnaz left his collection of paintings, pastels, aquarelles and drawings to the national museums (except for about forty works which remain at the Musée Bonnat). The Personnaz collection was exhibited at the Louvre from 1937 onwards.

One of the best-represented artists here is undoubtedly Pissarro, whose development may be traced with ease between 1870 and 1902. Attracted by the countryside, Pissarro first lived at Louveciennes, than at Pontoise, where he was joined by Cézanne. He quickly made a reputation for firmly-executed and composed paintings, using a rich palette based on browns, greens and reds *(Paysage d'hiver à Louveciennes – Winter Landscape, Louveciennes,* circa 1870). From 1884 to 1903, Pissarro was installed at Eragny-sur-Epte; by nature curious, he was always ready to try out new techniques such as the 'pointilliste' method invented by Seurat and Signac, which he adopted in 1885-1886 *(Femme dans un clos – Woman in a Small Field,* 1887). But he quickly abandoned 'Pointillisme' in favour of a supple, luminous approach of his own, using it to paint street themes in Paris, Rouen or Dieppe *(Dieppe, bassin Duquesne – Dieppe, the Duquesne Dock,* 1902).

Antonin Personnaz
1854-1936

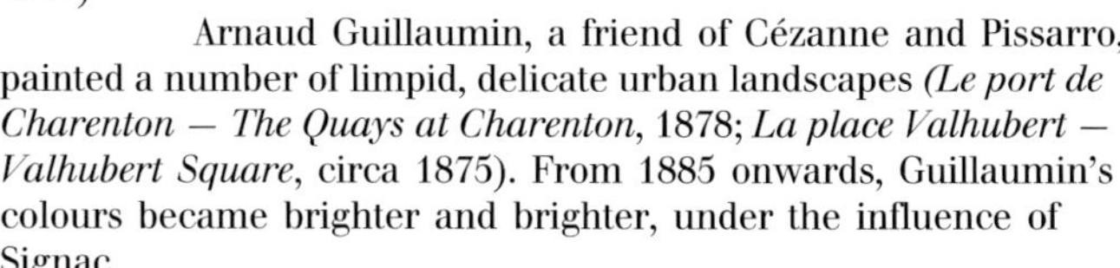

Arnaud Guillaumin, a friend of Cézanne and Pissarro, painted a number of limpid, delicate urban landscapes *(Le port de Charenton – The Quays at Charenton,* 1878; *La place Valhubert – Valhubert Square,* circa 1875). From 1885 onwards, Guillaumin's colours became brighter and brighter, under the influence of Signac.

Mary Cassatt, an American painter living in France, became the friend and pupil of Degas. The human figure and the ordinary gestures of day-to-day life rendered with versimilitude *(Femme cousant – Woman sewing)* were her favourite subjects. The collection of Antonin Personnaz also included one or two of Toulouse-Lautrec's more celebrated pictures, such as *Jeanne Avril dansant (Jeanne Avril dancing)* or *Le lit (The Bed)*, which for the safety of their colours are displayed with the painter's other works in a special dimly-lit room.

Mary Cassatt
1844-1926
Jeune fille au jardin
(Young girl in a Garden)
Circa 1880-1882
Oil on canvas
92 / 65 cm

C. Pissarro
1830-1903
Femme dans un clos,
soleil de printemps
dans le pré à Eragny
(Woman in a Small
Field, Spring Sunshine
in the Meadow
at Eragny)
1887
Oil on canvas
54.5 / 65 cm

Armand Guillaumin
1841-1927
Quai de la Gare,
effet de neige
(Paris, Quai de la Gare,
Snow Study)
Oil on canvas
50.5 / 61.2 cm

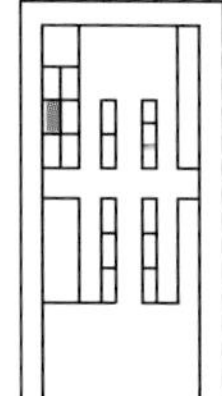

Eduardo Mollard Collection

This collection, donated by Doctor Eduardo Mollard, an Argentine living in France, includes an important ensemble of landscapes from Corot and the Barbizon school (Rousseau, Diaz), to the precursors of Impressionism (Boudin, Jongkind and Lépine) and finally, the Impressionists themselves, as represented by Sisley and above all, Pissarro. In accordance with the wishes of Doctor Mollard, the pictures donated are displayed in a single room which bears his name.

Jongkind frequently turned to urban landscapes; *La Seine et Notre-Dame de Paris* and *Rue de l'Abbé de l'Epée*, 1872, are both paintings that shimmer with the light suggested by the artist's fragmentary brushwork. Eugène Boudin, though on occasion he traveled further afield, remained firmly installed on his native Normandy coast. *(Port de Bordeaux*, 1874 – *Venise, Quai des Esclavons*, 1895). Conveying the artist's love for rainy skies, greenish or milky sea, and gay, elegant crowds, Boudin's *La plage de Trouville* (1864) has the ephemeral quality of a blustery summer day.

At the first Impressionist exhibition in 1874, Pissarro showed his *Gelée blanche, ancienne route d'Ennery, Pontoise (Hoar Frost by the Old Road to Ennery, Pontoise)* a painting which provoked a huge scandal. "Furrows and frost? Why, they're no more than scrapings from the palette, uniformly plastered on to a grubby canvas. The picture has no head, no tail, no up, no down, no front and no back." The critics were baffled by the meagreness of Pissarro's subject-matter; in effect, he scorned the picturesque and anecdotal approach, preferring a careful, subtle treatment of reflected light on the earth and in the sky. With this passionate interest in new techniques, Pissarro quickly made the acquaintance of Seurat and Signac, making his first attempt at 'pointilliste' painting towards the end of 1885 *(Femme au fichu vert – Women with Green Scarf*, 1893).

Alfred Sisley, an Englishman living in France, was always deeply attracted by the landscapes of the Ile-de-France. He settled at Moret-sur-Loing in 1880 after which he applied himself essentially to views of the village. *Le pont de Moret (The Bridge at Moret)*, 1893, is a good example of Sisley's painting method, which consists in depicting familiar, understated subjects by way of monumental compositions.

Camille Pissarro
1830-1903

Gelée blanche
(Hoar Frost)
1873
Oïl on canvas
65 / 93 cm

Johan-Barthold
Jongkind
1819-1891

La Seine
et Notre-Dame de Paris
1864
Oil on canvas
42 / 56.5 cm

Eugène Boudin
1824-1898

La plage de Trouville
(The Beach at Trouville)
1864
Oil on wood
26 / 48 cm

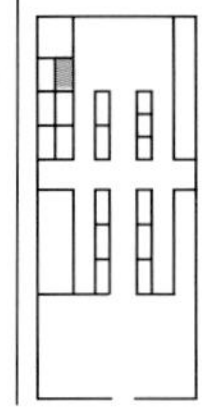

François Bonvin was associated with the realist movement, but took no real part in it; instead, he became the discreet chronicler of unruffled daily life *(Servante tirant l'eau – Servant Girl Drawing Water*, 1861). His technique was one of sober harmony, much influenced by the Dutch painters of the 17th century whom he loved to copy at the Louvre. His still lifes filled with animals *(Nature morte au canard, Nature morte au lièvre – Still Life with Duck, Still Life with Hare*, 1863) and his tranquil paintings of his studio *(Nature morte à la palette – Still Life with Palette*, 1863) show a measure of daring in their colours, emphasised by Bonvin's sure, subtle touch and steady treatment of light. By contrast Antoine Vollon, one of the best-known still-life painters of the second half of the 19th century, gives a totally realistic, even cruel rendering of fish dying out of water *(Poissons de Mer – Sea Fish*, 1870).

Théodule Ribot was influenced by 17th century Spanish painting in general, and by Ribera in particular. He specialised in religious themes, such as *Saint-Sebastien* (1865), in which the dramatic nature of the work is heightened by powerful and skilful contrasts of light and shade. Ribot was also much impressed by Dutch 17th century painting, to which his intimist work owes much *(Le sermon – The Sermon*, circa 1890).

Alphonse Legros, a disciple of Courbet, friend of Fantin-Latour and admirer of Spanish painting, was attracted to a kind of mystical realism; *L'Amende honorable (Making Amends)*, 1867.

Adolphe Monticelle concentrated on painting a magical, mysterious world of his own, using thick, superimposed touches *(Don Quichotte et Sancho Pança*, circa 1865). He also shows a fine realist touch in his portraits (Mme Tessier, 1872) and in the handling of brightly-coloured still lifes *(Nature morte au pichet blanc – Still Life with White Jug)*. Monticelli was a complex personality, whose subjects were mainly a prolongation of romanticism. Nonetheless, his robust colours and his taste for thick paint application impressed and influenced Van Gogh. In his early Dutch period, the latter executed sombre impasto paintings that featured peasants from the Borinage region in Belgium *(Paysanne près de l'âtre – Peasant Woman near the Hearth)*.

Adolphe Monticelli
1824-1886

*Nature morte
au pichet blanc
(Still Life with white
Jug)*
Circa 1878-1880
Oil on wood
49 / 63 cm

Vincent Van Gogh
1853-1890

*Paysanne près de l'âtre
(Peasant Woman near
the Hearth)*
1885
Oil on canvas
29 / 40 cm

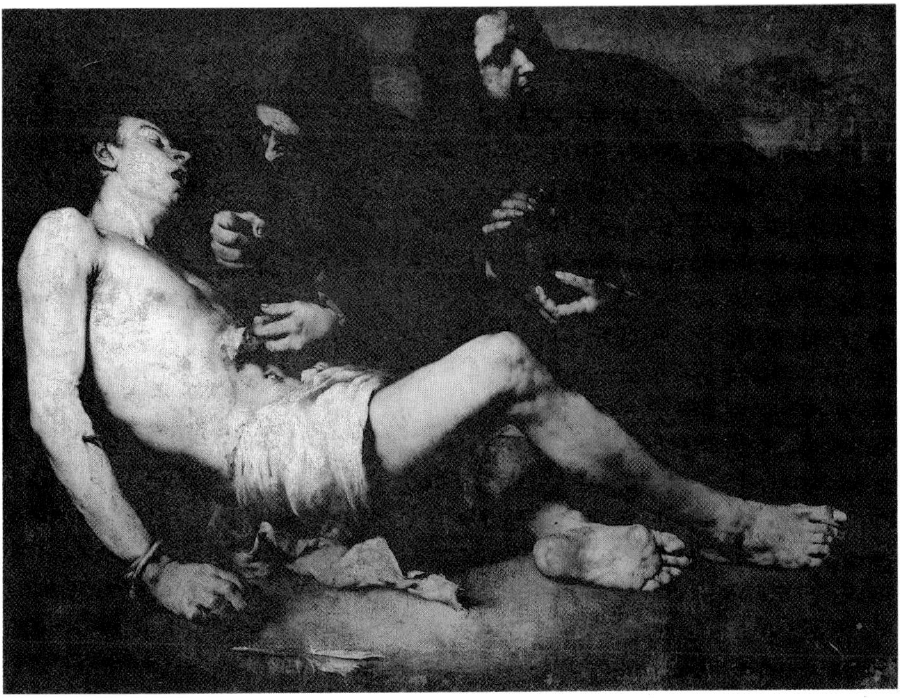

Théodule Ribot
1823-1891

Saint Sébastien, martyr
1865
Oil on canvas
97 / 130 cm

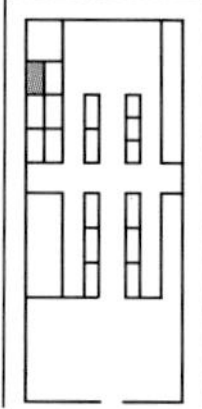

Orientalism

The orient has always intrigued Westerners; but it was not until the 19th century, and Bonaparte's Egyptian campaign, that these mysterious countries began to be truly accessible. After the unreal fantasies of odalisques produced by Ingres, the romantic generation set out to discover a panoply of new peoples, landscapes and colours. Some, like Gérôme, worked with meticulous realism from memories of their travels; others, like Fromentin, Guillaumet and Belly, were seduced by the beauty of the sites and colours. The latter painters set out to convey the charm and sometimes the disquieting nature of what they saw. Fromentin travelled in Algeria, published two books of memoirs and painted fantasy scenes and picturesque reconstitutions; but from time to time he was able to convey his sense of the desert's utter solitude *(Au pays de la soif – The Land of Thirst).* Guillaumet, working with limited skills and harsh colours, was nonetheless able to assemble a series of images whose grandeur astonished and delighted his contemporaries *(Prière du soir dans le Sahara – Evening Prayer in the Sahara,* 1863). He was obsessed with Algeria, travelled there on many occasions, and painted canvases which combine the picturesque with an atmosphere of sincerity. *(Les tisseuses-fileuses à Bou-Saada – Weavers at Bou-Saada).* Guillaumet was also capable of conveying the deadly natural violence of these parched regions *(Le désert – The Desert,* 1867). Belly, who was at first attracted to the Barbizon school, travelled to the Orient in 1840 and visited the Lebanon, Palestine and Egypt, where he stayed on two subsequent occasions. In his painting *Pèlerins allant à la Mecque (Pilgrims to Mecca),* 1861, the bold effect produced by the caravan advancing toward the onlooker was not universally appreciated, but nonetheless this painting was an immense success at the 1861 Salon. It was considered as "...one of the most remarkable of our contemporary paintings, unquestionably the most striking and true-to-life canvas yet inspired by the Orient". Tournemine, another dedicated orientalist, used bright, vivid colours to depict the exotic subjects and scenes described in travel stories *(Eléphants d'Afrique – African Elephants).*

Gustave Guillaumet
1840-1887

Le désert (The Desert)
1867
Oil on canvas
110 / 200 cm

Charles de Tournemine
1812-1872

Eléphants d'Afrique
(African Elephants)
1867
Oil on canvas
88 / 178 cm

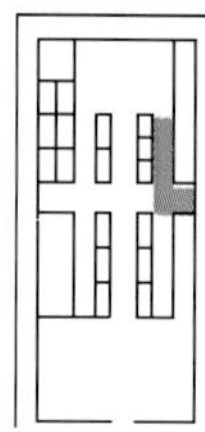

In the late 19th century, the arts as applied to industry tended to be dominated by eclecticism; constant reference to the styles of the past, already a feature of the era of Louis-Philippe, was later reinforced by the creation of museums, private collections of old masters, and the researches and discoveries of archaeologists, historians and scholars. Meanwhile, a new class of buyer had appeared, the rich bourgeois, uncertain of his judgement yet craving legitimacy and roots of his own. This infatuation with a wide range of styles was also favoured by the processes of exploration and colonisation, along with the Universal Exhibition, at which the arts of the West were juxtaposed with those of the Mediterranean Orient and Asia.

The new industrial firms recruited leading artists, with a view to combining the Beautiful with the Useful, in other words Art and Industry. Architects, decorators, sculptors, painters and designers furnished models, both for mass production and for the manufacture of single pieces. Thus industrial and commercial art contributed to the spread of eclecticism. *La toilette de la Duchesse de Parme (The Duchess of Parma's Dressing Table)*, the grand-daughter of Charles X, was one of the first examples of this burgeoning trend, which was commissioned in 1845, completed in 1851 and sent to the Universal Exhibition in London. The 'Toilette' was made of silver, bronze and iron and decorated with inlaid enamelwork and gemstones; it was the fruit of a joint effort by the silversmith Froment-Meurice, the architect Dubau, the sculptors Feuchère and Geoffroy-Dechaume, and the ornamentalist Liénard. The resultant ensemble is an astonishing blend of influences from Islam, the Middle Ages, the Renaissance and Baroque Italian.

The Middle Ages, and especially the Gothic style, were major sources of inspiration for contemporary silverwork and religious furnishings, the specialities of the firm of Poussielgue-Rusand. With the collaboration of architects and restorers like Viollet-le-Duc, Duthoit, Sauvaghe and Corroyer *(Ostensoir – Ostensory)*, this establishment published a sales catalogue offering a wide choice of mass-produced objects made of more or less precious materials, combined in different proportions according to order.

The firm of Christofle emerged as the leading manufacturer of lay gold and silverwork, by the use of new silver-plating techniques. These enabled the manufacturer to maintain a constant level of production while at the same time preserving the tradition of luxury silverware. Some remarkable pieces were made for the Universal Exhibition. An example is the *Vase de l'éducation d'Achille (Vase depicting the Education*

Maison Poussielgue-Rusand
after a design by
Edouard-Jules Corroyer
(1835-1904)
Ostensoir (Ostensory)
Circa 1865
Gilded silver and gemstones
70 cm

Maison Barbedienne
after a model by
Ferdinand Levillain
(1837-1905)
Medusa cup
Circa 1873
Patinated bronze, ivory, ebony
18.2 / 55.5 ∅38.5 cm

Christofle et Cie,
directed by
Henri Bouilhet (1838-1907)
and Paul Christofle (1830-1910)
Vase de l'éducation d'Achille
(Vase depicting the
Education of Achilles)
1867
Silver, partially gilded
75 cm

François Désiré
Froment-Meurice
(1802-1855)
Coffret
(Casket)
Circa 1847-1849
Gilded silver,
painted enamel, emeralds
and grenadines
42.6 / 35.8 /27.5 cm

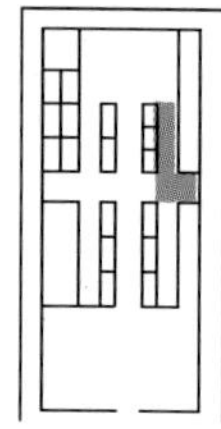

of Achilles), by the sculptor Mathurin Moreau and the ornamentalist Auguste Madroux, in which mannerist reminiscences are blended with innovative naturalist motifs.

Ferdinand Barbedienne managed France's principal bronze factory, which won regular medals and honorary distinctions at international exhibitions. His artistic director, Constant Sévin, was mainly inspired by Greek art and the Renaissance (patinated bronze cups, gilded or silvered, decorated with fruits, insects or child-motifs). In a slightly more austere neo-Grecian style, the sculptor and medallion maker Ferdinand Levillain invented the *Méduse (Medusa)* cup for Barbedienne. The décor of this original cup compliments the head, with its inlaid eyes, and the ornate handles. The neo-Grecian or neo-Byzantine furniture of the cabinetmaker Diehl, aided by the sculptors Braudely, Fremiet and Guillemin, was perhaps the most interesting contribution of Paris workshops to the 1867 Exhibition; the subject matter of their *Médaillier (Medal Cabinet)* was borrowed from France's Merovingian past, and gave Frémiet an opportunity to work with two of his favourite themes, animals and soldiers.

Jules Desfossé was another manufacturer who was eager to promote an alliance between Industry and the Beaux-Arts. He employed the painters Thomas Couture and Edouard Muller, among others, to design his extraordinary wallpapers. Le *Jardin d'Armide (Armide's Garden)*, 1854, which was the centrepiece of a Muller décor, is a masterwork of the naturalist movement in the decorative arts.

Certain artists reacted strongly against the dehumanising influence of mechanisation and refused to collaborate with industrialists. Instead, they sought to rediscover the humanist ideal of the Renaissance embodied in the rapport between artist and artisan. Charles-Jean Avisseau rediscovered the techniques of Bernard Palissy and sparked a revival of ceramic art. Rejecting the concept of the division of tasks, Avisseau fashioned, painted, fired and sold his work himself. In the same way, Claudius Popelin followed the tradition of the 16th century Limousin enamellers; his painted enamels testify to a lively concern for the past, which was shared by many other artists and art-lovers of the time.

Philippe-Joseph Brocard Known from 1865 to 1896 *Bouteille (Bottle)* 1867 Tinted glass, enamelled and painted decoration 41.5 / 20.5 cm 	Charles-Jean Avisseau 1796-1861 and Guillaume de Rochebrune 1824-1900 *Coupe et bassin* (Goblet and Bowl) 1855 Polychrome decorated porcelain, sculpted and inlaid Goblet: 34.5 ∅ 26.5 cm Bowl: 8 ∅ 51.5 cm 	Théodore Deck 1823-1891 *Coupe monumentale* *(Monumental Cup)* Circa 1870 Faience 58.5 ∅ 40.2 cm 

Charles-Guillaume Diehl
1811-circa 1885
E. Brandely,
Emmanuel Fremiet
1824-1910
Médaillier
(Medal Cabinet)
1867
Cedarwood, ebony and ivory, silver-plated bronze and copper
238 / 151 / 60 cm

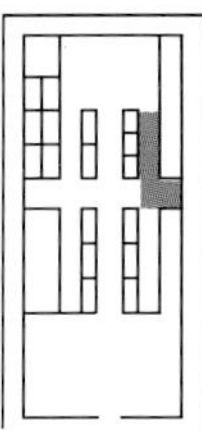

The vogue for the Orient also breathed new life into the crafts of glassmaking and porcelain manufacture. Joseph Brocard and Theodore Deck, among others, were inspired by Islamic decorative methods. Brocard revived the public taste for enamelled blown glass, while the more eclectic Deck contrived to produce perfect imitations of gleaming Iznick porcelain and Chinese ceramics. At the same time, he did not foresake the decorative repertoire of the XVIth century *(Vasque soutenue par une sphynge – Basin supported by Sphinx).*

Later, however, Japan began increasingly to dominate the artistic scene, especially after the 1867 Universal Exhibition, at which the Japanese arts section caused a sensation. The first western attempts at cloisonné enamelwork (underwritten by the firms of Barbedienne and Christofle) date from this time. Appointed in 1865 as head of Christofle's design studio, Emile Reiber developed within the firm a new and original line of production, which basically drew inspiration from Japan: polychrome bronze revived both table and furniture decoration *(Jardinière – Window Box*, 1878 model).

A remarkable example of Japanese influence on the contemporary decorative arts is given by a set of fine porcelain crockery, consisting of over 200 pieces, originally ordered from the painter-engraver Félix Bracquemond by the artist-dealer Eugène Rousseau. Rousseau himself was the author of similarly-inspired glassware. Bracquemond chose his motifs from albums of Japanese prints and illustrated books: they seem to lie almost at random in the white porcelain dishes.

The Japanese vogue took rather longer to reach French furniture. Duvinage's cabinet (c. 1877-1878) with its ivory marquetry and rare woods, including both cloisonné and rehaussé inlays in the form of flowers and insects, is an early example; as is the armoire designed by Edouard Lièvre, which incorporates a portrait of a Japanese warrior by Edouard Detaille. Both of these pieces display a remarkably uninhibited attitude towards elements borrowed from an imaginary Orient.

Eugène Rousseau
1827-1890
Vase (Modèle 'à larmes' Model with "tears")
Created circa 1875-1878
Tinted glass, overlays, engraved, painted, enamelled and gilded
25.8 / 23 cm

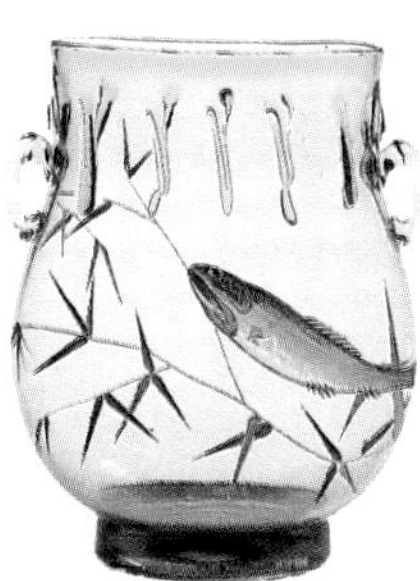

Félix Bracquemond
1833-1914
Eugène Rousseau
1827-1890
Creil et Montereau factory

Plat à poisson (Fish Platter)
Created in 1866, produced from 1866 to 1875
Fine porcelain, décor printed and painted under glaze
69.4 / 27 cm

Edouard Lièvre
1829-1886
Edouard Detaille
1848-1912
House of l'Escalier de Cristal, manufacturer
Meuble à deux corps : armoire sur table d'applique (Piece of Furniture composed of two Parts: Cabinet mounted on Bracket table)
1877
Brazilian rosewood, Indian ebony, gilded bronze, pitted iron, glass
210 / 110 / 57 cm

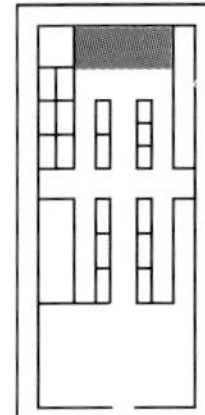

The Opera

The Second Empire was a period of massive redevelopment in Paris, under the aegis of Baron Haussmann. One of the city's largest projects was the construction of the Nouvel Opera, which was launched by Napoleon III in 1860; the works were to last for fifteen years, employ an entire generation of artists and make a lasting influence on subsequent Western architecture. The small existing opera-house in Rue Peletier had always been considered temporary premises, but until December 1860 no project for a replacement had been found acceptable. A contest was organised for the contract in that month, of which the eventual victor was Charles Garnier, an unknown young architect. The first stone of the new Opera was laid in 1862, and by 1867 the façade had been completed; but the war of 1870 brought the works to a halt, and the building could not be inaugurated till the 5th of January 1875.

A room has been set aside at the Musée d'Orsay to cover every aspect of this great monument, describing the problems of urban planning, architecture and decoration encountered by the Opera's builders, as well as the theatrical events that later took place within it. The display has been organised by Richard Peduzzi.

A scale model (1/100) of the entire Opera quarter as it was in 1914 shows some of the obstacles that Garnier had to face. The main problem lay in siting his construction within Haussmann's street plans. How was the architect to deal with the tall surrounding buildings and lack of open space around the site? He would have to work with grey, tightly-packed, regular façades and straight avenues, whereas Garnier had always favoured gardens, porticoes, low houses and narrow, winding streets. Though he had to bow to the rules of Haussmann's redevelopment, he rejected its architectural norms. In Garnier's Opera, curves were used instead of straight lines and ornemental exuberance was preferred to austerity. The regular gave way to the picturesque; the building was laden with coloured marbles, green and pink porphyry and shiny bronzes, while the great copper dome gleamed above the sober grey of Haussmann's townhouses. Today, ironically, the Opera epitomises the Second Empire and Haussmann's Paris.

Delimited to the north by the rue de Provence, to the east by the rue de Choiseul, to the south by the rue Saint-Augustin and to the west by the rue Caumartin, the scale model shows the complex links between the administrative centre (the new Louvre), the Opera, the Grands Magasins (department store) area, the headquarters of the banks and the Gare Saint-Lazare.

The scale model of the Opera quarter exhibited in the Musée d'Orsay was built by Rémy Munier, assisted by Eric de Leusse. The length-ways cross section of the Opera was built in Rome by L'Atelier, under the direction of Richard Peduzzi.

Aerial view of the Opera Quarter

Jean-Baptiste Carpeaux
1827-1875
Charles Garnier (1825-1898)
1869
Bronze
76 / 54.5 cm

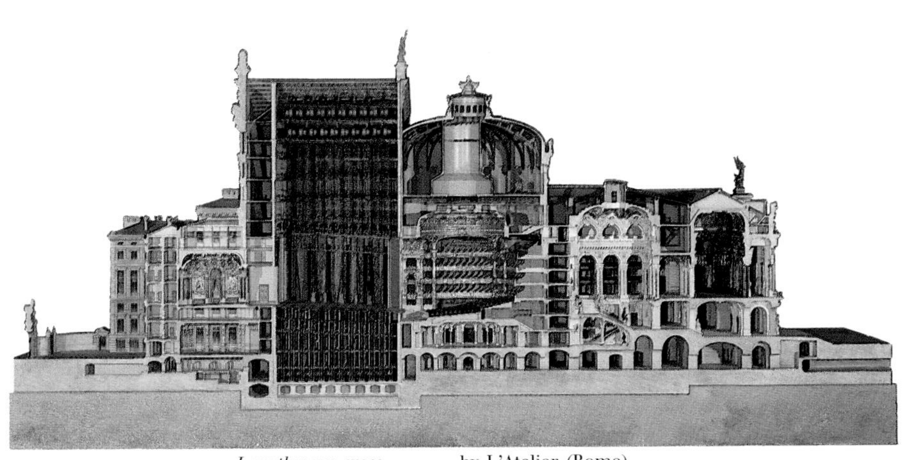

Lengthways cross-section of the Opera
Plaster

by L'Atelier (Rome)
directed by
Richard Peduzzi

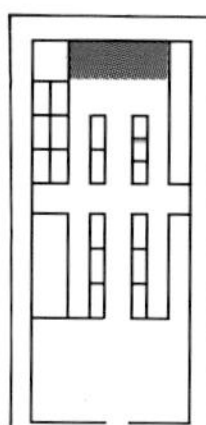

The cross-section of the Opera shows how carefully Garnier organised its various areas. He wanted anyone who passed by to know immediately what building this was; without being an architect, the visitor should be able to "identify the foyer, the spectator galleries, the stage and the administrative offices, whose shape and character, far from being masked, are bold and obvious, and all under the same roof". The scale model also shows the importance of the painted and sculpted décor, every element of which was supervised by Garnier, along with the constituent parts of the polychrome façade.

Viollet-le-Duc, one of the losing candidates in the 1860 competition, was highly critical of Garnier's interior, in which the auditorium is treated with maximum simplicity, so as not to distract spectators' attention from the music. Instead, Garnier concentrated his attention on the stairway and foyer of the building: here, the spectators themselves become actors, on a stage set by the architect. They arrive from the side through one of the pavilions, then cross the low, sparsely-decorated central vestibule. Then they are suddenly confronted with the soaring grandeur of the main staircase, after which they finally arrive at the auditorium.

A large number of works in the Musée d'Orsay are connected in some way with the Opera. Among them are sketches by Carpeaux for *La Danse (The Dance)*, along with the original group in stone (replaced on the main façade of the Opera by a plaster copy). There are also a number of maquettes of sculptures and decorative elements lent by the Opera's architectural agency, a maquette of the stage built for the 1900 Universal Exhibition (lent by the Musée de l'Opéra) and a rotating exhibition of maquettes of décor (also lent by the Musée de l'Opéra).

Albert-Ernest
Carrier-Belleuse
1824-1887
Torchère (Candelabra)
Study for the
main staircase
Circa 1872
Plaster
53.1 / 26.2 cm

Eugène Lequesne
1815-1887
Renommée retenant Pégase
(Fame Restraining Pegasus)
Study for the gable
of the auditorium
1866-1867
Plaster
62.8 / 44 cm

Jean-Baptiste
Carpeaux
1827-1875
La danse (The Dance)
Model for
original relief
1867-1868
Plaster
232 / 148 cm

Maquette of the Opera stage
built for the 1900 Paris
Universal Exhibition

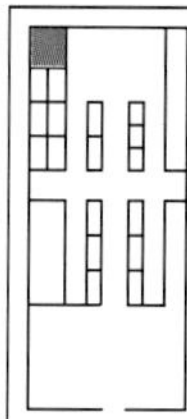

A display of the architecture of the second half of the 19th century has been installed in one of the clock rooms of the old Gare d'Orsay. The broad and vertical nature of this space and its uncovered metal structures make it ideal for an exhibition of architecture as related to sculpture and the decorative arts. It was obviously impossible for the museum planners to deal with all the problems of architecture and redevelopment in France and abroad, and difficult (to say the least) to cover the great modernising transformations of Paris carried out by Napoleon III and Haussmann. For example, how to describe in museum terms the reorganisation of the capital, the annexation of the suburban communes, the creation of the 20 arrondissements in 1860 and the building of three new road networks to open up the quartiers and link them to one another? And how to trace the subsequent development of the new quartiers, the laying out of parks, throughfares and sewage systems? The scale model of the Opera quarter shows some of the problems involved in Haussmann's planning — arrangement of roads, typology of buildings, handling of façades — while the mezzanine is reserved for an explanation of the transformation of Paris. Victor Navlet's great painting shows the pre-Haussmann capital in 1855, as viewed from a captive balloon. The countryside is still very close, and the future 13th, 14th, 5th and 6th arrondissements are clearly discernible. A series of independent communes stretch away from the centre, and outside Ledoux' tollgates Paris is still a labyrinth of trees and lanes. Rustic buildings surround isolated constructions like the Salpêtrière hospital, and the first factories and wharves are visible by the Seine at Javel.

Charles Garnier
1825-1898
Jean-Charles-Auguste
Coulon
1804-1861
*House for rental,
2nd class,
details of façade*

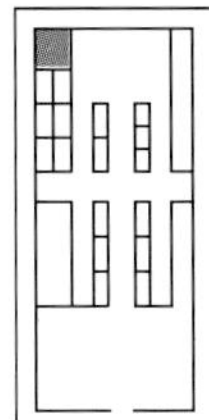

The Second Empire was gripped by architectural fever, and architects, though officially enjoined to abide by strict decorative rules (the ideal Haussmann building was described as 'surveyor' architecture') managed all the same to produce highly individualised work. To illustrate this, the museum planners have brought in pieces of exterior architecture such as one might see today on a walk through Paris or through one of the great principal towns. The motifs were selected from various contemporary publications devoted to recent construction work. Perspectives, elevations, cross-sections and details of this type served to propagate basic architectural models; these are displayed at the Museum in the form of polychrome reliefs fixed to Richard Peduzzi's tower construction, the aim of which is to retrace the history of contemporary architecture and decorative ornamentation.

Apart from the variety of their decorative vocabulary (caryatids, piers, chains, pilasters etc.), these reliefs give us an idea of the various schools they represent: rationalist, like Henri Labrouste (1801-1875) builder of the Bibliothèque Sainte-Geneviève (1843-1856), or Anatole Baudot (1834-1915) builder of the Lycée Lakanal; classical, like Duc (1802-1879) who designed the Palais de Justice in 1868, or Alfred Napoleon between 1856 and 1858.

The diversity of new programmes and use of new materials such as bricks, ceramics or mosaics, are also illustrated on the tower. Schools and lycées (Aillant-sur-Tholan and Sceaux); hospitals (Berck-sur-Mer); markets (the central Halles and the Marché des Martyrs in Paris); stations (project by Formigé); churches (Nœux-les-Mines, Marseille Cathedral); factories (the Menier factory at Noisiel, factory chimneystacks). Brick had a resounding success at the 1889 Universal Exhibition (Palais des Beaux-Arts, by Formigé) and soon began to be blended with stone.

Louis Clémentin
Bruyerre
1831-1887
Décor for a hallway

Victor-Marie-Charles
Ruprich-Robert
1820-1887
Private townhouse,
2nd class,
decoration for
a pier between
two windows

Jules Amoudru
House for rental,
2nd class,
detail from façade

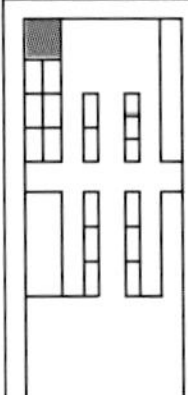

Viollet-le-Duc

For many, the name of Viollet-le-Duc is synonymous with misplaced restoration work; he is still ignorantly (and wrongly) accused of disfiguring old buildings, despite the fact that his first concern was always to understand their construction, equilibrium, originality and historic interest. We need only look at the masterly restoration, not to say creation, of the Château de Pierrefonds, to grasp not only Viollet-le-Duc's perfect knowledge of mediaeval architecture, but also his astonishing formal imagination. He was also modestly responsible for many country churches, manors and houses, in which he proved his ability to adapt and blend décor with function. Moreover, Viollet-le-Duc was a staunch opponent of the Ecole des Beaux-Arts and the architecture of the Grand Prix de Rome, which he considered unfit for human habitation. While his own work forcibly demonstrates that the Gothic style was well suited to 19th century buildings, it never overflows into anecdote, picturesqueness or sentimentalism about the past. On the contrary, Viollet-le-Duc's architectural principles were carefully grounded and reasoned; as he explains in one of his most extraordinary books, *Entretiens sur l'architecture (Conversations about architecture)*, 1863, his goal was a form of rationalised modernity. 'Entretiens sur l'architecture' expresses his vision of an architecture in which shape and substance are one, superfluous decoration is dismissed, and materials and their possibilities are respected to the utmost. This book is generally viewed as a seminal work of modern architecture; and even the champions of Art Nouveau such as Guimard and Sullivan acknowledged their debt to it.

Viollet-le-Duc first participated in, then overtook and enriched the ideas of Labrouste and Hittorf on the use of coulours in architecture. Later, he developed a theory of his own on the concept of painted decoration, especially after 1840 when he was engaged in the restoration of the Sainte-Chapelle with Duban and Lassus. For him, colour was not merely an accentuation of structures and forms, but also a vehicle, like light, for manipulating space. The décor of the chapel in the choir of Notre-Dame (c. 1866-1867) is still the best example of Viollet-le-Duc's thinking in regard to monumental polychromy, despite its lamentable condition. Working from plates from the architect's book *Peintures murales des chapelles de Notre-Dame (Mural Paintings in the Chapels of Notre-Dame)*, the Musée d'Orsay has reproduced plaster reliefs of these designs, which show how bright and fresh Viollet-le-Duc's colours originally were.

Painted mural design
from the chapels of Notre-Dame
Chapelle Saint-Vincent-de-Paul,
altar pillar

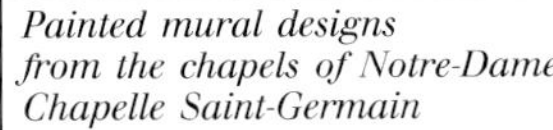

Painted mural designs
from the chapels of Notre-Dame
Chapelle Saint-Germain

Painted mural designs
from the chapels of Notre-Dame
Chapelle Saint-Guillaume

Painted mural designs
from the chapels of Notre-Dame
Chapelle Sainte-Geneviève

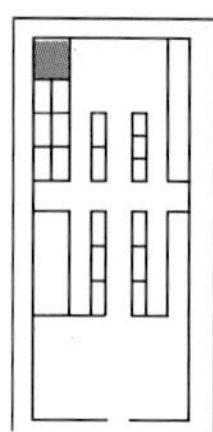

He sought an effect based on mat colour harmonies, using flat tints contoured with black lines to inhibit any blurring of tones. The coloured surfaces are broken up by highly varied motifs, such as flowerets, foliated scrolls, ribbons and chevrons, and this coloured ornamentation offsets the basic architectural forms of pillars, colonnettes, niches, etc.

From Viollet-le-Duc and William Morris to Art Nouveau, one of the main preoccupations of the second half of the nineteenth century was the idea of a composite architecture which would cover interior design, giving the same attention to plans, elevations, and wallcoverings as to the smallest detail of furniture. In Viollet-le-Duc's view, decoration was the greatest of all the arts. He developed his theories not only in his *Entretiens* but also in his didactic works for young people. *Histoire d'une maison (Story of a House)*, which was published by Hetzel in 1873, concerns a boy of sixteen who, with the help of his cousin, an architect, draws up plans and directs the building of a house down to the last detail. The architect suggests printed wallpapers which are cheap and "substantial to look at", with the "warm, velvety tones of tapestries... the coarse grain of the fabric resembles tapestry stitching, and the distempered colours have the same mat tones as wool". Here Viollet-le-Duc is harking back to a mediaeval technique, whose originality he extols: "That way, one can be sure of not seeing one's wallpaper reproduced in everyone else's house."

The plaster reliefs in the Pavillon Amont were manufactured in Rome by Enzo Ellardelli; relief painting and wall paper printing was carried out in the Nanterre-Amandiers workshops, under the direction of Richard Peduzzi

Ruprich-Robert, like Viollet-le-Duc, was never content to make sterile copies from the past. He invented a kind of ornamental vocabulary which was directly inspired by nature, with a range of compositions, friezes, panels, capitals and floral rosettes for decorating houses and buildings. Architects, painters, sculptors, ornamenters and industrial artists drew inspiration from his *Flore Ornementale,* examples of which can be seen on many Paris façades, as well as in the works of Grasset and Mucha.

Printed wallpaper for
Histoire d'une maison
The Billiard Room

Printed wallpaper for
Histoire d'une maison
The Salon

Printed wallpaper for
Histoire d'une maison
The Dining Room

Victor-Marie-Charles
Ruprich-Robert
1820-1887
Floral rosette,
potato flower
and Virginia
tulip-tree
Plaster
∅ 53 cm

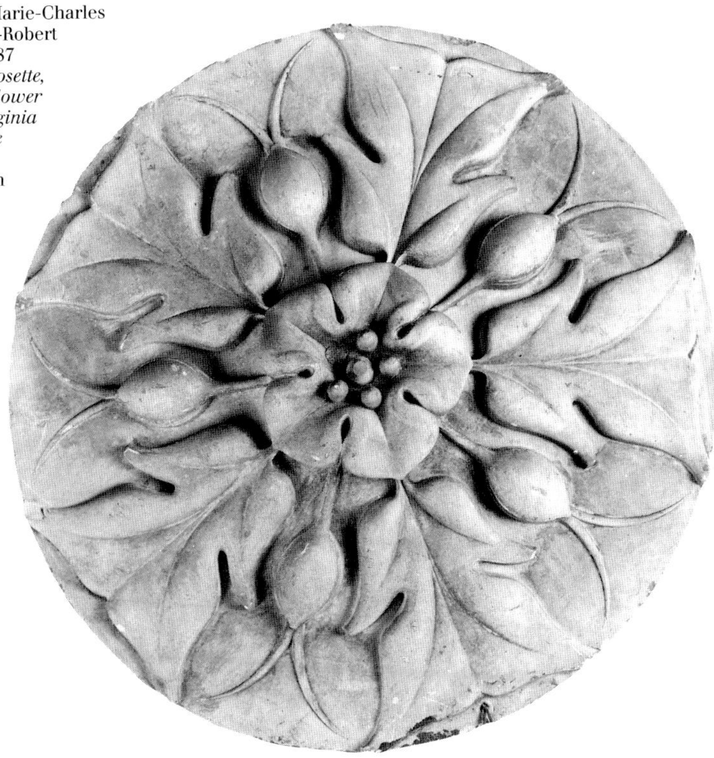

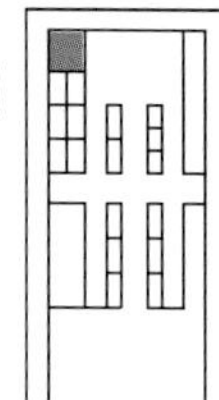

Pugin, Morris, Webb, Mackmurdo, Jeckyll, Godwin, Sullivan

In Great Britain, the process of industrialisation begun in the second half on the 18th century brought about a reaction against the dehumanising effects of factory labour. The theoretical reaction was led by John Ruskin, who rejected industrial work and dreamed of a return to the Middle Ages. A more conciliatory, pragmatic approach was that of Henry Cole, the organiser of the first Universal Exhibition in London in 1851, who was the instigator of reforms aimed at bringing art and industry into alliance.

The main initiator of this movement was the architect A.W. Pugin, who worked out a form of architecture based on a close partnership between arts, crafts and technical progress. Pugin advocated a return to Gothic styles, and gradually moved towards rational art, in much the same way as Viollet-Le-Duc. He designed simple, well-constructed furniture, which did not attempt to hide modes of assembly such as tenons, mortises and pins. In general the rôle of Arts and crafts movement was vitally important: professionals like Pugin, Webb, Burges, Mackmurdo, Godwin, Gimson and Voysey were all looking for a form of total art. They believed what what was necessary to daily life must be intrinsically beautiful, and that everything should be examined with the same attention to detail: wallpapers, printed or woven textiles, plain or painted furniture, ceramics (faïence and stoneware rather than porcelain), practical copper utensils and glass.

William Morris, who created the firm of William Morris and Co. in 1861, was the only individual who contrived to reconcile craft work with industrial distribution. Morris began as a painter, and was closely linked to pre-Raphaelites like Rossetti and Burne-Jones with whom he often collaborated. Morris also worked in perfect accord with the architect Philip Webb, who designed the 'Red House', which Morris fitted out for his own use in 1859. The solid wood sideboard built by Morris and Webb shows their partiality for furniture inspired by the Middle Ages, heavy in form and richly coloured. For the Earl of Carlisle, Morris designed an interior décor with a floral frieze by Burne-Jones depicting the legend of Psyche. Plant and flower motifs of this type, endlessly reproduced on fabrics and wallpapers, remain the best-known element of Morris' work. In 1876-1877, with the skilful help of William de Morgan, he transferred them onto brilliant glazed earthenware panels, to decorate the walls of Membland Hall.

Christopher Dresser
(1834-1904)
Hukin and Heath,
Birmingham

Soup Turen
Patent 1880
Silver plate and ebony
21 / 31 cm ∅ 23.5 cm

William de Morgan
1839-1917

Plat aux aigles
(Eagle plate)
Circa 1880-1885
Earthenware,
copper glaze
∅ 41 cm

Morris and Company
after William Morris
(1834-1896)

Painted wood-work
(detail)
1880

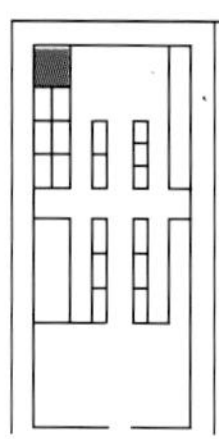

The contradiction inherent in the *Arts and Crafts* movement was its desire to inject beauty into all objects, whatever the cost. The result was expensive work which only rich people could afford. Following Morris' example, a number of artists formed craft guilds; these proved mostly ephemeral, because they rejected industrial techniques on principle. A.H. Mackmurdo, one of the most original personalities in the movement, formed his *Century Guild* in 1882 with William de Morgan, Selwyn Image and Voysey.

The *Century Guild* first came to public notice at the International Exhibition in Liverpool, where Mackmurdo presented a high-backed, corniced chair, along with the cabinet now in the Musée d'Orsay. The spare lines and rectilinear structure of this piece testify to Japanese influence; the paintwork on the two leaves is probably by Selwyn Image. William de Morgan's flamboyant glazed faïence owes much to Persian and Islamic techniques. Voysey, the last member of the Guild, spent over fifty years designing patterns for wallpapers and textiles, and used skilful blends of stylised and natural forms for his silk hangings.

By contrast, Jeckyll, Godwin and Dresser set out to be the servants of industry. The discovery of Japanese decorative art allowed them to introduce light, angular, stripped-down forms (see Godwin's *Hanging Shelves*). Dresser spent many years in Japan; his silverware designs are astonishingly modernistic, rigorous and pure.

In the United States, Louis Henry Sullivan was the pioneer of 20th century American architecture and the master of Frank Lloyd Wright (with whom he later collaborated). The décor of the Trading Room of the Chicago Stock Exchange (1984) is perhaps the outstanding example of the interior work of the first Chicago school; here Sullivan expressed his concept of organic decoration, which forms an integral part of the structure itself.

Edward Welby Pugin
1834-1875
Chair
Oak, bronze, velvet
86 / 51 / 53 cm

Arthur Heygate Mackmurdo
1851-1942
Chair
Circa 1886
Mahogany, wool and silk
127 / 46.5 / 59 cm

Edward William Godwin
1833-1886
Hanging shelves with glass-doored cabinet
Circa 1877
Mahogany, glass
132 / 69.5 / 23.5 cm

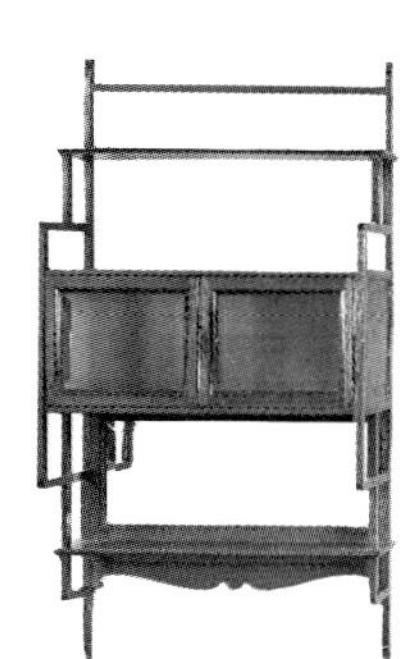

Philip Webb
1831-1915
Morris, Marshall, Faulkner and Co.
Work Bench
Circa 1860-1868
Oak, brass
73 / 167 / 61 cm

Upper level, second part of the visit

Moreau-Nélaton Collection

Daumier, Fantin-Latour, Manet, Monet, Pissarro, Sisley

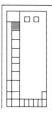

Etienne Moreau-Nélaton (1859-1927) was not only a painter, but also one of the great art historians of his time and an incomparable patron. To the best paintings he inherited from his grandfather, Adolphe Moreau (1800-1859), he added major works from the 1830s and began assembling the Impressionist sector of the collection. After 1906, he gave the Louvre what was qualitatively the most beautiful ensemble of 19th century works in existence: 100 canvases, including 37 Corots, 11 Delacroix, works by Decamp, Géricault, Daumier *(La République – The Republic)*, Puvis de Chavannes *(Le rêve – Dream)*, Manet, Monet, Morisot, Sisley, Pissarro, Fantin-Latour *(Hommage à Delacroix)*, Maurice Denis, Helleu, Besnard and Maillol. There was also a magnificent collection of drawings and aquarelles (about 3,000 sheets and 100 sketchbooks), along with many autographs (600 by Millet). To the Bibliothèque Nationale, the great collector left a considerable fund of engravings and documents relative to the artists he had studied. The ensemble of Moreau-Nélaton's Impressionist paintings are exhibited at the Musée d'Orsay, while a group of rooms at the Louvre is reserved for the canvases by the "1830 school" (Corot, Delacroix, etc.). Daumier's career as a painter began when he was about forty. *La République (La République nourrit ses enfants et les instruit – The Republic (The Republic nourishing and teaching her Children)* was chosen from five hundred-odd other entries to a contest organized by the provisional republican government, to celebrate its victory over Louis-Philippe. The project was never completed; but Daumier's sketch remains remarkable for its monumental construction, its expressive power, and its warm tones of red, brown and slightly transparent green. The brushwork is broad and decisive, whilst the composition is inspired by allegories of Charity from antiquity and the Renaissance.

In his first great painting, *Hommage à Delacroix*, Fantin-Latour recalls the collective portraits of 17th century Holland, in the group of figures and the muted russets, blacks and whites. Intended to render tribute to Delacroix, who had died unacclaimed in 1863, the painting includes the artist himself, Whistler with his curly hair, the fairhaired Manet and the ravaged features of Baudelaire. Critics saw this painting as no more than a manifesto for the realist painters, or a collection of good likenesses. They had expected a heroic work, an apotheosis, and instead were presented with images of contemporary life. The group was condemned for its lack of unity, its brutal colours and its photographic immobility.

Le déjeuner sur l'herbe is unquestionably the "historical" centrepiece of the collection. When he presented this canvas for the 1863 Salon, Manet was already considered by artists and critics as the head of a group in search of a new direction in

Claude Monet
1840-1926

Les coquelicots
(Poppies)
1873
Oil on canvas
50 / 65 cm

Edouard Manet
1832-1883

La blonde aux seins nus
(Blonde Woman with
Bare Breasts)
Circa 1878
Oil on canvas
62.5 / 52 cm

Edouard Manet
1832-1883

Le déjeuner sur l'herbe
(entitled *Le bain,*
Bathing in 1863)

1863
Oil on canvas
208 / 264.5 cm

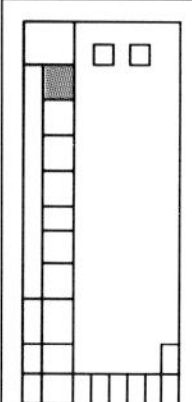

II

painting, whilst others reproached him, with some justice, for his free, rapid technique, his "mania for seeing things in patches", and his subject matter drawn from modern life. Although it was full of references to the old Masters (Titian's *Le concert champêtre – Open Air Concert* at the Louvre, and an engraving after Raphaël), *Le déjeuner* was turned down by the jury; however, the decisions were generally so injust that year that Napoleon III decided to open an annex, the famous "Salon des Refusés". *La Blonde aux seins nus (Blonde Woman with Bare Breasts)*, painted in bright light with a fluid, rapid style, shows how Manet drew closer to the Impressionists after the war of 1870. Monet, after travelling first to London, then to Holland *(Zaandam*, 1871) eventually settled in Argenteuil. Here he produced his vague, dreamlike vision of flowering lilacs *(Lilas, temps gris – Lilacs, Grey Weather*, 1872) and embarked on his investigation of the fleeting changes in water surfaces and the atmosphere *(Chasse-Marée à l'ancre – Coasting-Lugger at Anchor*, circa 1871). *Les coquelicots (Poppies)* also from this period, has become one of the most famous of all Impressionist paintings. Here Monet evokes the vibrant feel of a summer's day using scattered patches of colour; while the later *Le pont du chemin de fer à Argenteuil (The Railway Bridge at Argenteuil)*, circa 1873, is painted with quick, fragmented brushstrokes. This painting is in strong contrast to the sensitive, Corot-like vision of Alfred Sisley at this time *(Passerelle d'Argenteuil – Footbridge at Argenteuil*, 1872).

Honoré Daumier
1808-1879

La République
(The Republic)
Sketch for
the 1948 contest
Oil on canvas
73 / 60 cm

II

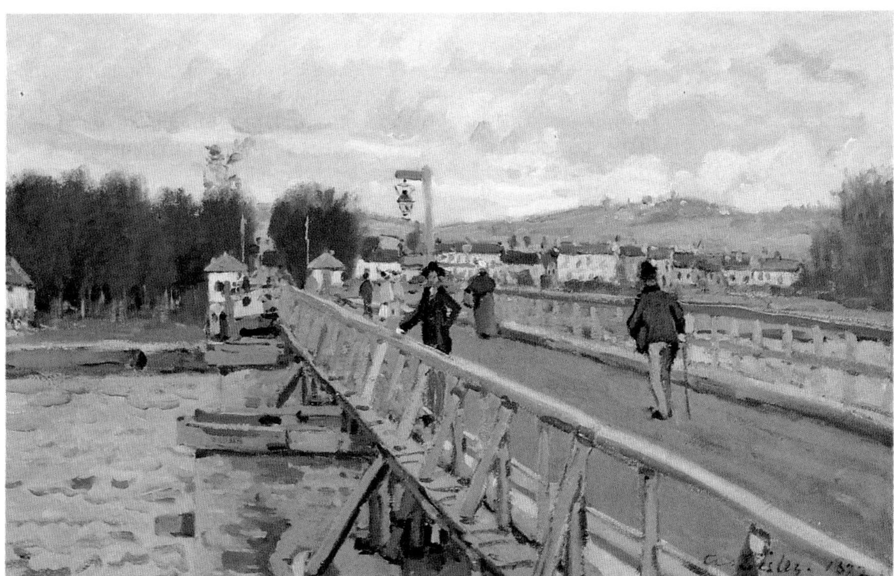

Alfred Sisley
1839-1899

Passerelle d'Argenteuil
(Footbridge at
Argenteuil)
1872
Oil on canvas
39 / 60 cm

Whistler, Caillebotte, Morisot, Degas, Manet, post 1870

James MacNeil Whistler, an American painter who divided his time between London and France, was closely associated with Fantin-Latour and the realist followers of Courbet. The official establishments of both England and France were suspicious of Whistler, whose taste for Japanese art attracted him to simple lines and refined neutral-tinted harmonies, as in his portraits and famous views of the Thames. *Arrangement in Grey and Black N° 1* or *The Artist's Mother* acquired for the national collection on the initiative of the poet Mallarmé and the critic Théodore Duret, is one of Whistler's most universally admired works. Spare lines, simple forms and limited colour range constitute his pictorial technique in this painting, of which he wrote, "For me, it is interesting because it is a portrait of my mother, but can or should the public be concerned with the model's identity? A painting should stand purely on the merits of its composition."

Gustave Caillebotte, collector and patron, also started out as a realist, with scenes of contemporary life *(Les raboteurs de parquet – Planing the Floor)* and views of Paris.

Berthe Morisot, Manet's pupil and sister-in-law, took part in most of the Impressionist exhibitions; she specialized in painting in the open air, but continued to paint portraits and interior scenes. *Le berceau (The Cradle)*, presented in 1874 at the first Impressionist exhibition, attests to her great subtlety and harmonious use of luminous, fresh colours.

"No art could be less spontaneous than mine. What I do is the result of careful reflection and a study of the great masters", wrote Degas, whose genius lay in creating the illusion of immediacy by way of painstaking research and careful construction. Degas constantly returned to his compositions; he was never satisfied, a perfectionist of line and draughtsmanship who remained independent and apart from the mainstream of the Impressionists. He did not share their obsession with landscapes and light changes, but this did not prevent him from exhibiting his paintings alongside theirs in the common cause of artistic freedom.

Berthe Morisot
1841-1895
Le berceau
(The Cradle)
1872
Oil on canvas
56 / 46 cm

James Mac
Neil Whistler
1834-1903

Arrangement in Grey
and Black n° 1
or *The Artist's Mother*
1871
Oil on canvas
144.3 / 162.5 cm

Gustave Caillebotte
1848-1894

Les raboteurs
de parquet
(Planing the Floor)
1875
Oil on canvas
102 / 146.5 cm

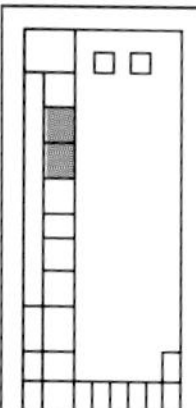

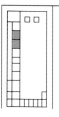

"Your need is for natural life; mine is for artificial", he explained to Pissarro. Intrigued by Baudelairian 'modernity' and by the search for new subject matter, Degas turned to the lively world of the racecourse and the closed environment of the Opera. Both gave him an opportunity to study movement closely, and to produce original, asymmetrical compositions. Like Manet, whom he met at the Louvre, Degas was interested in the cafés; *L'absinthe (Absinthe)*, apart from its naturalist theme, reveals an aspect of ordinary life which was taken up in litterature by Zola *(L'Assommoir – The Bludgeon)*. This canvas also attests to Degas' inventive approach to space, which he suggests rather than depicts by placing his figures off-centre, a fluid perspective being created by tables in the foreground.

II

Whether viewed from below *(Répétition d'un ballet sur la scène – Dress Rehearsal for a Ballet*, 1874), in accelerated, receding perspective *(La classe de danse – Dancing Class*, 1873-1875/1876) or within an animated space varied by the play of doors and mirrors *(Le foyer de la danse à l'Opéra – Backstage at the Ballet at the Opera*, 1872), the world of the dance allowed Degas to use the colours of his palette with sometimes acid effect. He observes, with irony and lucidity, what goes on behind the scenes: tired dancers relaxing, stretching, scratching their backs, in graceless poses. After 1880, colour began to assume greater importance in Degas' paintings and pastels. Gradually, colour began to dictate form, completing and supplanting draughtsmanship and line. This is true of *Danseuses bleues (Blue Dancers)*, whose daring composition and glittering artificial light rendered with touches of intense blue, green, yellow and pink, reflect the excitement of an enchanted world.

Racecourses were places of special importance for Degas, where he could paint the bright colours of the jockeys' shirts, along with the shining, lathered coats of the horses and their almost unbalanced motions.

Degas was also an attentive portraitist of the bourgeoisie, whom he observed at work *(Portraits à la Bourse – Portraits at the Stock Exchange)* or at home *(Mme Jeantaud au miroir – Mme Jeantaud before her Mirror*, circa 1874).

Edouard Manet
1832-1883
Georges Clemenceau
(1841-1929)
Politician
1879
Oil on canvas
94.5 / 74 cm

Edgar Degas
1834-1917
Le champ de courses. Jockeys amateurs près d'une voiture
(The Racetrack, Jockeys near a Carriage)
1876-1887
Oil on canvas
66 / 81 cm

Edgar Degas
1834-1917
Portraits à la Bourse
(Portraits at the Stock Exchange)
Circa 1878-1879
Oil on canvas
100 / 82 cm

Edgar Degas
1834-1917
Dans un café,
dit aussi *L'Absinthe*
(In a Café, also known as *Absinth)*
1875-1876
Oil on canvas
92 / 68 cm

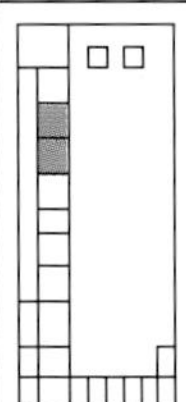

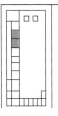

Other favourite subjects were workshops where women worked, such as fashionhouses or laundries. *Les repasseuses (Women Ironing)*, c. 1884-1886 took up a theme previously attempted by Daumier; here Degas uses a synthetic approach to the canvas itself, leaving certain zones uncovered by paint and shrouding others, so as to suggest a grey, humid atmosphere.

After 1881, Degas turned to sculpture. "I make wax models of people and animals, purely for my own satisfaction; I do this not to relax from painting and drawing, but in order to give my paintings and drawings more expression, ardour, life... these are exercises to get me going; they're my working documents." On Degas' death, about 150 sculptures were found in his studio, mostly in wax or clay; about 73 were recovered and handed over to the sculptor Bartholomé, an intimate friend of the artist, who restored and made casts in bronze of them in 1920-1921. In his horse series, Degas has left a meticulous study of equine movement based on Muybridge's photographs, while he handles *Danseuses (Dancers)* and *Femmes à leur toilette (Women washing)* in a free, spontaneous fashion. *La petite danseuse de 14 ans (Young Dancer of Fourteen)*, with her real hair, her tutu and her ballet slippers, was first exhibited to the public at the 1881 Impressionist exhibition, where one of the very few people to notice it was Karl-Joris Huysmans. Struck by its "terrible reality", Huysman referred to this little statuette as "... the only truly modern attempt at sculpture that I know of."

After 1870, Manet drew closer to Monet and Renoir, working in the open air with them at Argenteuil. His palette quickly acquired a new luminosity, as *Sur la plage (On the Beach)* attests. This painting was done at Berck-sur-Mer, in the summer of 1873, probably from life. It clearly demonstrates Manet's original temperament, in treating a favourite Monet or Boudin subject with complete disregard for the picturesque. To the distant, overshadowed ocean of ultramarine and emerald green, are contrasted the two silhouettes in the foreground, which are handled in classic harmonies of black and grey. The work also shows a Japanese influence, with its high horizon accentuated by dark blue and its flat colouring. Manet attempted the sea again in his *L'Evasion de Rochefort (Clearing Rochefort)*, 1880, but here the whole canvas is given over to the vivid green 'plaine marine', which is evoked with passionate strokes of the brush. *La dame aux éventails (Lady with Fans)*, 1873-1874, makes reference to an exotic, antiquarian Japan. This painting features Nina de Callias, a generous, whimsical personality who maintained a highly-valued artistic and literary salon frequented by Verlaine and Leconte de Lisle, among others. It was here that Manet and Mallarmé first met, after which they saw each other almost daily

Edgar Degas
1834-1917
*Danseuse,
grande arabesque,
premier temps
(Dancer, Arabesque,
first attempt)*
Bronze, 49 / 38.5 cm

Edgar Degas
1834-1917
*Femme surprise
(Woman caught
unawares)*
Bronze
41 / 28 cm

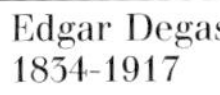

Edgar Degas
1834-1917
*Cheval faisant
une descente de main
(Horse being led)*
Bronze
18.6 / 9.5 cm

Edgar Degas
1834-1917
*Danseuses bleues
(Blue Dancers)*
Circa 1893
Oil on canvas
85 / 75.5 cm

for ten years. The portrait of *Stéphane Mallarmé*, 1876, gives us an insight into the intellectual refinement, charm and elegance on which their friendship was based.

Georges Clemenceau was a staunch friend of the Impressionists. Manet's powerful portrait of him is painted with a speed, precision and simplicity of composition that accurately reflects the politician's energy, determination and penetrating humour.

In the 1880's, Manet turned more and more to small still-lifes. Some were sent to his friends *(L'asperge – Asparagus*, 1880); others were expressions of his simple joy in painting. *(Le citron – Lemon*, 1880; *Œillets et clématites dans un vase de cristal – Carnations and Clematis Blossoms in a Crystal Vase*, circa 1882).

Edouard Manet
1832-1883

Sur la plage
(On the Beach)
1873
Oil on canvas
59.6 / 73.2 cm

Edgar Degas
1834-1917
Patined bronze,
cotton skirt,
pink satin
ribbon
98 / 35.2 / 24.5 cm

Petite danseuse
de quatorze ans
(Young Dancer
of Fourteen)
or *Grande danseuse*
habillée

II

The War of 1870 dispersed most of the artistic fraternity. Bazille was killed, Renoir was called up for Military Service, Degas and Manet remained in Paris and Cézanne retired to l'Estaque. Monet and Pissarro went to London, where they discovered the English landscape painters and the quick, feverish brushwork of Turner. It was at this time that they met the great dealer and artlover Paul Durand-Ruel, who had supported Courbet and Manet. Durand-Ruel became the defender of the two controversial painters, who at that time were living in destitution; they owed their survival in these difficult years to a small group of artlovers and critics.

Weary of seeing their work refused time and again by the juries of the official Salons, they decided to form a group of their own to mount free exhibitions, with no juries and no prizes. Their first manifestation took place in 1874, and included some 165 canvases by thirty painters, among whom were Cézanne, Monet, Degas, Sisley, Berthe Morisot, Pissarro, Renoir and Boudin. One of Monet's works, *Impression, soleil levant (Impression: Sunrise),* suggested to a malevolent critic the adjective 'Impressionist' which immediately stuck. More Impressionist exhibitions were mounted in 1876, 1877, 1879, 1880, 1881, 1882 and 1886, despite various defections and quarrels: only Manet steadfastly refused to take part. The group was soon enriched by fresh personalities such as Gustave Caillebotte, who quickly became a major patron after participating in the 1876 Exhibition. On his death in 1894 Caillebotte bequeathed his collection of his friends' work to the state; among other paintings, it included *Le Bal du Moulin de la Galette (Dancing at the Moulin de la Galette), La Balançoire (The Swing)* and *La Liseuse (Woman Reading)*, by Renoir; eight Monets, including *La Gare Saint-Lazare (The Saint-Lazare Station)* and *Régates à Argenteuil (Sailing Boats at Argenteuil);* seven Pissarros, including *Les toits rouges (Red Roofs);* several works by Manet, Sisley, Cézanne *(L'Estaque)* and Degas. The third Impressionist exhibition in 1879 exhibited works by the American painter Mary Cassatt, Albert Lebourg and Gauguin, who was a close friend of Pissarro. Finally, the arrival in 1886 of Seurat and Signac heralded a new departure in painting.

Monet, who now became the titular leader of the Impressionist movement, settled in Argenteuil between 1872 and 1878, where he was quickly joined by the rest of the group, even Manet. Renoir, Sisley, Caillebotte and Monet regularly worked together and shared their creative researches whilst each blossomed in his own style.

Monet forsook large-scale figurative compositions and concentrated entirely on painting sky and water, along with

Claude Monet
1840-1926

La rue Montorgueil
Fête du 30 juin 1878
(Rue Montorgueil,
Decked out with Flags,
30 June 1878)

1878
Oil on canvas
81 / 50 cm

II

the atmospheric vibrations, subtle reflections and fleeting effects of light. His subject matter during this period was principally the Seine, with its sailing yachts; Monet, like Daubigny before him, usually worked from a boat which he had turned into a floating studio. *Régates à Argenteuil*, a painting he left deliberately at the sketch stage, gives a double image of reality and its reflections; the painter's fragmented brushwork intensifies vivid colour rapports of green and red, green and blue, white and blue, and suggests the luminous, shimmering surface of the water. *Le bassin d'Argenteuil (The Dock at Argenteuil)*, 1875, a lively, animated canvas, celebrates the sky and the flux of clouds, while *Les barques, Régates à Argenteuil (Boating at Argenteuil)*, circa 1874, depicts a stormy, turbulent atmosphere and a grey, troubled river. Renoir painted his *La Seine à Argenteuil (The Seine at Argenteuil)*, in 1873.

Le déjeuner (Lunch), which was painted by Monet around 1873, is one of the few large Impressionist paintings from this period. It conveys the charm of a scene from daily life, the family meal, with the little Jean Monet playing by the table and the hat hung on a branch. The intimist theme and composition of this work remind us of Bonnard and Vuillard. But Monet was also interested in urban scenes: he painted no less than seven canvases entitled *La gare Saint-Lazare (St. Lazare Station),* with locomotives obscured by clouds of blue-white smoke. Six of these views were exhibited at the third Impressionist exhibition, and Zola wrote a highly complimentary article about them. "Monet has contributed some superb railway station interiors this year. You can almost hear the rumble of the trains as they surge forward, and see the clouds of steam rolling under the broad sheds. This is what painting today is all about... our artists must find the poetry of the railway station, just as their fathers found that of the woods and rivers." *La rue Montorgueil pavoisée*, 1878, shows the mastery, the glorious freedom of Monet, who can suggest anything he chooses with a flash of colour and a rapid stroke of the brush: rippling flags, crowds, noise, confused movement.

Renoir concentrated on applying Impressionist principles to the study of the human figure. Some of his most famous paintings, such as *Le bal du Moulin de la Galette (Dancing at the Moulin de la Galette), La balançoire (The Swing),* or *Torse de femme au soleil (Nude in the Sunlight)*, were executed while he was living in his Montmartre studio. 'Torse de femme' aroused violent criticism; it was even described as a "... pile of decomposing flesh". Renoir's aim in this canvas was to transcribe the glint of sunlight falling through the leaves. The shadows are in various tones, ranging from pale pink to violet; the face, which seems almost dissolved by light, serves to dehumanise the model.

Camille Pissarro
1830-1903

Les toits rouges
(Red Roofs)
1877
Oil on canvas
54.5 / 65.6 cm

Claude Monet
1840-1926

Régates à Argenteuil
(Boating
at Argenteuil)
Circa 1872
Oil on canvas
48 / 75 cm

Claude Monet
1840-1926

La gare Saint-Lazare
(Saint-Lazare Station)
1877
Oil on canvas
75.5 / 104 cm

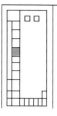

She is treated as an object of study, but infused nonetheless by Renoir's simple, characteristic sensuality. *La balançoire,* like *Le bal du Moulin de la Galette*, shows a similar intent: the figures and the ground shimmer with patches of light and shade. *Le bal du Moulin de la Galette* was painted on the spot, at a guinguette at the top of the Butte Montmartre, just under the famous windmill. Critics were baffled by Renoir's dissolving forms and vibrant colouring. "... the figures dance on a surface resembling the violet clouds that cover the sky just before a thunderstorm." Renoir was also an excellent portraitist, and earned his living at this profession. He received a number of commissions, notably *Mme Charpentier* 1876, the elegant wife of Georges Charpentier, publisher of Flaubert, Zola, Daudet and the Goncourts. Another fine portrait was *Claude Monet,* which shows the close ties between the two painters. *Alphonsine Fournaise*, 1879, is pictured in her father's restaurant at Chatou; this painting illustrates the bustling, friendly atmosphere along the banks of the Seine, just as described by Guy de Maupassant.

Pissarro settled at Pontoise in 1872; his *Coteau de l'Hermitage, Pontoise (Hermitage Hill, Pontoise)* displays a balanced equilibrium between light touch, refined colours and firm, structured framework. These principles were also adopted by Cézanne, who was working closely with Pissarro at that time. Pissarro's friendship with the painter Ludovic Piette gave him an opportunity to work in the Mayenne region, at Montfoucault: *La moisson à Montfoucault (The Harvest at Montfoucault)* is expansively handled, its subtle range of colours being applied with brush and palette knife. This work is in strong contrast to *Les toits rouges (Red Roofs),* whose solid composition, thick paintwork and high colours recall the first landscapes of l'Hermitage.

Sisley moved to the outskirts of Paris, between Louveciennes and Marly; here he painted landscapes etched by the perspective of a road *(La route, vue du chemin de Sèvres – Road, viewed from the Sèvres Footpath,* 1873), a subject which had inspired Corot before him; and his famous *Inondation à Port-Marly (Flooding at Port-Marly)*, a melancholy vision of a village transformed by a sheet of water and the presence of a grey, cloud-encumbered sky. *La Neige à Louveciennes (Snow at Louveciennes)*, 1878, is a fine example of Sisley's natural balance, discretion and sensitivity as an artist.

Pierre-Auguste Renoir
1841-1919
Claude Monet
1875
Oil on canvas
85.6 / 60.6 cm

Alfred Sisley
1839-1899
Inondation à Port-Marly (Flooding at Port-Marly)
1876
Oil on canvas
60 / 81 cm

Pierre-Auguste Renoir
1841-1919
Torse de femme au soleil (Nude in the Sunlight)
1876
Oil on canvas
81 / 64.8 cm

Pierre-Auguste Renoir
1841-1919
Le bal du Moulin de la Galette (Dancing at the Moulin de la Galette)
1876
Oil on canvas
131 / 175 cm

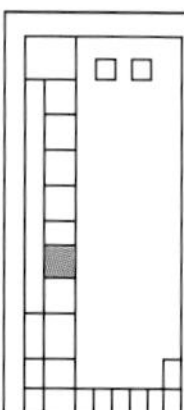

II

Monet's career, like Renoir's, continued full speed ahead into the 20th century, developing according to the houses and areas he inhabited. From 1878 to 1881, Monet lived at Vétheuil, where he depicted the atmosphere of the village *(Œglise de Vétheuil, neige – The Church at Vétheuil, Snowy Weather,* 1878-1879; *La Seine à Vétheuil,* circa 1879-1882), and notably the effects of the hard winter of 1879-1880, the frozen Seine, and the ensuing break-up of ice.

"I'm in ecstasy", wrote Monet in 1883. "Giverny is a wonderful place for me." Indeed, his arrival at this village heralded a new stage in his work. Giverny remained Monet's base for the rest of his life, a haven to which he constantly referred on his trips to Holland, the Normandy coast, Belle-Ile in Brittany (where he painted several pictures of the "unheard-of" marine colours), Antibes and the Creuse department of France. In Monet's two canvases entitled *Femme à l'ombrelle (Woman with Umbrella),* he attempted to represent figures in the open air, and to convey what he perceived as a luminous 'envelope' surrounding his instantaneous vision of them. The faces are scarcely drawn at all. Also at this time he had the idea of painting the same subject, turn and turn about, according to the changing seasons, times of day and prevailing qualities of light *(Meules, fin de l'été – Haystacks, End of Summer,* 1890). Other series followed, among them the *Cathédrales de Rouen (Rouen Cathedrals),* which were painted between 1892 and 1893 (though dated 1894). Five magnificent versions of this theme are exhibited in the Musée d'Orsay (from the bequest of Comte Isaac de Camondo, and from a purchase by the state from the artist in 1907). Monet did other series on London and Vétheuil, but the latter part of his work was totally devoted to Giverny. These "landscapes of water and reflected light" begin with clearly-outlined compositions, in which we recognise the *Pont japonais (Japanese Bridge)* which spans the pond; gradually, however, the canvases are invaded by a world of shifting, floating, captivating water-lilies, whose luxuriant colours finally exclude all else*. This phase of Monet's research reached its zenith in the decoration of two rooms in the Musée de l'Orangerie, a project conceived with the strong support of the artist's old friend and admirer, Georges Clemenceau. The museum was inaugurated in 1927, just after Monet's death.

* "Since the banks at that place were heavily wooded, the water depths would be stained a dark green by the mighty shadows of the trees, but sometimes, while walking there on clear evenings after stormy afternoons, I noticed the tone of the water had changed to a bright kingfisher blue, verging on violet, the colour of Japanese cloisonné. Here and there on the surface lay the strawberry blush of a waterlily bloom, with scarlet heart and white petals..." (Marcel Proust, *Du côté de chez Swann).*

Claude Monet - 1840-1926 - *La série des cathédrales de Rouen (Rouen Cathedral Series)*
1892-1893 - Oil on canvas

Le portail, Harmonie bleue (Main Door, Harmony in Blue) 91 / 63 cm	*Le portail Harmonie blanche (Main Door, Harmony in White)* 106 / 73 cm	*Le portail Harmonie bleue et or (Main Door, Harmony in Blue and Gold)* 107 / 73 cm	*Harmonie brune (Harmony in Brown)* 107 / 73 cm

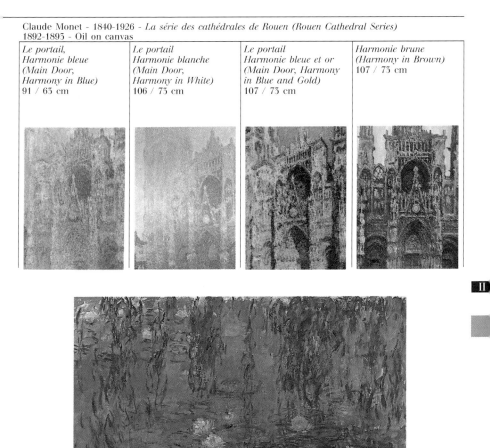

Claude Monet
1840-1926

Nymphéas bleus
(Blue Waterlilies)
Circa 1916-1919
Oil on canvas
200 / 200 cm

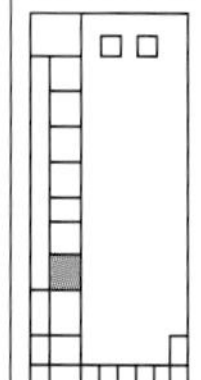

The beginning of the 1880's ushered in a period of reflection and crisis for all the artists of the Impressionist group. The expression of a new pictural manner which had the effect of dissolving forms seemed perfectly natural to Monet, but was perceived as a dangerous development by Renoir and rejected by younger artists. Renoir put the case bluntly to his dealer, Ambrose Vollard: "Towards 1883, I reached a crisis point in my work; I had followed Impressionism to its logical conclusion, and having done so I decided I could neither paint nor draw. In a word, I was stuck." For the first time in his life, Renoir had no material worries; he travelled to Algeria, where he discovered the Mediterranean light, the vivid colours and the motley animation of that country *(Fête arabe à Alger – Arab Celebration, Algiers,* 1881). In Italy, he rediscovered Raphaël and the Renaissance masters he had admired at the Louvre in his youth, and visited the great sites of classical antiquity: Naples, Pompeii and Sicily. He now paid much closer attention to draughtsmanship and line, as in *Danse à la ville (Dance in the City)* and *Danse à la Campagne (Dance in the Country)*, two large compositions from this time. Conceived as a pair, each of these paintings is made strongly individual by the use of simple structures and sharp contours; Renoir's range of colours is now more pure, with acidulated tones that are typical of the stage he was going through. Around 1888, he had another period of discouragement, rejected some of his work as 'too dry' and adopted a new approach, sometimes called 'nacré', or pearly, in which line gradually gives way to greater flexibility and warmer colours. *Les jeunes filles au piano (Girls at the Piano)*, which was the first of Renoir's works to be purchased by the state, on the initiative of Mallarmé in 1892, is executed in warm colours, golden light and soft, dainty brushwork. Another version on this theme, in colder and more contrasted tones, is found in the Walter-Guillaume Collection at the Musée de l'Orangerie.

Until his death Renoir continued to paint portraits, on an ever increasing scale, in vivid colours and whimsical costumes *(Monsieur et Madame Bernheim de Villers*, 1910). *Les baigneuses (Women Bathing)*, painted at Les Collettes, the artist's house in Cagnes-sur-mer, is an ambitious canvas, Renoir's last masterpiece. 'Les baigneuses' owes much to Rubens and the great Venetians; the figures are at one with the surrounding landscape, sharing in its warmth and sunlight. By now a martyr to arthritis, Renoir was heard to exclaim: "Now that I'm legless and armless, all I want to do is paint huge pictures. Veronese and weddings at Cana monopolise my dreams. Woe is me!"

Pierre-Auguste Renoir
1841-1919
Danse à la campagne
(Dance in the Country)
1882-1883
Oil on canvas
180 / 90 cm

Pierre-Auguste Renoir
1841-1919
Danse à la ville
(Dance in the City)
1883
Oil on canvas
180 / 90 cm

II

Gustave Caillebotte, in retreat in his house at Petit Gennevilliers, devoted himself to views of the Seine. *Voiliers à Argenteuil (Sailing Boats at Argenteuil)* circa 1888, testifies to Monet's influence in its handling of light and reflection, but Caillebotte's deeper attachment to reality is apparent in his precise observation of the design of the boats, their masts and their sails.

Pissarro too was a prey to doubt. Having been a landscape painter hitherto, he now paid more attention to human figures, which began to predominate in his work. *Jeune fille à la baguette (Young Girl with Stick)* is one of the main examples of this new approach, in which landscape is relegated to the background. The composition is both sensitive and structured, and the brushwork is sometimes fine and sometimes very thick, testifying to Pissarro's technical researches.

Camille Pissarro
1830-1903
La bergère (jeune fille à la baguette ; paysanne assise)
(The Shepherdess, peasant Girl with Stick)
1881
Oil on canvas
81 / 64.7 cm

Pierre-Auguste Renoir
1841-1919
Monsieur et Madame Bernheim de Villers
(Monsieur and Madame Bernheim de Villers)
1910
Oil on canvas
81 / 65.5 cm

Pierre-Auguste Renoir
1841-1919
Les baigneuses
(The Bathers)
Circa 1918-1919
Oil on canvas
110 / 160 cm

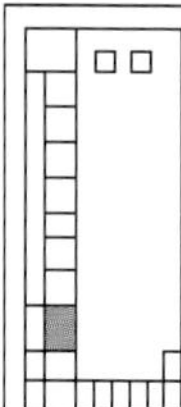

Cézanne

"Over the last 15 years, M. Cézanne has been more abused and maltreated by the public than any other artist. Every possible epithet has been attached to his name, and his works have been, and still are, greeted with gales of derisive laughter", wrote Georges Rivière after the third Impressionist exhibition in 1877, in which Cézanne took part. The artist's correspondence with his few faithful friends shows the depth of his isolation and self-doubt. After the publication of *L'Œuvre* in 1886, Cézanne thought he recognised himself in Zola's hero, Claude Rantier, characterized in the book as a 'failed genius' and 'self-consuming intelligence'. Cézanne's response was to break definitively with Zola, whom he had known since childhood in Aix, and with whom he had shared many hopes and dreams.

In 1861, Paul Cézanne announced to his father, a banker in Aix-en-Provence, that he wanted to be a painter. In the portraits of his uncle Dominique *(L'oncle Dominique en avocat – Uncle Dominique dressed as a Lawyer)* he uses new techniques: the canvas is covered in thick impasto, spread on with a knife, which enables him, through force of the paint alone, to convey relief, volume and intensity of colour without resorting to chiaroscuro. His earliest works were marked by his discovery of ancient and modern masters in the Louvre, especially the Venetians and the school of Caravaggio. Their influence is palpable in *La Madeleine (Mary Magdalen)*, circa 1868-1869, whose prostrate figure, grief-stricken attitude and dramatic intensity are heightened by the use of dark, powerfully-deployed colours. *Pastorale (Pastoral)* or *Idylle (Idyll)*, 1870, the theme of which foreshadows Cézanne's later research, betrays the same sources tempered by the romanticism and modernity of Manet's *Déjeuner sur l'herbe. Achille Emperaire*, a portrait verging on caricature of a crippled friend of his, also a painter from Aix, was rejected by the 1870 Salon.

In 1872, Cézanne came to live at Auvers-sur-Oise, where he worked with, and was influenced by, Pissarro. Two of his paintings were much ridiculed at the first Impressionist exhibition of 1874. *Une moderne Olympia (A Modern Olympia,* Gachet Collection), was an erotic, theatrical reinterpretation of Manet's original, which shows how Cézanne was moving towards higher key colours and technical brilliance. *La maison du pendu (The House of the Hanged Man)*, with its fragmented brushwork, clear tints, and choice of a simple motif, shows Pissarro's influence; but the firm touch and rigorous treatment of space are all Cézanne's own. It was with *L'Estaque*, a view of the coast near Marseille, that the artist imposed his own concept of space and perspective. The landscape in this painting is divided into three synthetic zones, which are very precisely demarcated by their contrasting colours.

Paul Cézanne
1839-1906

Les joueurs de cartes
(Card-Players)
Circa 1890-1895
Oil on canvas
47.5 / 57 cm

Paul Cézanne
1839-1906

L'Estaque
Circa 1878-1879
Oil on canvas
59.5 / 73 cm

Paul Cézanne
1839-1906

Pommes et oranges
(Apples and Oranges)
Circa 1895-1900
Oil on canvas
74 / 93 cm

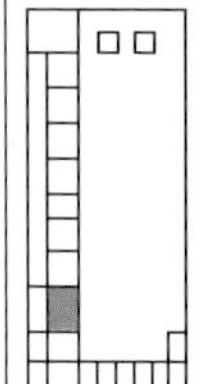

Le Pont de Maincy (The Bridge at Maincy), 1879, which was painted during a stay at Melun, marks Cézanne's definitive break with Impressionism, since it depicts a diffused landscape. Ever since 1870, Cézanne's work had been haunted by a need to integrate figures into his landscapes; again and again, in oils and aquarelles, he returned to the same figures in the same attitudes, usually inspired by drawings or sculptures. The result was that his work developed a special lyrical quality, exalting the harmony of man and nature with a predominant balance of blues and greens and a subtle interplay of space and volume. These works had a considerable influence on young artists like Maurice Denis, Matisse and Picasso, each of whom owned a version of *Les Baigneurs (Les Baigneurs – Men bathing*, 1890-1902, belonged to Maurice Denis).

The closed world described by *Joueurs de cartes (Card-Players)* was a pretext for a study in line and volume; of the five canvases Cézanne did on the subject, the version at the Musée d'Orsay probably displays his rendering of tension between forms and figures at its finest. *La femme à la cafetière (Woman with Coffee Pot)*, in which the subject is handled like a still life without emotion or sentiment, marks another point in the evolution of Cézanne towards geometrical figures with the aura of inanimate objects, and an approach to nature "...based on cylinders, spheres and cones".

From the beginning of his career, the still life was a favourite subject for Cézanne. *Le vase bleu (Blue Vase)*, circa 1885-1887, reveals one of his principal preoccupations, the study of light shed on objects and colours and the construction of space through the play of vertical and horizontal lines. Later, he adopted a fresh attitude to perspective, taking a bird's eye view of objects, often from several different angles at once *(Pommes et oranges – Apples and Oranges*, 1895-1900).

Cézanne's discoveries in regard to the simplification and synthesis of forms, the role of colour in the creation of space, and the perception of objects and figures from different vantage points, were later taken up, transformed and renewed by the Fauvist and Cubist painters.

Paul Cézanne
1839-1906
La femme à la cafetière
(Woman with
Coffee Pot)
Circa 1890-1895
Oil on canvas
130 / 96.5 cm

Paul Cézanne
1839-1906
L'oncle Dominique
en avocat
(Uncle Dominique
dressed as a Lawyer)
Circa 1866
Oil on canvas
63 / 52 cm

Paul Cézanne
1839-1906
Achille Emperaire
(1829-1898)
Circa 1868
Oil on canvas
200 / 120 cm

Paul Cézanne
1839-1906

Baigneurs
(Men Bathing)
Circa 1890-1892
Oil on canvas
60 / 82 cm

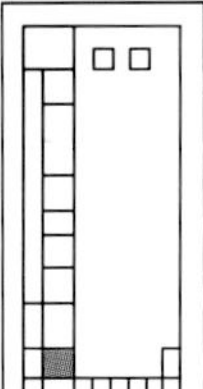

Toulouse-Lautrec

In 1895, La Goulue, a celebrated dancer at the Moulin Rouge music hall, commissioned Toulouse-Lautrec to decorate the booth she had rented at the Foire du Trône for her new Moorish dance routine. After the sale of the booth in 1896, the two canvases vanished until 1926, when they were discovered in a dealer's showroom, unwittingly cut up into eight pieces. They were subsequently bought by the state, and contain several of Toulouse-Lautrec's favourite models (eg. Jane Avril in her extravagant hat), along with famous personalities like Oscar Wilde and the critic Fénéon, depicted with the artist's customary verve.

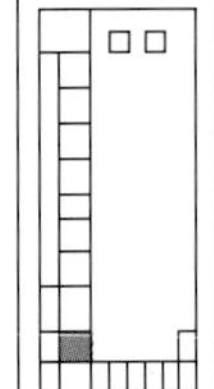

Pastels

Degas

Degas was a master of all the techniques of art: oils, pencil, water colours and charcoal. But he was also a genius of pastel, which he enriched by combining it with the others. He brought gouache, distemper and 'peinture à l'essence' (oils thinned with turpentine) to the aid of coloured crayons, transforming pastel into a richly transparent and profound medium. Degas also used pastel for monotypes*.

As time went by, pastel techniques acquired more and more importance in Degas' work. In 1869, after a visit to Boulogne, he painted a series of seascapes, recreating his impressions in the quiet of his studio, suggesting forms and outlines and conjuring up atmospheres from memory (*Falaises au bord de la mer; Marine*). Between 1873 and 1878, he turned to night time Paris, cafés, brothels and the ballet and opera for his subject matter.

Though sometimes pictured in repose (*Danseuse assise*, circa 1881-1883), Degas' dancers are usually captured in full movement (*L'étoile ou la danseuse sur la scène*, 1878, or *Fin d'arabesque*, circa 1877). The colours are flamboyant and

* Monotype: A one-off print from a metal plate on which a picture is painted, as in oil-colour or printing ink.

Henri de Toulouse-Lautrec
1864-1901
Panel for La Goulue's booth
at the Foire du Trône, Paris
La danse mauresque ou *Les Almées*
(Moorish Dance or *Dancing Woman)*
1895
Oil on canvas
285 / 307.5 cm

Henri de Toulouse-Lautrec
1864-1901
at the Foire du Trône, Paris
La danse au Moulin-Rouge
(Dancers at the Moulin Rouge)
(La Goulue and Valentin le Désossé)
1895
Oil on canvas
298 / 316 cm

II

Edgar Degas
1834-1917
Danseuse au bouquet saluant sur la scène
(Dancer on Stage with Bouquet,
Acknowledging Applause)
1878
Pastel on paper stuck to canvas
72 / 77.5 cm

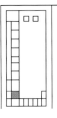

iridescent; their effect is strengthened by off-centre, abruptly cut-off compositions and powerful, mysterious light.

In 1886, at the last Impressionist exhibition, Degas showed a group of pastels entitled *Série de nus de femmes se baignant, se lavant, s'essuyant, se peignant ou se faisant peigner*. In this series, he used the same techniques as for his studies of dancers, with highly varied angles of view, multiple perspectives (sometimes foreshortened), and carefully gauged light heightened and varied by the use of rare colour tones. This emphasises the downy softness of the model's flesh, and *Le tub* is one of the most beautiful examples of this technique. Degas also used hatching, vertical lines in pastel which were more or less evenly spaced, to accentuate the luminosity and the forms of the bodies he was observing (*Après le bain, femme s'essuyant la nuque*, 1898; *La sortie du bain*, circa 1895-1898). Lastly, *Chez la modiste*, circa 1898, was the culmination of another series that was dear to Degas, which he had begun in 1879.

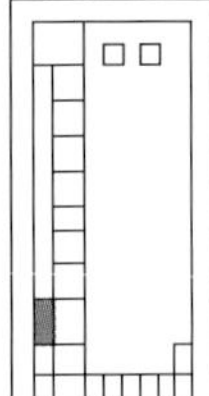

Rooftop Café
Consultation Room

The consultation room on the mezzanine of the Café des Hauteurs contains a number of information sources on the artistic period between 1848 and 1914. The bulk of these sources are Musée d'Orsay publications and essential catalogues, along with art films acquired of produced by the Museum which can be viewed in audiovisual cabins. Access is also provided here to a computer bank of images and texts, which may be consulted by author or title and offers a number of educational programmes on the second half of the 19th century. Here the visitor can pass easily from one field to the next, find out about works hitherto unknown to him, or even consult the museum's scientific database.

Edgar Degas
1834-1917
Le tub
(The Tub)
1886
Pastel on cardboard
600 / 830 cm

Degas' lucid, realistic and modern treatment of the female body.

The clock
from the Rooftop Café

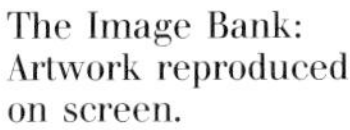

The Image Bank:
Artwork reproduced on screen.

Detail:
the image is analysed and preserved on a numbered optical disc.

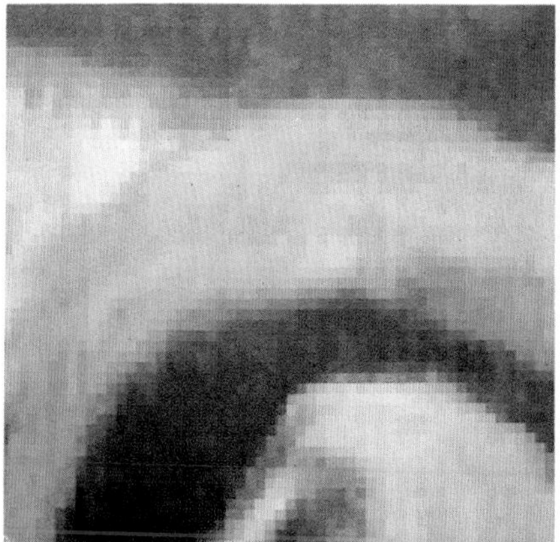

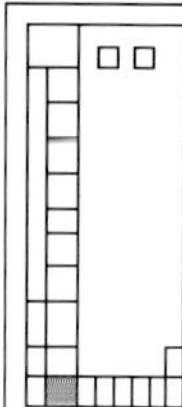

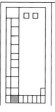

II

The life and the work of Vincent Van Gogh were intimately mingled. Every change or voyage he undertook, every whim of his anguished temperament, led him into some new period or fresh field of pictural investigation. Van Gogh was born in the province of Brabant; he was the son of a pastor and it was not until 1880, after his failure in a religious career, that he became a painter.

Van Gogh's first period in Holland is characterized by sombre works and thickly applied paint surfaces. The subjects tended to be peasants from the Belgian Borinage, a mining region where Van Gogh had tried to lead the life of a pastor.

In 1886, Van Gogh came to live in Paris, where his brother Théo was already installed as an employee of the picture-dealer Goupil. Théo's loyal affection and moral and financial support of his brother persisted throughout Vincent's short life; and it was to Théo that he unburdened his soul about himself and his work, in a copious, beautiful and sometimes heart-rending correspondence. Vincent's contacts with Pissarro, Gauguin, Emile Bernard and Toulouse-Lautrec were crucial to his art; from the Impressionists he learned the techniques of light and colour *(Le restaurant de la Sirène – The "La Sirène" Restaurant,* 1877). He frequented the 'Tambourin', a cabaret on the Boulevard de Clichy in Paris, and even organised an exhibition there. *L'Italienne (Italian Woman)*, no doubt a portrait of the patronne of this establishment, Agostina Segatori, is a heavily simplified image, with no shadows or perspective, off-centre and assertively rendered in broad, flat tints, intense and solid.

In February 1888, Vincent left Paris for Arles, where he discovered the light and heat of the South; his paintings from this period are dominated by colour and synthetic draughtmanship. Already drawn to portraiture, he found a model in his landlady, Mme Ginoux *(L'Arlésienne – The Woman of Arles)*: "I have finally done my Arlésienne... pale lemon-yellow background, the face greyish, the clothes black, black, black, straight Prussian blue. I have her leaning on a green table, and she sits in an orange-coloured chair." Vincent deeply admired Gauguin, and begged him to come to Arles: *La salle de danse à Arles (The Dance Hall of Arles)*, 1888, testifies to the influence of Gauguin and Emile Bernard, the co-discoverers of 'synthetisme' and 'cloisonnisme'. In 'La salle de danse', the forms are surrounded like elements of a stained glass window, painted in bright, flat colours, with very violent brushwork that brings the faces to the brink of distortion and caricature. The break with Gauguin, whom Van Gogh had physically attacked at the end of 1889, led him to cut off his left

Vincent Van Gogh
1853-1890
Portrait de l'artiste
(Portrait of the Artist)
1889
Oil on canvas
65 / 54.5 cm
Gift of Paul
and Marguerite Gachet, 1949

Vincent Van Gogh
1853-1890
L'église
d'Auvers-sur-Oise
(The Church at
Auvers-sur-Oise)
1890
Oil on canvas
94 / 74.5 cm
Acquired by
agreement with
Paul Gachet,
through an
anonymous Canadian
donation,
1951

Vincent Van Gogh
1853-1890
Le Docteur
Paul Gachet
(Doctor Paul Gachet)
(1828-1909)
1890
Oil on canvas
68 / 57 cm
Gift of Paul and
Marguerite Gachet,
1949

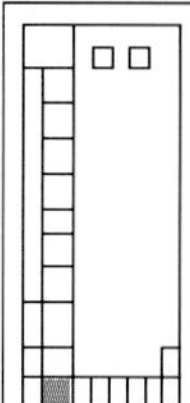

ear in a fit of madness. After this episode, he requested internment at the Saint-Rémy mental hospital. Here he painted a new version of *Chambre à Arles (Bedroom at Arles)*, in which colour completely predominates within a shifting perspective. Vincent's *Self-portrait* of 1889 is among the last of a series in which he anxiously examined his own image. The face rears up against a limpid background; it seems to shimmer and float, revealing Vincent's perfect self-control and lucidity between his raving crises. *La Méridienne*, or *La sieste (The Midday Siesta)* was also painted during this period of incarceration at Saint-Rémy, after a drawing by Millet. A propos of this calm, luminous canvas, Vincent wrote that it was an attempt "... to translate into another language, that of colour, impressions of light and darkness in black-and-white."

II

After a short stay in Paris, Van Gogh settled at Auvers-sur-Oise at the house of Doctor Gachet, who treated him, offered him friendship, and above all admired, respected and acknowledged his work. Vincent executed three portraits of Gachet, describing one of them to Théo, as he was doing it, in the following terms: "I'm working on his portrait — he has a white cap on his head, very blonde and light; the hands also very light flesh-tint. He wears a blue dress-coat and he is set against a cobalt blue background; he is leaning on a red table with a yellow book and a purple foxglove on it." Doctor Gachet had many friends in the artistic community, especially among the Impressionists. Guillaumin, Pissarro and Cézanne often visited him at Auvers, and he owned a number of their paintings (now in the Musée d'Orsay: see the rooms assigned to Cézanne and the Personnaz collection). But Van Gogh's *Self-portrait* of 1889, *Portrait du docteur Gachet*, and *L'église d'Auvers* were perhaps the most beautiful paintings in the Gachet collection, generously donated to the state in 1954 by the Doctor's children, Paul and Marguerite.

The twisting forms of *L'église d'Auvers*, with their "sumptuous expressive" lines, have the effect of transforming the peaceful village church into a violent motif. The heavy, nocturnal uneasiness somehow communicated by Van Gogh's colours and volumes was later to be echoed by the Norwegian painter Munch.

In an agony of despair and solitude, Van Gogh finally shot himself with a revolver on the 29th of July 1890.

Vincent Van Gogh
1853-1890

La chambre de Van Gogh à Arles (Van Gogh's Bedroom at Arles)
1889
Oil on canvas
57.5 / 74 cm

Vincent Van Gogh
1853-1890

La méridienne ou *La sieste (The Midday Siesta)*
1889-1890
Oïl on canvas
73 / 91 cm

II

Vincent van Gogh
1853-1890

L'Arlésienne (The Woman of Arles)
1888
Oil on canvas
92.3 / 73.5 cm

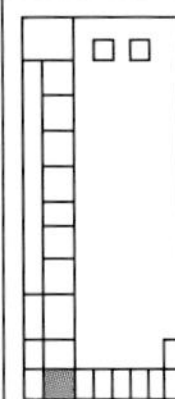

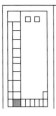

II

In 1859, Doctor Paul Gachet (1828-1909), a specialist in melancholia and other mental illnesses, settled in Paris, where he met such young artists as Courbet, Rodolphe Bresdin and François Bonvin. He moved to rue Rémy, Auvers, in 1872, and offered his warm hospitality to painters visiting the region, like Pissarro and Cézanne. The latter stayed in Auvers from 1872 to 1874, working alongside his friend and painting *La maison du docteur Gachet (Dr. Gachet's House)*. At the first Impressionist exhibition, *Une moderne Olympia (A Modern Olympia)* was met with derision; it was a theatrical, erotic interpretation of Manet's painting that revealed Cézanne's evolution towards luminous colours and brilliant technique. During his stay at Auvers, the artist worked on a theme he never abandoned, a series of still-lifes, painted here in a realist manner *(Pommes vertes – Green Apples; Bouquet au petit Delft – Bouquet with Delft Faience)*.

Pissarro, who settled in Louveciennes in 1869, confirmed his fondness for long perspectives traced by tree-lined roads *(La route de Louveciennes – The Road to Louveciennes*, 1872). Armand Guillaumin, who met Cézanne at the Swiss Academy in 1863, then later Pissarro, took part in the Salon des Refusés and most of the Impressionist exhibitions. He lodged with Cézanne in Auvers at Dr. Gachet's, and continued to paint in the Parisian region *(Soleil couchant à Ivry – Sunset at Ivry*, 1873).

Dr. Gachet, himself a painter and sculptor, exhibited at the 1891 Salon des Indépendants, and adopted the pseudonymn Van Ryssel in 1905. Most of his collection was generously donated to the State by his children, in 1954.

Camile Pissarro
1830-1903
La route de Louveciennes
(The Road to Louveciennes)
1872
Oil on canvas
60 / 73.5 cm

II

Paul Cézanne
1839-1906
Une moderne Olympia
(A Modern Olympia)
Circa 1873-1874
Oil on canvas
46 / 55.5 cm

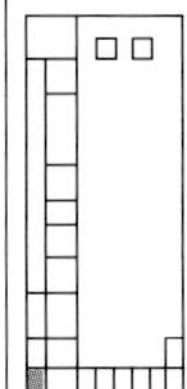

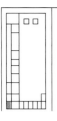

Redon

Redon was fascinated by dreams and the unconscious, and in his earlier work favoured charcoal drawing over oil painting. But from 1890 onwards he began to turn to colour, while retaining the originality of his style (even in portraiture – see the *Portrait de Gauguin*). Colour pastels proved to be the best vehicle for depicting Redon's ambiguous and fantastic visions (*Le Bouddha – Buddha*). In sharp contrast to this work, which is one of the richest expressions of symbolism in existence, Redon painted admirable bouquets of flowers and, for his own pleasure, a number of small landscapes of Brittany and his native Bordelais: all are simply, realistically and precisely observed. Thanks to the generosity of Suzanne and Ari Redon, the artist's son, the Musée d'Orsay possesses a superb collection of his pastels and landscapes. Elsewhere, graphic works by Redon, Bresdin, Bonnard and Daumier are displayed by rote in a glass-covered area devoted to the Claude Roger-Marx donation.

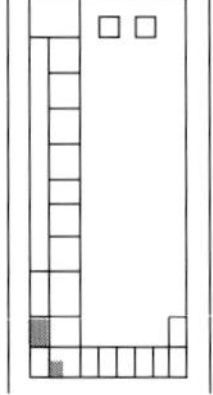

Pastels

The room devoted to Odilon Redon separates three other areas devoted to pastels, a technique mastered and brought to its apotheosis by great artists like Millet (*La baratteuse – Churning Milk,* 1866-1868; *Le Bouquet de marguerites – Bouquet of Daisies,* 1871-1874), Degas (*Le tub – The Tub,* 1878-1879), Manet (*Mme Manet sur un canapé bleu – Mme Manet on a Blue Couch*, 1874).

Landscapes, portraits, still-lifes and scenes from daily life were the most frequent themes. Open-air painters like Boudin, Monet and Guillaumin made use of the vaporous quality of pastel to depict fleeting impressions, while symbolists like Puvis de Chavannes, Redon, Lévy-Dhurmer, Ménard, the Italian Segantini, the Belgians Degouve de Nuncques and Spilliaert and the Dutchman Toorop all adapted the medium's strange nuances to their own visions. Lastly, masters of Art Nouveau like Chéret and Cappiello developed their taste for undulating lines and violent colours by experimenting with pastel.

Odilon Redon
1840-1916
Le bouddha
(Buddha)
Circa 1906-1907
Pastel on Belgian paper
90 / 73 cm

Odilon Redon
1840-1916
Portrait de Gauguin
Painted between 1903 and 1905
Oil on canvas
66 / 54.5 cm

This painting is displayed in the Gauguin room

II

Lucien Lévy-Dhurmer
1865-1953
Méduse (ou *Vague furieuse*)
(*Medusa* or *The Angry Wave*)
1897
Pastel and charcoal
on Belgian paper
59 / 40 cm

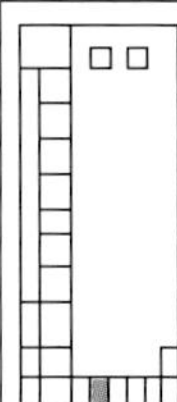

Douanier Rousseau

The mediocre, insecure life of Henri Rousseau – a clerk of the Paris 'octroi' (tollgates), hence his nickname of 'Douanier' – was in strong contrast with the strange world and original style of his paintings. Though an exact contemporary of the Impressionists, Rousseau occupies a place of his own in the history of turn-of-the-century art.

Over the years, he taught himself to paint, working as an amateur, but only gave all his time to the profession when he retired from his job in 1893. Rousseau always proclaimed his admiration for the 'official' masters Cabanel, Bouguereau and Gérôme, and felt no kinship with Impressionist and modern tendencies. In 1886, thanks to Signac, he exhibited his work for the first time at the Salon des Indépendants, and continued to do so until his death; he also took part in the 1905 Salon d'Automne, along with the Fauvists. *La guerre (War)*, which was presented at the Salon des Indépendants of 1894, depicts a fantastic scene with strong symbolist overtones. The horse and the heaps of bodies are described with extreme precision, while the powerful atmosphere of this strange work,with its fresh harmonious colours and weird light, unquestionably springs from an extraordinary imagination. Pissarro was stunned by the exuberance and sincerity of Rousseau's work, while his pictural daring, his modernity and his freedom of composition attracted the attention of Gauguin, along with poets and avant-garde painters such as Alfred Jarry, Guillaume Apollinaire, Robert Delaunay and Pablo Picasso, who possessed several of his paintings (now in the Picasso museum in Paris). In his large *Portrait de Femme (Portrait of a Woman),* the woman is posed full face with a fixed expression; the draughtsmanship and the forms are clearly outlined, the colours are vivid and the details tinged with Rousseau's characteristic humour.

Rousseau's greatest success came at the end of his life, when he began to paint large canvases with exotic motifs. The dreamy sumptuousness of his jungle scenes was based on magazine pictures and frequent visits to the Jardin des Plantes. This vegetable and animal world is treated with such astonishing audacity that it seems to herald the 'revolutionary' movements of the 20th century.

This is particularly true of *La charmeuse de serpents (The Snake Charmer)*. This is particularly true of *La charmeuse de serpents (The Snake Charmer)*, commissioned by Robert Delauney's mother, loved by Apollinaire, Picasso and the Cubists, and an invitation to mystery, dreams and the imagination...

Henri Rousseau,
called Douanier
Rousseau
1844-1910
Portrait de femme
(Portrait of a Woman)
Circa 1897
Oil on canvas
198 / 115 cm

Henri Rousseau
called Douanier
Rousseau
1844-1910
La charmeuse de serpents
(The Snake Charmer)
1907
Oil on canvas
169 / 189 cm

Henri Rousseau,
called Douanier
Rousseau
1844-1910

La guerre
ou *la chevauchée*
de la discorde
(War, or *the Onset*
of Discord)

1894
Oil on canvas
114 / 105 cm

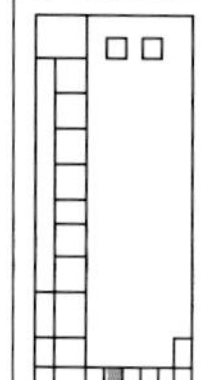

School of Pont-Aven

Gauguin, Emile Bernard, Sérusier

The life of Gauguin, who described himself as "urged onwards by a terrible itch for the unknown", was a kind of uninterrupted voyage which took him several times from Brittany to the Pacific, the two geographical poles of his existence. He exhibited with the Impressionists from 1880 onwards, but it was not until 1883 that he decided to stop being an amateur and "paint every day".

In 1886, Gauguin arrived at Pont-Aven, a picturesque Breton 'bourg' which ever since 1860 had attracted a cosmopolitan colony of artists with its slightly archaic charm, and the possibility of cheap living. *Les lavandières à Pont-Aven (Washerwomen at Pont-Aven)*, one of the artist's first Breton paintings, is executed with a clear, vibrant touch borrowed from the Impressionists. After a voyage to Martinique, where he discovered strong light and bright colours, Gauguin returned to Pont-Aven in February 1888. "I love Brittany", he wrote at this time. "I find it wild and primitive. When I hear my clogs knocking on the granite of Brittany, I hear the muted, muffled, powerful sound that I am searching for in paint." His meeting with Emile Bernard at Pont-Aven was a turning-point: the dialogue between these two strong personalities was fruitful and stimulating, enabling them to develop their new *cloisonniste* techniques (the use of black outlines) with great rapidity.

Pot de grès et pommes (Jug and Apples) carries an inscription on the back, written by Emile Bernard: "Premier essai de synthétisme et de simplification, 1887" (First attempt at synthetism and simplification, 1887). While Bernard's admiration for Cézanne is immediately obvious from this painting, his technical researches had an almost purifying effect on the master's discoveries, which served to set in motion a process of simplification. This method of eliminating details in order to retain essential forms is evident in *Madeleine au Bois d'Amour (Madeleine in the Bois d'Amour)*. Madeleine was Emile Bernard's sister, the 'mystical muse' of Pont-Aven. She is portrayed lying beside the river Aven, in a forest of column-like trees.

La fenaison en Bretagne (Haymaking in Brittany), 1888, shows that Gauguin, during this second spell at Pont-Aven, had renounced Impressionism for a firmer, more heavily contrasted form of art. In October of that year, he dictated a rough sketch to Sérusier, with simplified forms and flat, bright tones: *Le Talisman*. Sérusier was to pass this lesson on to the young Nabis.

Paul Gauguin
1848-1903
La belle Angèle
(The Beautiful Angèle)
1889
Oil on canvas
92 / 73 cm

II

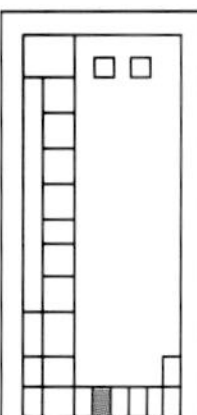

In october 1888, Gauguin joined Van Gogh at Arles and together they painted *Les Alyscamps*. Gauguin created a monumental, static work, heightened with intense colours. But this southern episode ended suddenly with a dramatic separation, and Gauguin hurried back to Paris. Here he painted a portrait of the painter Schuffenecker *(Schuffenecker et sa famille – Schuffenecker and his family)* in his studio; the bird's eye vantage point and the daring foreshortenings in this painting, like the print on the wall, reflect the art of Japan.

Gauguin returned to Pont-Aven once again in 1889, where he painted his great masterpiece, *La belle Angèle (The Beautiful Angèle)*. Angèle Satre is pictured in a circle 'as in Japanese crepons'; her headdress is used for decorative purposes, and the title is placed in the canvas itself, which is something of a novelty. The presence of one of Gauguin's pre-Columbian style ceramics on the left of the canvas has the effect of signing his painting twice over. *Les meules jaunes (Yellow Haystacks)*, 1889, is composed of ringed, flat tints, and may be compared with Emile Bernard's *Moisson au bord de la mer (Harvest by the Sea)*, 1891, which testifies to Bernard's development towards a more geometric art, influenced by Cézanne.

In general, the Pont-Aven painters rejected the analytical, imitative approach of the naturalists and Impressionists; they themselves set out to eliminate detail and simplify forms with flat colours.

The work of Sérusier is particularly well-represented at the Musée d'Orsay, thanks to the recent donations of Mlle Henriette Boutaric. During his spells in Brittany, Sérusier painted a series of vivid canvases, often marked by the influence of Gauguin, several of whose favourite subjects he attempted. This was the case of *La barrière fleurie (Gate and Flowers)*, 1889, and *La lutte bretonne (Breton Wrestlers)*, 1890-1891, which are like muffled echoes of Gauguin. In *L'Averse (The Cloudburst)*, 1893, Sérusier draws closer to the tones of his Nabi friends.

Gauguin and his group organised an exhibition at the Café Volponi in 1889, which had a profound effect on the young Nabis. For many of the participants in this exhibition, the Pont-Aven period represented the summit of their achievement. For Gauguin, still questing after the new and the unknown, it was no more than a temporary phase.

Paul Sérusier
1864-1927
L'averse
(The Cloudburst)
1893
Oil on canvas
73.5 / 60 cm

Emile Bernard
1868-1941

Madeleine au bois d'Amour
(Madeleine in the
Bois d'Amour)

1888
Oil on canvas
137 / 164 cm

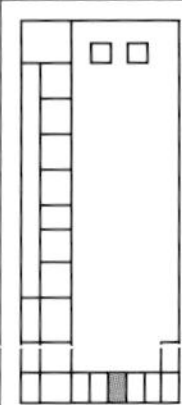

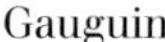

In his unwillingness to admit of boundaries between the different areas of art, Gauguin rapidly branched out into other forms. From 1886 onwards he experimented with pottery *(Vase à quatre anses, sujet breton — Four Handled Pitcher, Brittany)*, and learned the technique of glazed earthenware from Chaplet *(Pot à tabac en forme grotesque — Grotesque Tobacco Jar*, 1889). Symbolist influences appear in his highly original woodcarvings; the bas-relief *Soyez mystérieuses (Be Mysterious)*, which was conceived as a pair for *Soyez amoureuses et vous serez heureuses (Love, and you will be Happy)*, 1889 (Boston Museum), shows that Gauguin was already striving for the freshness of primitive art. This piece was executed in Brittany in 1890 and has overtones of both Japan and Art Nouveau; the beauty of the wood and the subtlety of the carving make it one of Gauguin's most important pre-Tahiti sculptures.

In 1891, Gauguin successfully auctioned his paintings (on this occasion, Degas purchased *La Belle Angèle*) and set sail for Tahiti with the proceeds. As soon as he arrived, he became fascinated by the lazy charm of the local beauties. In *Femmes de Tahiti (Women of Tahiti)*, massive, serene forms are placed in surroundings which have been reduced to a few deep-toned planes, one above the other, while the stylisation of the red and white skirt adapts well to Gauguin's decorative researches. At Mataïea he lived with Tehura, the Tahitian woman whose characteristic features he sculpted, expressing his admiration for the "most beautiful race in the world", and achieving a kind of synthesis between the smooth, stylised face on one side and the roughly-hewn 'exotic Eve' on the other. His idols, which he described as "barbaric knick-knacks", were inspired by Tahitian mythology. In the ironwood *L'idole à la coquille (Idol with Shell)*, several different materials are used; the back of this piece is heavily influenced by traditional Marquesan tikis. Many of Gauguin's sculptures are functional objects, like canes or decorated cups.

In *Le repas (The Meal)*, 1891, the sumptuous coloured fruits in the foreground are contrasted with a motionless frieze of young Tahitians; the door at the side suggests the blinding sunlight outside. A similar mysterious charm is perceptible in *Arearea (Joyeusetés)*, 1892, better known as *Le chien rouge (The Red Dog)* because of its arbitrary colours, which intrigued the Fauvists.

Here, in a masterly synthesis, Gauguin blends the different influences of Egyptian, Javanese, Japanese and Polynesian art which he had seen at the Universal Exhibitions or elsewhere. When in 1894 he returned to Pont-Aven for the last

Paul Gauguin
1848-1903
Idole à la coquille
(Idol with Shell)
1893
Wood, mother of pearl for the halo, incrustations of bone for the teeth
27 cm

Paul Gauguin
1848-1903

Soyez mystérieuses
(Be Mysterious)
1890
Wood
73 / 95 cm

Paul Gauguin
1848-1903

Femmes de Tahiti
(ou *Sur la plage*)
(Women of Tahiti
or *On the Beach*)
1891

Oil on canvas
69 / 91.5 cm

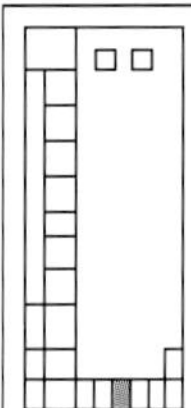

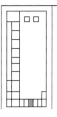

time, his Tahitian experience had renewed his vision and enriched his colours: in *Le Moulin David*, 1896, the tones are positively saturated, far more violent than in his earlier Breton landscapes.

In July 1895, he returned to Tahiti and completely repudiated the Western world. His *Autoportrait (Self portrait)* of 1897 is dedicated to Daniel de Monfried, whose protective friendship was an indispensable support for Gauguin, isolated as he was in the Antipodes. Morice described de Monfried as follows: "A large, massive, bony face, with a narrow forehead and a nose not hooked, not curved, but broken-looking".

In the manuscript of *Noa Noa*, in which Gauguin describes the pantheon of "Tahiti, faithfully imagined", he recounts the legend of *Vaïrumati*, 1897. "She was tall, and the fires of the sun burned in her flesh, whilst all love's mysteries slumbered in the night of her hair." Tahiti had the enchantment of myth, and the secret of Gauguin's art (like that of Mallarmé) lay in his ability to suggest, rather than state that myth. Gauguin's painting is like a return to the very sources of art: "I have gone far, far back, farther than the horses of the Parthenon, to the rocking-horses of my childhood" *(Le cheval blanc – The White Horse*, 1898).

In September 1901, Gauguin retreated to "a simpler country, to simpler, wilder elements"; this was Hiva Oa, one of the Marquesa Islands, where he bought a plot of land near the mission, built a large hut on piles out of wood, palm-branches and bamboo, and provocatively called it *La Maison du jouir (The House of Pleasure).* The imported sequoia door jambs were carved all over by the artist... After his death on the 8 May 1905, the five panels were put up for sale in Tahiti, where Victor Ségalen, a young Navy doctor and admirer of Gauguin, was living. He bought four of the panels, which his children sold to the national museums in 1952; the fifth one came to France, in 1990, to complete Gauguin's greatest carved, decorative ensembles.

The work of Georges Lacombe constitutes a link between the school of Pont-Aven and the Nabis, through its Breton subject matter. Lacombe was introduced to the group in 1892, and subsequently became the 'Nabi sculptor'. His *Isis*, 1895, is an evocation of the mother goddess, symbolic of life and harmony, in triumphant polychrome.

Paul Gauguin
1848-1903
Le cheval blanc
(The White Horse)
1898
Oil on canvas
140 / 91.5 cm

No-one has ever understood Gauguin's painting better than Mallarmé: "It is extraordinary", he wrote, "to place such mystery within such radiance."

Paul Gauguin
1848-1903
Oviri
1894
Enamelled ceramic
Stoneware
75 / 19 cm

Oviri, denoted "La Tueuse" (The Killer) by Gauguin, was the primitive god of death and bereavement. The artist was extremely proud of this mysterious, powerful statuette, the largest ceramic he ever made; on this death, he requested that it be placed on his grave.

II

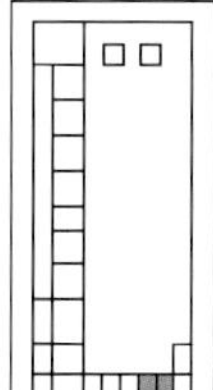

Neo-impressionism

Seurat, Signac, Cross

II

The term Neo-Impressionism was coined by the critic Félix Fénélon in his account of the eighth Impressionist exhibition of 1886. On this occasion, Georges Seurat, the originator of this new technique, exhibited his *Un dimanche à la Grande-Jatte (Sunday at Grande-Jatte Island)* (Chicago Art Institute); but he had already caused a sensation with *Une baignade, Asnières (Bathers at Asnières)*, 1883-1884 (London, Tate Gallery) which was refused by the official Salon and subsequently exhibited at the Salon des Indépendants founded in 1884. These two works are represented at the Musée d'Orsay by small, rapidly executed studies.

The technique invented by Seurat (which was also called 'pointillisme' or 'divisionisme') consisted in dotting pure colours on the canvas, carefully juxtaposed to reinforce the richness, solidity and brilliancy of the overall tone. An optical blend of these pigments take place in the eye of the observer, where a synthesis of elements serves to reconstruct the ensemble. This way of painting is an extension of the experiments made by Delacroix, as developed by the Impressionists, as well as an application of the scientific theories applied to colour by Chevreul and Charles Blanc. Before he was able to master this method, Seurat painted a number of open-air studies, such as *Le petit paysan en bleu (Peasant Boy in Blue)*, an imposing figure despite his small size. The three advanced studies for the large canvas *Les Poseuses (Nude Models*, Merion Foundation, Pennsylvania) are an admirable introduction to Seurat's densely-packed world; they show the same nude model in three different poses, seeming to be made of nothing but air and light, though somehow her shape remains visible *(Poseuse debout — Model standing; Poseuse assise de profil — Model Seated in Profile; Poseuse de dos — Model from Behind*, 1886).

Seurat spent the summer of 1888 at Port-en-Bessin, a village on the Normandy coast discovered by his friend Signac, and came back with a groupe of landscapes. *Port-en-Bessin*, 1888, is a play of lines and rhythmic colours — horizontal piers offset by curving cliffs — which leaves the greater part of the canvas to the calm, poetic sea and sky. The dotted border of this picture, like that of *Les poseuses (The Models)* was put in by the painter himself to achieve a harmonious transition between canvas and frame. Seurat's final work, the strange, unfinished *Le cirque (The Circus)*, suggests the gaiety and excitement of the spectacle by the use of ascending colour rhythms of red and yellow (for the ring and the performers). The background spectators are placed in straight horizontal rows, which evoke calm and stability in tones of yellow and violet. This painting echoes one of Charles Henry's theories on the dynamics of line.

Georges Seurat
1859-1891
Poseuse de dos
(Model from Behind)
1886
Oil on canvas
24.5 / 15.5 cm

Georges Seurat
1859-1891
Cirque
(Circus)
1891
Oil on canvas
185.5 / 152.5 cm

Georges Seurat
1859-1891
Port-en-Bessin
avant-port, marée haute
(Port-en-Bessin,
Outer Harbourg,
High Tide)
1888
Oil on canvas
67 / 82 cm

II

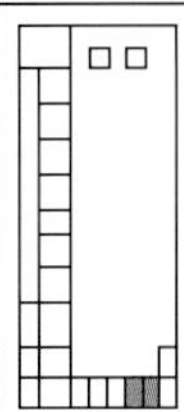

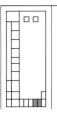

The flat, simplified silhouettes and sinuous arabesques denote an overwhelmingly decorative intent (a smaller oil study close by shows how the painting was developed). Meanwhile, the members of Seurat's group, Signac, Cross, Angrand and Dubois-Pillet, used the same divisionist approach each according to his own temperament and sensibility.

Signac was aligned with the Impressionists for the early part of his career (*La route de Gennevilliers – The Road to Gennevilliers*, 1883) before participating actively in the divisionist experiment. After the death of Seurat, he travelled south and discovered Saint-Tropez and Antibes. *Les femmes au puits (Women at the Well),* 1892 was preceded by a number of sketches, brightly-coloured and with supple, sinuous lines like those of Art Nouveau; this painting is an example of the pointillist theory pushed to extremes. *La bouée rouge (Red Buoy)*, 1895, is more free of scientific constraints and is handled with broader brushstrokes, while the glittering colours are broken up into multiple patches of reflected light. *Le château des Papes (The Papal Château)*, 1900, confirms this use of a 'touch proportionate to the size of the painting', which eventually gave Signac's canvases the appearance of mosaics *(L'entrée du port de la Rochelle – Entrance to the Port of La Rochelle*, 1921), along with a growing attention to light and colours. Cross, by contrast, painted harmonious, pure compositions, such as *Les îles d'or (The Golden Isles)*, 1891, an almost abstract exercise in coloration; his larger landscapes are sometimes tinged with the idealism of Puvis de Chavannes and the Nabis *(L'air du soir – Evening Breeze*, 1893-1894) or pretexts for the exaltation of colour for its own sake *(Les cyprès à Cagnes – Cypresses at Cagnes*, 1908). Meanwhile, the realist sensibility of Luce attracted him to scenes of ordinary daily life *(Le quai Saint-Michel et Notre-Dame).*

Signac made friends with the Belgian painters Théo van Rysselberghe *(Voiliers et estuaire – Sailing Boats and Estuary*, circa 1892-1893; L'homme à la barre – The Steersman, 1892), and Georges Lemmen both active members of the XX group which published Impressionist theories. Around 1898 saw Lemmen's first Neo-Impressionist paintings, which were deeply influenced by Seurat in their range of colours and the care taken in framing the compostion with a border of small dots *(Aline Maréchal)*. However, some canvases allowed more room for motif or Art Nouveau's sinuous line *(Plage à Heist – Beach at Heist*, 1891).

II

Paul Signac
1863-1935
La bouée rouge
(Red Buoy)
1895
Oil on canvas
81 / 65 cm

Maximilien Luce
1858-1941
Le quai Saint-Michel
et Notre-Dame
1901
Oil on canvas
73 / 60 cm

Henri Edmond Cross
1856-1910

L'air du soir
(Evening Breeze)
1893-1894
Oil on canvas
115.6 / 163.2 cm

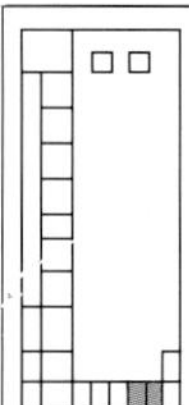

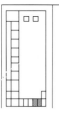

II

Henri Matisse is said to have started *Luxe, calme et volupté (Luxury, Calm and Delight)* while staying with Signac in Saint-Tropez, during the summer of 1904. Taking as his theme a verse from Baudelaire's *L'invitation au voyage (Invitation to a Voyage)*, Matisse created a paradisiac vision of a "Golden Age" already evoked by Puvis de Chavannes, Cross and Signac. This theme also owes much to the *Bacchanalia, Rustic Concerts,* and *Pastorales* of the great Venetian painters or Poussin, and to the modern *Déjeuners sur l'herbe.* Before the major innovation of *La joie de vivre (The Joy of Living)*, in 1906, Matisse gave a very free interpretation of Neo-Impressionism and was already using the range of bright colours to be found later in his Fauve works. In 1899, Signac brought out his *D'Eugène Delacroix au Néo-Impressionisme*, a book that remains crucial both to the understanding of divisionist theories and of the fauvist, cubist and abstract movements that stemmed from them.

Georges Lemmen
1865-1916
Aline Maréchal
1892
Oil on canvas
60 / 51 cm

II

Henri Matisse
1869-1954

Luxe, calme et volupté (Luxury, Calm and Delight)
1904
Oil on canvas
98 / 118 cm

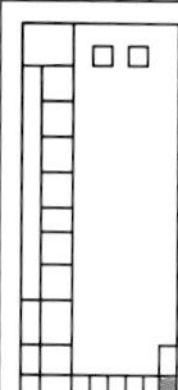

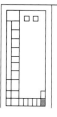

Toulouse-Lautrec came from an old aristocratic family in which drawing was a popular pastime, but after two accidents which left him a cripple, painting became the central motivation of his life. In 1882 he frequented the studios of Bonnat and Cormon; two years later he moved to Montmartre, where he began painting scenes of contemporary Paris life. Toulouse-Lautrec was a passionate devotee of the theatre, and in 1889 he executed a portrait of the actor *Henry Samary* of the Comédie Française, posing in highly original fashion on the stage itself. Paris nightlife and the world of entertainment were always a source of fascination to him, from circus to cabaret: and from this unfashionable raw material he created his own "personal Olympus". One of his favourite models was the dancer *Jane Avril*, 1892, whom he made a star with his posters. As in many other cases, he placed special emphasis on the legs of this elegant creature, whom he outlines firmly and cursively, while at the same time capturing the strange, absent-minded charm of her expression. The incisive draughtsmanship and off-centre composition that characterise Toulouse-Lautrec's work attest to his admiration for Japanese art. In the *Clownesse Cha-U-Kao*, a cunning and arbitrary arrangement presents the model without showing her face. Here, Lautrec comes close to the art of the captured instant, by rendering the exact gesture of the woman adjusting her yellow ruff amid a symphony of violent colours.

"Artist's models always look stuffed, but these girls are alive", he noted of his prostitute subjects, drawn from life in brothels *(Femme tirant son bas) — Woman pulling her Stocking*, 1894, or *Femme sur le dos: lassitude — Woman Lying on her back — Lassitude*, 1896). Lautrec produced a series of lithographs on this theme, entitled *Elles*. By contrast, both the subject and the perspectives of *La toilette* carry echoes of Degas.

"Only form exists", proclaimed Lautrec, who disapproved of accessories and only included them in his paintings when he thought them essential and meaningful. His friend *Paul Leclerc*, who sat for his portrait in 1897, recalled Lautrec's 'phenomenal facility', and stated categorically "... that he had not posed for more than two or three hours". Lautrec's principal concern was for psychological truth, and in *Paul Leclerc* he produced an exact rendering of his relaxed model, one of the founders of *La Revue Blanche*, of which the artist was an habitué.

Lautrec died prematurely at 37, leaving an abundant and extraordinary body of work, which had a profound influence on the Expressionists and on Picasso.

Henri
de Toulouse-Lautrec
1864-1901
Jane Avril dansant
(Jane Avril Dancing)
Circa 1892
Oil on cardboard
85.5 / 45 cm

Henri
de Toulouse-Lautrec
1864-1901
La clownesse Cha-U-Kao
(The Lady Clown Cha-U-Kao)
1895
Oil on carboard
64 / 49 cm

II

Henri
de Toulouse-Lautrec
1864-1901
La toilette
(Red-head, Washing)
1896
Oil on cardboard
67 / 54 cm

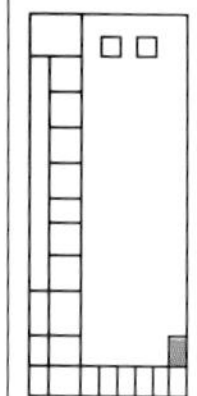

This room is reserved for small paintings that are mostly works of the Nabi group, though less exclusive painters are also represented; naturalist Cottet was attracted to subjects treated by Degas and Lautrec *(Le cirque – The Circus*, 1913), while Albert André *(Le serin – The Canary*, circa 1894) was influenced by Bonnard's intimism and Japanese art.

The Nabi movement began in October 1888, when Sérusier was working at Pont-Aven. "How do you see that tree?" Gauguin said one morning, at a corner of the Bois d'Amour. "Green? Well, paint it green, the most beautiful green on your palette. And that shadow? I would call it blue. Don't be afraid of painting it as blue as you possibly can."

The vivid landscape that resulted, painted by Sérusier on the instructions of Gauguin, was baptised *Le Talisman*. It was a revelation for Sérusier's friends at the Académie Julian, namely Ranson, Denis and Bonnard, who in turn recruited Vuillard and Roussel. 'Le Talisman' is displayed at the Musée d'Orsay beside two 'tachiste' works by Maurice Denis; together, they demonstrate the importance of Gauguin's teaching, in that they seem to be "formless landscape, because synthetically formulated", hence nearly abstract and rendered in pure, juxtaposed colours. *La montée au Calvaire (The Ascent to Calvary)*, 1889, Maurice Denis' earliest religious composition, and above all his *Taches de soleil sur la terrasse (Sunlight on the Terrace)*, 1890, are spectacular proofs that art is a "transposition", "the impassioned equivalent of a received sensation".

These young artists formed a kind of brotherhood, calling themselves (some ironically, others with conviction) the nabis (or 'prophets' in hebrew). They were united by ties of friendship and by their common ambition to create a new brand of art, and they constitued the avant-garde of Paris painters in the last decade of the 19th century.

Paul Sérusier
1863-1927
Le talisman
(The Talisman)
1888
Oil on canvas
27 / 22 cm

Pierre Bonnard
1867-1947
Le corsage à carreaux
(The Checked Blouse)
1892
Oil on canvas
61 / 33 cm

II

Maurice Denis
1870-1943
Le calvaire
ou *Montée au calvaire*
(Calvary or *The Road to Calvary)*
1889
Oil on canvas
41 / 32.5 cm

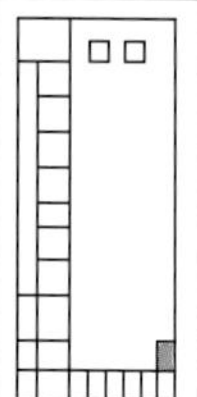

Nicknamed the "Nabi japonard" (The Japanese Nabi), Pierre Bonnard admitted his checked motifs were inspired from Japanese art *(Le corsage à carreaux – The Checked Blouse*, 1982). From 1894 onwards, the artist seemed more attracted to interiors and family scenes, using artificial light *(Sous la lampe – Under the Lamp*, 1899). At first very close to the Nabis, the Swiss painter Félix Vallotton treated landscape with subtlety; the sinuous lines, the hint of symbolism and atmosphere of silence and mystery in *Clair de lune (Moonlight)* make it a rare, exceptional canvas, since the artist only developed this theme in 1910-1911. Edouard Vuillard painted small panels full of imagination and caricatural verve *(Femme de profil au chapeau vert – Profile of Woman with Green Hat*, 1891), with wide stretches of colour superimposing the silhouette on a neutral background, and a taste for synthesis found also in *Le Sommeil (Sleep)*, 1891.

Edouard Vuillard
1868-1940
Femme de profil au chapeau vert (Profile of Woman with Green Hat)
Circa 1891
Oil on cardboard
21 / 16 cm

Félix Vallotton
1865-1925

Clair de lune (Moonlight)
Circa 1895
Oil on canvas
27 / 41 cm

Press Passage

"Opinion is made in Paris: it is made with paper and ink!" exclaimed Balzac in 1840. Not without reason! The press had become the "fourth power in the state" and continued to develop throughout the century. It was muzzled by the law of the 9th of September, 1835; freed in 1848; muzzled again in 1850; and freed again, this time for good, by the law of the 29th of July, 1881. Its authors and journalists (Girardin, Villemessant, Veuillot, Prévost-Paradol, Léo Lespés, Zola, Vallès, Rochefort) were influential men whose power grew as the press changed. First of all, it became democratic. In 1936, Girardin launched subscriptions at 40 francs per year, instead of 80, and invented an advertising system; in 1863, Moïse Millaud started the *Petit Journal* at five centimes a copy. This was a "price for people who have no money", and it effectively brought the press into the poor man's orbit. Later, newspapers began to diversify: politics and society columns gave way to 'faits divers', reportages from distant countries, sport, gastronomy and above all serialised stories. The serial was an unprecedented social phenomenon which guaranteed the success of the non-political press of the Second Empire and the Third Republic, along with that of its authors; Eugène Sue's *Les Mystères de Paris* and Ponson du Terrail's 'Rocambole' were instant triumphs. Above all, the press became more and more heavily illustrated. Fashion magazines, satirical publications, geographical, scientific and travel press and papers for children, proliferated throughout France. A wide variety of images poured into every home, from the richest to the poorest; in short, a new collective imagination was created which also influenced the century's writers, musicians and artists.

By way of images and texts, the 'Passage de la Presse' traces the metamorphosis of a political, Paris-based and scantily-illustrated press, to the century's principal vehicle for information.

Le Petit Journal

ADMINISTRATION
61, RUE LAFAYETTE, 61
Les manuscrits ne sont pas rendus
On s'abonne sans frais
dans tous les bureaux de poste

5 CENT. SUPPLÉMENT ILLUSTRÉ 5 CENT.

25me Année — Numéro 1.219

DIMANCHE 29 MARS 1914

ABONNEMENTS

SEINE et SEINE-ET-OISE	2 fr.	3 fr. 50
DÉPARTEMENTS	2 fr.	4 fr. »
ÉTRANGER	2 50	5 fr. »

Tragique épilogue d'une querelle politique

Mme CAILLAUX, FEMME DU MINISTRE DES FINANCES, TUE A COUPS DE REVOLVER M. GASTON CALMETTE DIRECTEUR DU " FIGARO "

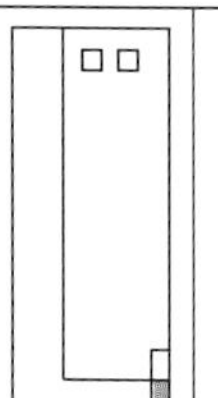

Max and Rosy Kaganovitch Collection

Gauguin, Van Gogh, Derain, Vlaminck

The Max and Rosy Kaganovitch collection was given to the state in March 1973 by Max Kaganovitch (1891-1978), and named after himself and his wife. It comprises some 20 canvases, judiciously chosen by an enlightened dealer and amateur with a view to one day handing them over to the state. In accordance with the donor's desire, the paintings must be exhibited in a room bearing his own and his wife's names. The collection spans the development of Impressionist and post-Impressionist painting, along with the birth of Fauvism.

The great Impressionists, Monet *(Eglise de Vétheuil – The Church at Vétheuil*, 1879), Sisley, Renoir *(Marine, Guernesey – Seascape, Guernesey*, 1883) and Pissarro are well-represented; Sisley's *La route de Versailles (The Versailles Road)* is executed with a quivering touch, while the landscape of *La route d'Ennery (The Road to Ennery)*, 1874, by Pissarro, a serene, slow-paced compostion, is rendered in broad and powerful strokes.

By contrast, in his *Coin de jardin à l'Hermitage (Corner of a Garden at l'Hermitage)*, 1877, Pissarro uses a fragmented technique like that of Monet. Van Gogh's *L'Hôpital Saint-Jean* is a tormented work, painted with quick, feverish touches. Gauguin's *Paysannes Bretonnes (Breton Peasant Women)*, which was completed during the artist's final period in Brittany, attests to the influence of Tahitian features and colours, within a synthetic, monumental composition.

Marx Kaganovitch
1891-1978

Bonnard's *Nu Bleu (Blue Nude*, circa 1899-1900) echoes the sinuous lines of *L'indolente (Lazy Nude)*, seeming to melt into elegant harmonies of grey and blue.

Derain and Vlaminck, who were close friends, used the same kind of pure, flamboyant colouring in their work; the yellows, greens, blues and pinks of Derain's *Pont de Charing Cross (Charing Cross Bridge)* radiate harsh light. Moreover, the curving waterfront confers a special dynamism on every element of this painting, which was one of the most successful Fauvist compositions.

André Derain
1880-1954

Pont de Charing-Cross
(Charing Cross Bridge)
Circa 1906
Oil on canvas
81 / 100 cm

Paul Gauguin
1841-1903

Paysannes bretonnes
(Breton Peasant Woman)
1894
Oil on canvas
66 / 92.5 cm

Middle level, last part of the visit

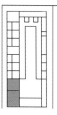

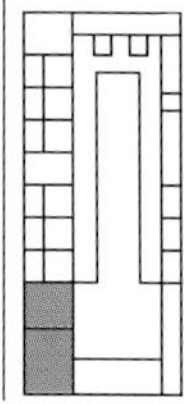

Arts and Décors of the Third Republic

The proclamation of the Third Republic, on the 4th of September, 1870, produced no real rupture in the artistic domain. On the contrary, it stimulated a wide campaign of official commissions for the decoration of reconstructed buildings, along with monuments dedicated to the new régime. The government remained unstable until 1877, but the patronage of a Republican state had replaced the imperial will; the Republican ideal had to be popularised, and it needed traditional iconography in order to be understood. Some of the resultant works recalled the Franco-Prussian war and the Commune, like Meissonier's *Le siège de Paris (Siege of Paris),* a sketch painted with feverish speed in the emotion of defeat, or the later *Cimetière de Saint-Privat (The Saint-Privat Cemetery)*, 1881, by Alphonse de Neuville. In sculpture, this sentiment was echoed by Cabet's desolate allegory *Mille huit cent soixante et onze (Eighteen Seventy One), 1877*, and Mercié's insolent *Gloria Victis*, while the first stirrings of revanchism may be discerned in Falguière's *Resistance* and *Défense de Paris (Defense of Paris).*

Sculptures appeared all over Paris. Public monuments, busts and statues dedicated to the glory of France were erected in every corner, including a *Monument to Gambetta* by the sculptor Aubé and the architect Boileau, in the Cour Napoléon at the Louvre. This large, heavy sculpture was selected after an open competition in 1884; its bronze sections were eventually melted down during the Occupation, and the final stones dismantled in 1954. The model at the Musée d'Orsay shows how pedagogical this piece was, with its blend of inscription and show tableau vivant. (See also the corner room, which contains a number of sketches for public monuments.)

The Salon, which dominated artistic, cultural and social life, gave its blessing to the kind of official art and processes of selection illustrated in Henri Gervex' painting, *Un jury de peinture (A Painting Jury)*, 1885. Included in it, as jury members, are J.P. Laurens, Léon Bonnat, Alexandre Cabanel and Jules Lefebvre, along with other more independent personalities like Puvis de Chavannes or Cormon.

These artists were jealous guardians of the various 'genres' in painting of which history, mythology and allegory remained firmly paramount. These genres were used as pretexts for the female nudes so beloved of contemporary collectors; especially in sculpture, as we see from the nudes displayed in the Salle des Fêtes (*Jeunesse – Youth,* 1885, a marble by Carlès; *Eve*, 1891, a marble by Delaplanche; and *Bacchante couchée*, 1892, a marble by Moreau-Vauthier).

Victor Ségoffin
1867-1925
Danse guerrière
(ou *Danse sacrée*)
(*War Dance*
or *Sacred Dance*)
1903-1905
Bronze and marble
250 / 140 cm

Louis-Ernest Barrias
1841-1905
La Nature se dévoilant à la Science (Nature revealed to Science)
1899
Polychrome marble
and Algerian onyx
200 / 85 cm

Charles-René
de Saint-Marceaux
1845-1915
Génie gardant le secret de la tombe (Genius protecting the Secret of the Grave)
1879
Marble
168.5 / 95 cm

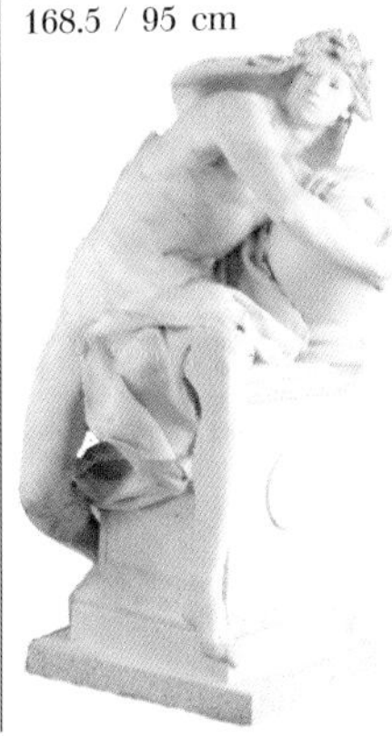

Jean-Léon Gérôme
1824-1904
Tanagra
1890
Marble
154.7 / 56 cm

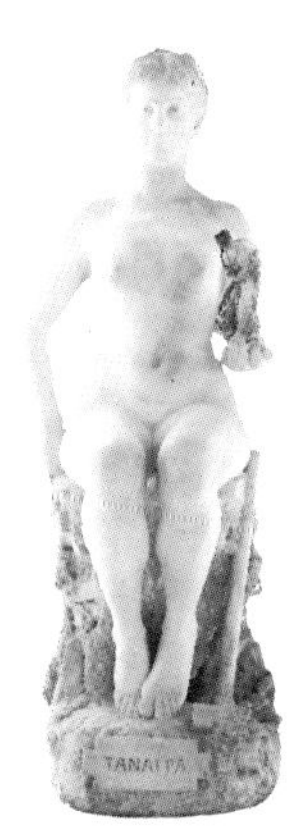

William Bouguereau
1825-1905

La naissance de Vénus
(Birth of Venus)
1879
Oil on canvas
300 / 218 cm

III

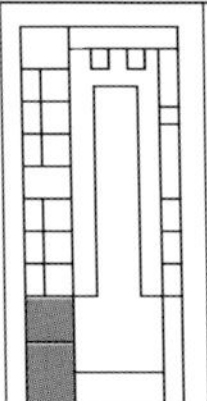

The painter and sculptor Gérôme celebrated the Greek ideal of beauty in his *Tanagra*, which created a sensation at the 1890 Salon because a part of it was coloured in imitation of the painted statues of antiquity. (This part is now lost.) Meanwhile, Louis-Ernest Barrias affirmed the current taste for mixed materials (already exploited by Cordier under the Second Empire) by using coloured marbles, onyx, lapis-lazuli and malachite for his allegory *La Nature se dévoilant devant la Science (Nature revealed to Science)*. Saint-Marceaux' *Le Génie gardant le secret de la Tombe (Genius protecting the Secret of the Tomb)* and Segoffin's *Danse guerrière (War Dance)* achieve strength and force with baroque interpretations of movement.

Bouguereau used mythology as a vehicle for a return to Raphael's draughtsmanship and respect for form. *La naissance de Vénus (Birth of Venus)* is an example of this quest for a decorative ideal, approached by way of Ingres's *La source (The Spring)*, from which Bouguereau borrowed the pose for his Venus. Jules Lefebvre, by contast, was a traditional academic painter; his Vérité *(Truth)*, presented at the 1870 Salon, was acquired by the state. The Salon also exhibited society portraits, like Bernard's *Mme Roger Jourdain*, which reflect the brilliant social scene of the epoch.

The sculptor Aubé's *Surtout de table (Table Centrepiece)*, in silver and rock crystal, is an allegorical commemoration of Tsar Nicolas II's visit to Paris in 1896 and the rapprochement between France and Russia. This piece, which represents the four continents participating in the apotheosis of Paris, was exhibited at the 1900 Universal Exhibition.

A large number of other painters produced virtuoso decorative work, which (with the exception of Luc Olivier Merson's décors from the demolished hôtel Watel-Dehaynin), is represented at the Musée d'Orsay by only a few sketches. Benjamin Constant's ceiling for the Opéra Comique (1898), and Besnard's for the Comédie Française, create an elegiac, brilliant world of images based on the baroque; while clear composition, sober colour harmonies, powerful draughtsmanship, and precise figurative attitudes characterize the work of Elie Delaunay, Laurens and above all Puvis de Chavannes at the Panthéon.

Alphonse de Neuville
1835-1885
Le cimetière de Saint-Privat
(The Saint-Privat Cemetery)
1881
Oil on canvas
236 / 344 cm

Emile Thomas
1817-1882
L'Air (Air)
1877
Plaster study for a statue in stone at the Palais du Trocadéro
44.2 / 23 cm

Jean Benjamin-Constant
1845-1902
First sketch for the ceiling of the Opéra Comique (Glorification of Music)
1898
Grisaille on paper
∅ 56 cm

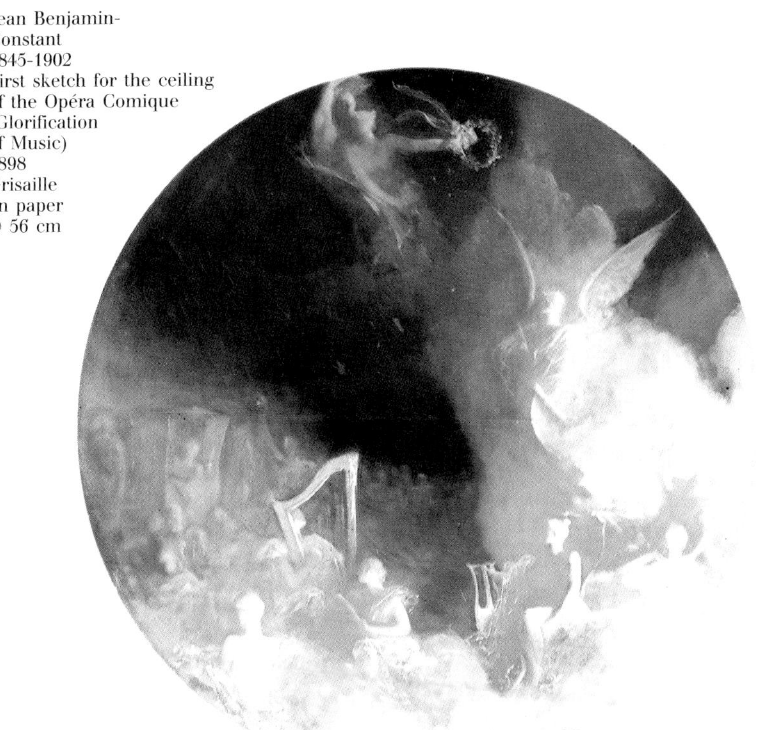

III

The monumental sculpture of the IIIrd Republic, represented at the Musée d'Orsay by reliefs, groups and statues, testifies to a rediscovery of the baroque style, which is characterized by expansive gestures and wild expressions.

The high reliefs of Barrias and Coutan for the exterior of the paleontology gallery of the Museum of Natural History (built by Dutert in 1894-1895), were intended to evoke mankind's brutal early existence *(Chasseurs d'alligator – Alligator Hunters or Les Nubiens – The Nubians*, 1894, by Barrias; *Chasseurs d'aigles -Eagles Hunters*, 1900, by Coutan). The Musée d'Orsay possesses the two original models of these reliefs, bronze versions of which may be seen on the Natural History Museum façade.

The work of Deloye was also influenced by baroque art, but in his case the reference was to central Europe, with its tormented, theatrical style. His curiously-composed group at the Musée d'Orsay bears witness to the desire for grandiloquence which seems to have gripped sculptors at the turn of the century.

Fremiet was mainly concerned with historical realism, as his huge *Saint Michel* shows. This statue is a copper replica of the oriflamme weathervane that has crowned Mont-Saint-Michel ever since 1897. Fremiet's respect for traditional iconography is evident here, as is the careful research behind his rendering of St. Michael's armour. The original plaster model was presented at the 1896 Salon and the cast was made by the Monduit foundry, which had acquired an international reputation for the finesse, precision and soundness of its reproductions. Thanks to the generosity of Mme G. Pasquier-Monduit, the Musée d'Orsay now possesses a large number of studies and sketches and archives from the firm, which also produced the casts for the quadrigae of the Grand Palais, along with many elements of the Pont Alexandre III, Bartholdi's statue of *Liberty* (New York) and the *Lion* of Belfort.

The same taste for extreme realism and historical veracity may also be found in Gérôme's astonishing group *Gladiateurs (Gladiators)*, his first sculpture. This piece, which for many years was believed lost, was actually included in Aimé Morot's homage to Gérôme, his father-in-law, which represents Gérôme sculpting *Gladiateurs*.

Emmanuel Fremiet
1824-1910

Saint Michel
Beaten copper
617 / 260 cm

Gustave Deloye
1838-1899
Saint Marc
1878
Plaster
205 / 145 cm

III

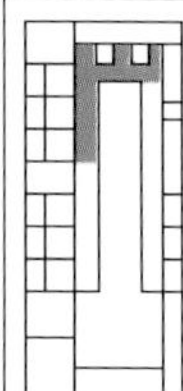

Rodin

More than a quarter of the terrace is devoted to Rodin, in recognition of his major importance in the history of 19th century sculpture. Rodin's development may be traced from the early *L'Age d'Airain (Bronze Age)*, which was thought so natural when it was exhibited at the 1877 Salon that the sculptor was accused of moulding it from a real human body – through to *La Muse*, part of his *Monument to Whistler* (1902) which was constructed with extreme freedom, of scarcely connected elements and drapery dipped in plaster and left to harden.

After *L'Age d'Airain, Saint Jean-Baptiste* and *L'Homme qui marche – Man walking* (the latter was a 1905 enlargement of a study for Saint Jean done around 1877-1878), Rodin's talent as a portraitist is demonstrated by a gallery of busts. Society portraits as well as faces from the artistic and literary worlds feature here. They include the elegant *Mme Vicuña*, wife of the Chilean ambassador to Paris; a symbolist portrait of Camille Claudel, *La pensée (Thought)*; heroic busts of *Hugo and Rochefort*; the famous mask of *L'Homme au nez cassé (The Man with the Broken Nose)*; and heads of a series of personalities linked to the arts, such as the critic Geoffroy and the artists *Puvis de Chavannes, Eugène Guillaume, Jean-Paul Laurens* and, finally, bare-chested *Dalou*, whose rigorous conception and precise modelling bear witness to Rodin's admiration for the Florentine Renaissance.

The years 1880-1890 saw the assembly of Rodin's *Porte de l'Enfer*, which was commissioned by the state in 1880 for a new Museum of Decorative arts. This museum was planned for the site of the former Cour des Comptes, but the project was abandoned and the Gare d'Orsay was built in its place. The theme of *Porte d'Enfer* is Dante's *Divine Comedy*, and Rodin was originally inspired to do it by the Gates of the Baptistry at Florence. The piece mostly consists of sculptures that were already independent entities such as *Le Penseur (The Thinker), Le Baiser (The Kiss), Fugit Amor,* and *Ombres (Shadows)*. In the resultant tangle of bodies driven by passion to the abyss "grasping, anxious, significant, full of pathetic clamour", the two main episodes concern Paolo and Francesca (embracing at left), based on the famous Baiser (Kiss), and, leaning to the right, the figures of Ugolin and his children. The latter group, slightly altered and enlarged in 1906, produced the Ugolin group displayed nearby. Note the drapery around the bodies, moulded from real fabric which appears under the plaster.

Ugolin was inspired by Canto 33 of Dante's *Hell*: "... already blind, I went groping from one to the next: for three days after they were dead. I called to them. Then my hunger grew stronger than my pain..." Not far from the *Porte d'Enfer* is the famous *Fugit Amor*: the young man being whirled away by a woman is Rodin's answer to *L'Age mûr (Maturity)* by Camille Claudel. *L'Age mûr* was executed when the relationship between

Auguste Rodin
1840-1917
Pensée (Thought)
1886
Marble
74 / 55 cm

Auguste Rodin
1840-1917
Mme Vicuña
1888
Marble
57 / 49 cm

Camille Claudel
1864-1943
L'âge mûr (Maturity)
1899-1905
Bronze
114 / 166 cm

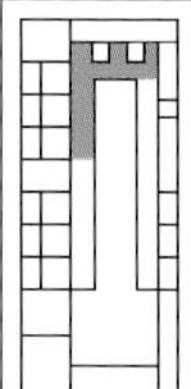

the two sculptors was disintegrating; it symbolises Rodin's hesitation between his old mistress, Rose Beuret, and Camille, who leans forward in the attitude of *L'Implorante*, almost losing her balance in the hopeless effort to retain her lover. The three figures are placed on a plinth in the shape of a curling wave, which echoes the sinuous lines of the Art Nouveau objects occuping domed rooms further on.

With *Balzac*, Rodin moved towards a more abstract form of sculpture. The 'Société des Gens de Lettres' (Society of Authors) wished to erect a monument to the man who had been their second president, and after the death of Chapu, who was originally given the commission, Zola secured it for Rodin. Working from a series of realistic, almost visionary nude studies, which he then simplified and deformed, Rodin produced a pyramidal silhouette which laid strong emphasis on the disproportionately large head. "In my opinion", he declared. "modern sculpture shoud exaggerate forms from a moral standpoint".

His *Balzac* is an almost abstract study of the novelist's raw power; it completely revolutionised the concept of the public monument, which hitherto had been confined to precise physical description, accompanied by allegories, of the person it was intended to honour. The plaster cast caused such a scandal at the 1898 Salon that the commission was taken away from Rodin and given to Falguière instead. Not until 1939, long after Rodin's death, was *Balzac* erected in the Boulevard Raspail in Paris: today it is considered to be one of the great masterpieces announcing the dawn of the 20th century.

Auguste Rodin
1840-1917
Balzac
1897
Plaster
300 / 120 cm

Auguste Rodin
1840-1917
Porte de l'Enfer
(Gate of Hell)
1880-1917
Plaster
635 / 400 cm

Auguste Rodin
1840-1917
Ugolin
1882
Plaster
140 / 140 cm

III

It was Rodin's opinion that a sculpture should not be approached from any particular vantage point, since it represents the sum of all the contours resulting from the play of light on the model. Medardo Rosso's work offers many points of comparison with the Impressionist painters; he pushed their researches to logical extremes by attempting to 'suggest' the atmosphere around his figures, while disintegrating their shapes. His *Ecce Puer*, a portrait of *Alfred Mond at the age of six*, depicts a face whose features seem to have been smoothed away by the effect of light.

At the height of his fame and success, Rodin was obliged to surround himself with assistants, many of whom went on to have successful careers of their own. Some, like Desbois, were permanently marked by the master's influence: other, like Schnegg and Bourdelle, joined the early twentieth century movement that sought to revive the qualities of strength, balance and clarity exemplified by antiquity.

Bartholomé was an acknowledged pioneer in this field. In his *Monument aux Morts*, 1889-1899 (Père Lachaise cemetery), of which *Fillette pleurant* is a fragment, this sculptor attained a form of universal symbolism whose technique and style were in direct contrast to those of Rodin. Again, in the neo-Hellenist *Monument à J.J. Rousseau*, Bartholomé attempts to express his own original perception of rhythm.

Bourdelle also imposed 'constraints of style' on himself in the early 1900's, by gradually curbing the expressive romanticism of his youth: though this quality is still visible in his *Tête de combattant (Head of a Soldier)*, a theme taken up again in 1905 from the original *Monument aux Morts (Monument to the fallen)* at Montauban. Bourdelle became interested in the archaic style, with influenced his *Tête d'Apollon (Head of Apollo)* (1900-1909) and *Pénélope* (1905-1908) whose monumental nature does not exclude a certain dreamy grace. *Héraklès archer (Hercules the Bowman)*, 1909, shows Bourdelle's extraordinary mastery of composition, tension and the arrangement of empty spaces. "The movement embodied in this archer, who is suspended in mid-air yet at the same time balanced, is one of astonishing audacity. He is braced against a rock; though motionless, he seems to be coiled like a spring; his physical features are succinct, exact, full and vibrant. *Héraklès archer* is one of the most prodigious achievements of living art, in which realism verges on the ideal..."

Medardo Rosso
1858-1928
Ecce Puer
1906
Bronze
44 / 37 cm

Emile-Antoine
Bourdelle
1861-1929
Héraklès archer
(Hercules the Bowman)
1909
Bronze
248 / 247 cm

III

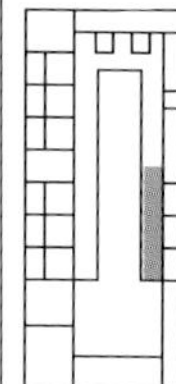

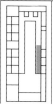

Having begun as a painter, glazer and ceramist, Maillol began to work in sculpture around 1895. While the rippling lines of his *Danseuse (Girl dancing)* carry overtones of Art Nouveau, he quickly evolved towards the more restrained style of the two *Baigneuses (Women bathing)* exhibited on the console.

In 1900, Maillol began the first of his large sculptures, *Méditerranée (Mediterranean)*, the plaster model for which was exhibited at the 1905 Salon d'Automne. (The marble version at the Musée d'Orsay was sculpted from this original.) A comparison of the final version and the 1902 scale model, which is more naturalist in conception, shows the drift of Maillol's thought at this time: "It is not enough", he used to say, "to have a model and copy it. Nature may provide the basis for work, but art does not consist in merely copying nature". Working from a given theory, he set out to simplify physical features, allowing nothing to interfere with their regularity. He also pared down composition to bare essentials with no parallel limbs, no contorsions, nothing but a self-evident geometrical framework. *Désir* (*Desire*), 1907, is a fine example in relief of this rigorous quest for perfection. For Maillol, beauty was to be found in harmony, in the balanced, controlled gestures of the body untroubled by passion.

This concept led him to reject thematic sculpture; for example, his *Monument to Cézanne*, 1912-1925, which was commissioned but refused by the town of Aix-en-Provence, consisted of a simple, clothed female figure bearing an olive branch. For Maillol, this classical composition was the most fitting way to evoke the painter.

At the outset of his career as a sculptor. Maillol, like Gauguin and Lacombe, devoted himself to woodcarving. It was Joseph Bernard who made the decisive step forward, attacking large blocks of stone and wood with a view to "freeing the imprisoned nymph" within. Because this procedure eliminated all intermediaries between the artist and his work, it answered a crying need for strength and sincerity felt by modern sculptors, who were tired of the sterile academic approach to their art. Both the title and the massive aspect of Bernard's *Effort vers la nature (Effort toward Nature)*, 1906-1907, testify to a desire for unity of form and matter. *La danse (The Dance)*, 1911-1913, was executed in the same fashion, with the difference that the original desire for simplification is replaced with a rhythmical quality (also perceptible in *La Porteuse d'eau – The Water Carrier*, 1912). This quality establishes a certain kinship between Bernard's work and that of Maurice Denis.

Joseph Bernard
1866-1931
Effort vers la nature
(Effort Toward Nature)
1906
Stone
32 / 23 cm

Aristide Maillol
1861-1944
Désir
(Desire)
1907
Lead
120 / 115 cm

Aristide Maillol
1861-1944
Danseuse
(Dancer)
1895
Bois
22 / 24 cm

Aristide Maillol
1861-1944
Méditerranée
(Mediterranean)
1905
Marble
110 / 117 cm

III

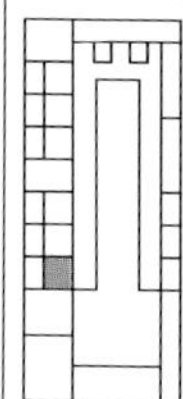

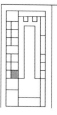

Naturalism

This room contains paintings of the type that were officially approved under the Third Republic; at the time they were widely known even to the ordinary populace, and were reproduced in dictionaries and schoolbooks all over France. Then, from the 1920s onward, they were abruptly and totally forgotten. Despite their wide variety of subject matter, they illustrate the naturalist trends which developed strongly in France between 1880-1890.

Jules Bastien-Lepage specialised in the illustration of peasant life and farm work: he was highly attuned to contemporary sentiment. His work is vividly painted, with a freedom of treatment learned from Manet and his friends. *Les foins (Haymaking)* assured him of a place in the first rank of official naturalist painters, along with Alfred Roll, whose large, skilful, fresh renderings of country scenes were greatly appreciated *(Manda Lamétrie, fermière – Manda Lamétrie. Farmwife*, 1887). Lhermitte's valiant, determined peasants introduce a social tone to painting of the agricultural world and *La paye des moissonneurs (Harvesters' Wages)*, purchased by the State, added to the painter's fame.

Another aspect of modern life was dealt with by Cormon in *La forge (The Forge)*, 1894, a painting in muted colours lit by fleeting gleams of light. But Cormon's real specialities were prehistoric and religious scenes. For his *Cain*, the lynch-pin of the 1880 Salon, Cormon painted each figure from life, and gave proof of a profound concern for archaeological realism in his rendering of primitive existence. This canvas was widely acclaimed and subsequently purchased by the state.

Jean-Paul Laurens was a painter of scenes from French history: *L'excommunication de Robert-le-Pieux (Excommunication of Robert the Pious)*, 1875, is typical of his dramatic work.

Léon Bonnat began as a history painter, then turned to portraiture, becoming the official painter of all the main personalities of the Third Republic. In his rendering of *Madame Pasca* the actress imposes her personality by the reality of her presence, which is accentuated by colour and light.

From France, the naturalist trend spread throughout Europe; Marie Bashkirtseff, a painter who came to study in Paris, was greatly influenced by her teacher Bastien-Lepage *(Le meeting*, 1884).

Léon Bonnat
1833-1922
Portrait
de Madame Pasca
1874
Oil on canvas
222.5 / 132 cm

Edouard Detaille
1848-1912
Le rêve
(The Dream)
1888
Oil on canvas
300 / 400 cm

Jules Bastien-Lepage
1848-1884
Les foins (Haymaking)
Oil on canvas
180 / 195 cm

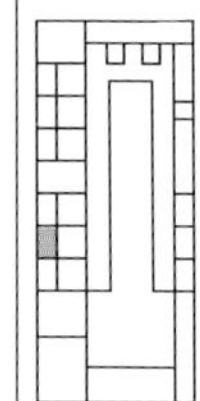

Fernand-Anne Piestre,
also known as Cormon
1845-1924

Caïn
1880
Oil on canvas
584 / 700 cm

Cormon's theme for this painting was taken from Victor Hugo's poem *La Conscience*, in *La Légende des siècles.*

« Lorsque avec ses enfants vêtus de peau de bêtes.
Echevelé, livide au milieu des tempêtes,
Caïn se fut enfui de devant Jéhovah,
Comme le soir tombait, l'homme sombre arriva
Au bas d'une montagne en une grande plaine... »

III

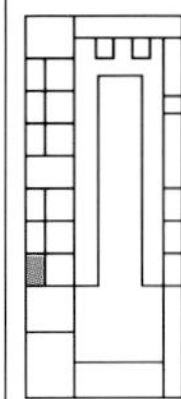

In the wake of painting, sculpture too rediscovered the qualities of realism which had always characterised the French tradition. Vincenzo Vela in Italy, Constantin Meunier in Belgium and Jules Dalou in France turned for subject matter to workers and peasants, thus freeing their work of historical, mythological and religious overtones.

Dalou, whose sympathy for the Republican party is evident in his passionate bust of *Henri Rochefort*, 1888, had been an active participant in the Paris Commune. Having succeeded in escaping to England with his family, he sent his project for Le *Triomphe de la République (The Triumph of the Republic)* from London in 1879, the year of the amnesty. Dalou's *Le forgeron (The Blacksmith)* nearby pushes the wheel of a waggon; he wears wooden clogs and a leather apron and carries his hammer on one shoulder. Nobody could mistake this blacksmith figure for Vulcan; Dalou planned to use him again for a *Monument au travail (Monument to Work),* which was never realised though the artist accumulated quantities of preliminary sketches from 1889 and in the meantime completed *Le Grand paysan (The Peasant),* 1889-1899.

Although Dalou's attention to day-to-day reality is evident from his choice of subject matter — women at their toilet, workers — it is also displayed in his talent as a modeller and his refusal to make the smallest concession to the idealism of academic art. The nude study for *La République* brings into focus all the strengths and weaknesses of a body which is that of a real woman, not merely an allegory.

Constantin Meunier's preferred themes were coalminers, stevedores, rough peasants and industry in general, which was the source of much misery but also of the massive economic progress then taking place in Europe. Aware of the strength embodied in these workers, which he symbolised in his *Débardeur du Port d'Anvers (Stevedore at the Port of Antwerp),* 1890, Meunier endowed them with a dignity and monumentality which raised them to the level of mythological heroes. From 1885-1890, Meunier, like Dalou, dreamed of creating a *Monument de Travail*, which was only realised in 1929-1930, long after his death. With this in mind, he sculpted a number of reliefs depicting the *Human Machine*, also evoked by Hoetger in a powerful composition (*Machine humaine*, 1902).

Bernhard Hoetger
1874-1949
Machine humaine
(Human Machine)
1902
Bronze
44 / 37.5 cm

Constantin Meunier
1831-1905
Puddleurs
(Puddlers)
1893
Bronze
50 / 49 cm

Jules Dalou
1838-1902
Forgeron (Blacksmith);
one of the figures
in his project
for a monument
to the *Triumph*
of the Republic.
1879-1889
Plaster
67 / 37 cm

Brittany, with its melancholy and passion, became the chosen refuge of a group of artists known as 'la bande noire' (the black group), who were inspired by the violent contrasts of the region. Charles Cottet and Lucien Simon painted dark-tinted realist canvases in the tradition of Courbet, depicting the harsh lives of Breton seafaring folk. In Cottet's work, the colours are shadowy, the gestures apparently frozen, and the forms are simultaneously grief-stricken, resigned and fatalistic *(Au pays de la mer*, 1898; *Douleur au pays de la mer – Grief by the Sea*, 1908).

The naturalist movement had by now extended all over Europe. The German painter Max Liebermann, whose work is akin to Impressionism, uses vivid brushwork to depict sunlight filtered through foliage *(Brasserie de campagne à Brannenburg – Country Brewery at Brannenburg*, 1893). The same influence is apparent in the intimist, refined portrait of *M*[me] *Lwoff*, 1895, by the Russian, Valentin Serov: here, the light seems to cling in waves of colour to the face and the bodice.

Research into the nature of light was also under way in Scandinavia, where the Dane Kroyer introduced a taste for open-air painting into his country. Kroyer lived by the sea at Skagen, where he produced paintings that captured the lively, fresh, translucent quality of the coastal atmosphere *(Bateaux de pêche – Fishing Boats*, 1884). Light of a similar naturalness and warmth may be found in the paintings of the Spaniard Sorolla y Bastida *(Retour de la pêche, halage de la barque – Return of the Fishermen: Hauling up the Boat).*

Meanwhile, the Dutch artist Breitner continued in the realist tradition: much influenced by Courbet, Millet, Manet and the naturalist writings of Zola, he set out to be a witness of his own time. Breitner settled in Amsterdam in 1886, where he painted scenes of daily life using broad brushwork to create sombre, harmonious effects, as in *Chevaux tirant des pieux à Amsterdam (Horses hauling Logs, Amsterdam).*

In Switzerland, Eugène Burnand's naturalist bent found an outlet in his religious compositions. *Les disciples Pierre et Jean courant au sépulcre (The Disciples Peter and John Hastening to the Sepulcre),* one of his most famous works, creates a powerful atmosphere of dramatic intensity with a combination of light, shrewd composition and facial expression.

Finally, the Belgian painter Léon Frédéric, in his triptych *Ages de l'ouvrier (Workman's Ages)* 1895-1897, contrived to associate an almost hyper-realist treatment of his subject with cold colours and social symbolism. A similar approach is adopted by Eugène Laermans in his *Fin d'automne (Last Days of Autumn),* 1899.

George-Hendrik Breitner
1857-1923
Deux chevaux blancs tirant des pieux à Amsterdam (Two White Horses Hauling Logs, Amsterdam)
Circa 1897-1898
Oil on canvas
100 / 152 cm

Eugène Burnand
1850-1921
Les disciples Pierre et Jean courant au sépulcre le matin de la Résurrection (The Disciples Peter and John Hastening to the Sepulchre on the Morning of the Ressurrection)
1898
Oil on canvas
82 / 134 cm

Charles Cottet
1863-1925
Douleur au pays de la mer (Grief by the Sea)
1908
Oil on canvas
264 / 345 cm

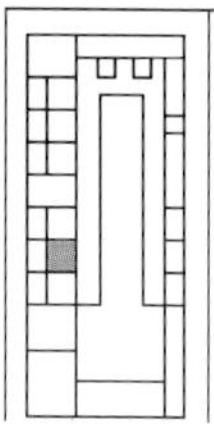

Lionel Walden
1861-1933

The Docks of Cardiff
1894

Oil on canvas
127 / 193 cm

Valentin Alexandrovitch
Serov
1864-1955
Madame Lwoff
the artist's cousin
1895
Oil on canvas
90 / 59 cm

Blanche, Boldini, Helleu, Troubetzkoy

Brilliant, elegant and cosmopolitan, the Parisian society which frequented the theatres, cafés and salons of the capital quickly became a favourite theme for painters and sculptors, impregnating the world of literature with its light and witty atmosphere, and captured so well by Marcel Proust (1871-1922). In 1891, Jacques-Emile Blanche met the writer and executed the famous portrait in which Proust's face stands out against a sombre background, thus enhancing the light shades of the orchid and the author's shirt. One of the most conspicuous characters of the time was Count Robert de Montesquiou, an aesthete, symbolist writer and man of the world. The main characters in Proust's *Remembrance of Things Past* were modelled on members of Montesquiou's circle, while de Monstesquiou himself was the original for Baron Charlus. The Russian sculptor Troubetzkoy created a bronze statuette of the writer seated with "head held high, his look commanding; his right hand rests on a cane that supports his outstretched arm; his left hand holds a wide—brimmed hat; a cloak is draped to one side, its folds falling around a fine recumbent Russian hound..."

Boldini, who settled in Paris in 1872, began his celebrated series of Parisian portraits of society women and demi-mondaines like *Madame Max*. Sarah Bernhardt, the current queen of the theatre, was one of the "muses" of this Parisian society; Gérôme sought to reconcile a tranquil image with an evocation of the actress's dramatic talent (*Sarah Bernhardt*, 1890).

With Devambez, however, the outlook on life in the capital became more disturbing. Painted with the liveliness and dynamism of a journalist used to capturing a scene very quickly, *La Charge — The Charge*, 1902, is a reminder that the "Belle Epoque" was also a period of social unrest before the slaughter of the Great War.

Jacques-Emile Blanche
1861-1942
Portrait of Marcel Proust
1892
Oil on canvas
73.5 / 60.5 cm

Giovanni Boldini
1842-1931
Madame Max
1896
Oil on canvas
205 / 100 cm

Paul Troubetzkoy
1866-1938
Robert de Montesquiou
(1855-1921)
1907
Bronze
56 / 62 cm

Symbolism was an international trend, of which France was one of the most active centres. It gathered momentum as a reaction against Realism and Impressionism; rejecting a world dominated by science and machines, symbolist intellectuals and artists set out to translate the untranslatable, meaning their thoughts and dreams. Hence the wide diversity of symbolist themes and modes of expression.

One of the first symbolist movements appeared in Great Britain. The pre-Raphaelite brotherhood, founded in 1848, stood for a rejection of realism in favour of Gothic art, 15th century Italian painting, in fact everything prior to Raphaël. Edward Burne-Jones, a fervent admirer of Botticelli and Michelangelo, transformed a traditional subject, *The Wheel of Fortune*, into a monumental work peopled by ideally beautiful, pensive figures which were noticed and admired by Puvis de Chavannes and his contemporaries. Odilon Redon's *Les yeux clos (Closed Eyes)*, 1890, neatly illustrates one of his principal tenets: "In art, everything is achieved by docile submission to the unconscious". His bent head, with half-closed eyes in the style of Michelangelo's *Dying Slaves* can only have emerged from the painter's inner world. Meanwhile, Gustave Moreau was inspired by the Bible and mythology; in his work, the main rôle is given to woman, perverse and heavily adorned, whom he portrays as a hieratic figure without action or movement.

Carrière, in complete contrast to Moreau's iridescent style, chose to evoke his world of family and childhood in strict shades of brown; a misty veil seems to permeate his paintings, creating an atmosphere that is at once familiar and unearthly. Carrière's portrait of *Paul Verlaine* is a homage to the writer, who was the precursor and master (with Mallarmé) of a generation of symbolist poets.

The landscape was another favourite symbolist theme; handled lyrically and romantically in the work of the Swiss painter Arnold Böcklin (*La chasse de Diane – Diana the Huntress*, circa 1896), it became merely bucolic in Ménard's enormous canvases. Ménard depicted mystical scenes of ancient Greece, with temple colonnades and pine trees blurring into dusk and silence (*L'Age d'Or – The Golden Age*, décor for the Law faculty at Paris). Close to Böcklin, but without resorting to mythology, the German Hans Thoma took up Poussin's theme of the inhabited landscape (*Siesta*, 1889).

Eugène Carrière
1849-1906
Paul Verlaine
1890
Oil on canvas
61 / 51 cm

Sir Edward
Burne-Jones
1833-1898
The Wheel of Fortune
1883
Oil on canvas
200 / 100 cm

Gustave Klimt
1862-1918
Rosiers sous les arbres
(Roses under the Trees)
1905
Oil on canvas
110 / 115 cm

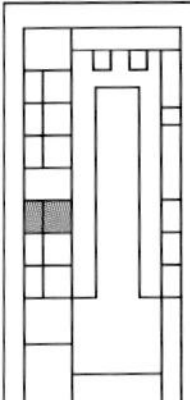

In Italy, Pellizza da Volpedo, another follower of Seurat, used the 'divisionist' technique to emphasize the play of light and convey the mysteries of life and death *(Fleur brisée – Crushed Flower*, circa 1896-1902).

Symbolism also flourished in Belgium, though it varied widely according to the temperament of each artist. Ferdinand Khnopff, who was generally accepted as the leader of the Belgian symbolist school, has left us a vision of a silent, melancholy world, in his portrait of *Marie Monnom*, wife of the painter Théo van Rysselberghe. In contrast to Knopff, Ensor's *Dame en détresse (Lady in Distress)* shows a bourgeois bedroom that has become a place of grief and pain: the furniture, curtains and carpets, all in muted colours, create an oppressive, unsettling atmosphere. Jean Delville, with his *Ecole de Platon (School of Plato)* 1898, offers an extravagant, idealistic, intellectual brand of symbolism, which is well-served by his precise graphics and his cold, lavish palette.

Lastly, the American painter Winslow Homer's *Summer Night* is an evocative image of the mysterious ocean, and the obscure influence it exercises on the destiny of mankind. New trends were announced at the close of the century by Gustave Klimt, Edvard Munch and Ferdinand Hodler, all firmly associated with symbolism and attracted to landscape. The Austrian Klimt was one of the founder members of the Viennese Secession movement that stood against academicism and historicism. His style constantly evolved; after painting dark, sentimental landscapes, he began representing nature as a protective tissue. *Rosiers sous les arbres (Roses under the Trees)*, a decorative landscape which is almost mosaic-like in aspect, breathes this essential, organic vitality the artist sought to convey. Although Munch still met with adverse reaction in Norway, his reception was favourable in Berlin, Prague and Paris, where he exhibited at both the 1903 and 1904 Salons des Indépendants; he presented several views of Asgarstrand, a village on the Oslo fjord. *Summer Night at Asgarstrand* is a highly structured work with simplified geometrical forms, a long diagonal line rendering depth, and vivid, contrasting colours. The Swiss painter Ferdinand Hodler rejected picturesque landscape, and used diversified brushwork to express the strength and eternity of the Bern Alps in *Schynige Platte*, 1909.

Winslow Homer
1836-1910
Nuit d'été
(Summer Night)
1890
Oil on canvas
76.7 / 102 cm

Edvard Munch
1863-1944
Nuit d'été à
Asgarstrand
(Summer Night at
Asgarstrand)
1904
Oil on canvas
99 / 103 cm

III

The last 30 years of the 19th century saw a profound renewal of architecture and the arts of decoration. Everywhere in Europe a need for emancipation and originality was emerging, which culminated in the 1890s with the appearance of Art Nouveau. In the history of forms, Art Nouveau may be described (at least theoretically) as the first conscious attempt to create a radically new style, totally divorced from anything that had gone before.

The architect and the decorator Victor Horta put the new ideas into practice from 1892 onwards, beginning with his Hôtel Tassel in Brussels. Similar disciplines of unity and harmony were paramount in the residence built by Horta for the industrialist Octave Aubecq (between 1899–1904), but the style had by then become more restrained. The characteristic ribbing which outlined the woodwork, articulations of windows and furniture, was refined, with the result that the ensemble acquired greater sobriety and the structures themselves were clarified. Paul Hankar, one of the most brilliant representatives of Belgian Art Nouveau, together with Horta and Van de Velde, favoured flat surfaces, drawings and restraint, to enhance the structure of both his architecture and his furniture. Gustave Serrurier-Bovy, who had been influenced by the English Arts and Crafts movement, abandoned curves and inflections after 1901 in favour of rectilinear forms which emphasised the natural qualities of wood.

Henry Van der Velde operated within the same tradition of craftsmanship. In 1893, he abandoned painting in order to build and decorate his house at Uccle near Brussels. Rejecting everything that was artificial and useless, he designed a chair with pure, dynamic forms which was successfully marketed and contributed widely to the spread of the new ideas throughout Europe. Likewise, an armchair design created for the banker Biart in 1896 later made its way into many Belgian and German interiors. Van de Velde's desire for harmony of form and décor reached its peak of perfection in his large *Desk*, with its flowing rhythm, its vigour, its abstract and dynamic lines, and whose only ornaments – gilded bronze mouldings and handles – highlighted its functional value.

René Lalique 1860-1945 *Flacon à odeur* *(Scent-bottle)* Circa 1900-1902 Blown and moulded glass using lost wax process; cast, chased gold, 10.5 cm	Georges Bastard 1881-1939 *Eventail "Epis d'orge"* *(Fan: Ears of Barley)* 1911 Horn and mother of pearl 21.4 / 38.7 cm	Eugène Feuillâtre 1870-1916 *Drageoir* *(Comfit box)* Circa 1903-1904 Silver, enamel and crystal H 8.3 cm ∅ 14,5 cm
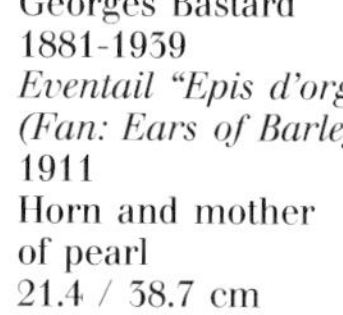	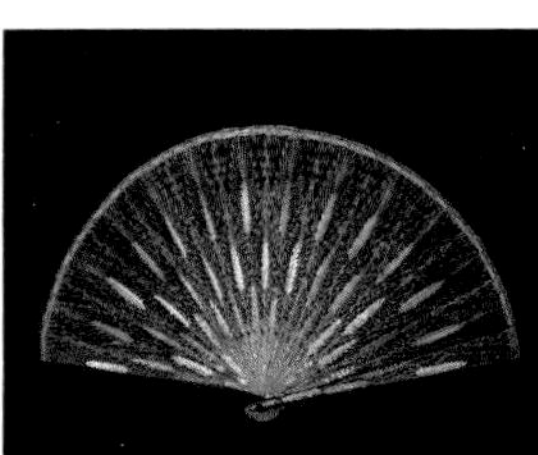	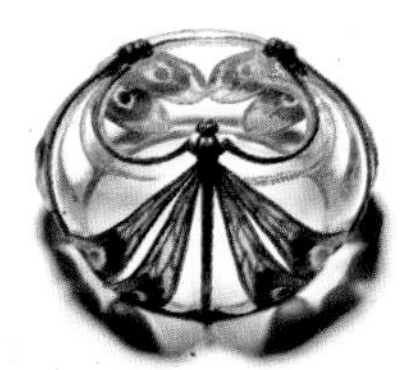

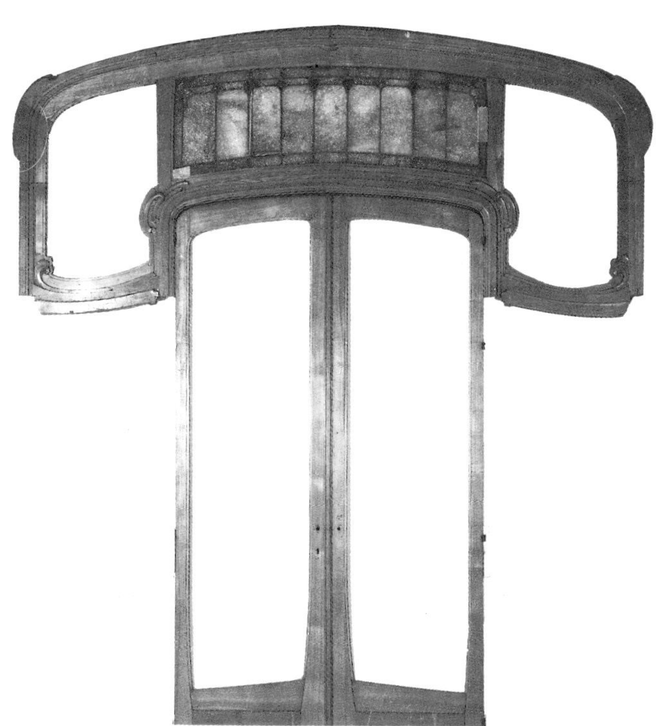

Victor Horta
1861-1947

Boiserie, for the Hôtel Aubecq, 520, avenue Louise, Brussels, 1902-1904

Ash wood, chenillé 'American' glass
415 / 353 cm

III

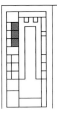

Around 1895-1898, in Amsterdam, Hendrikus Petrus Berlage invented a chair that clearly showed the way it was made, in the manner of British designers like A.W.N. Pugin. The same influence underlies the early creations of the German Richard Riemerschmid, in the mid-1890s, but he rapidly moved on to design mass-produced furniture that would be solid, inexpensive and unadorned; this attempt, however, was unsuccessful (*Chair*, 1902 model). In Norway, Johan Borgersen produced plain oak furniture, carved with traditional Scandinavian, abstract motifs that intertwined and undulated, evoking waves, ropes and sea monsters (*Bench*, circa 1899-1900).

In the field of decorative arts, Belgium was again a source of astonishing creations. For the 1857 Brussels Universal Exhibition, at Tervueren, in the rooms of the Congo pavilion, whose entire interior decoration had been entrusted to Hankar, Léopold van Strydonck, jeweller of the Belgian court, presented an extraordinary composition, "The Struggle between Good and Evil", arranged around one of the elephant tusks sent from the Congo and laid at the artists' disposal by King Léopold II. Van Strydonck contrasted the purity of the tusk with a furious entanglement of bronze serpents...

According to his own definition, Hector Guimard was an 'architectural artist'. He pursued the same utilitarian ideal as Victor Horta, whose Hôtel Tassel in Brussels he visited in 1894. At this time, Guimard was building a block of rental apartments at No. 16, rue de la Fontaine in Paris, the 'Castel Béranger'; in 1898, he received a prize from the City of Paris for its façade. This building was the blueprint for what became known at the 'style Guimard' (an expression which first appeared in 1903); the gist of it is a predilection for asymmetry, arabesque and long vegetable curves fashioned from a wide range of different materials.

Richard Riemerschmid
1868-1957
Dresdener Werkstätten
für Handwerkskunst
Chair
1902
Oak, straw-bottom
82.5 / 43 / 48 cm

Gustave Serrurier-Bovy
1858-1910
Pair of Chairs for the
"Réséda" Dining-room
Circa 1905-1908
Oak, brass, original velvet
upholstery
93.8 / 48 / 44 cm

Hendrikus Petrus Berlage
1856-1934
Chair
Circa 1895-1898
Oak, modern leather
upholstery
94 / 44 / 56 cm

Henry Van de Velde
1863-1957
Writing-desk
1898-1899
Oak, gilded bronze,
copper, leather
128 / 268 / 122 cm

III

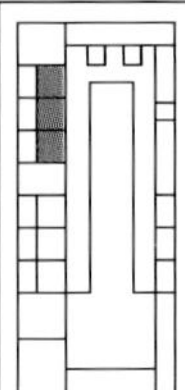

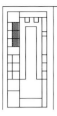

For the billiard room and "petit salon" of the Roy property at Les Gévrils (Loiret), Guimard referred back to his original Castel Béranger models – *Chimney-piece, Smoking-room sofa, Banquette-chest, Stained glass windows* – running through which was a movement inspired from the plant world, the stem and its vital principle, and whose branching off points were highlighted by knots of abstract motifs. The early years of the 20th century marked a development in Guimard's style, as may be seen in *Armchair*, designed for the Castel Val at Chaponval and built in 1902-1905; the artist abandoned his play on lines in favour of opposing full and empty space, emphasized the functional aspect of the piece through the concave form of the seat, back and arms, and relegated ornamentation to the ends of the armrests.

Around 1903-1905, the architect designed a series of decorative cast-iron pieces that were produced by the foundries at Saint-Dizier, and were intended to feature on both town buildings and suburban villas. This attempt to commercialize elements connected with architecture, or decoration of parks and cemeteries, was a failure, because of their intensely personal character and the difficulty of integrating them with work by architects other than Guimard himself.

Jewelry and costume accessories supplied a wide field of decorative research for Art Nouveau. René Lalique blended the subtle colour range of precious stones and cloisonné enamels with horn, ivory and glass, for his naturalist and symbolist designs; then, no doubt stimulated by Emile Gallé's success, he created a glassware workshop in 1898. Inspired by marine fauna and flora, his *Flacon à odeur – Scent-bottle* also referred to certain 18th century creations. Henri Vever collaborated with Eugène Grasset, who invented a style of 'Merovingian' jewelry for him. At the same time, Fernard Thesmar created a line of jewels in iridescent enamel and gold cloisonné, along with gold appliqué on soft-paste porcelain.

The sculptor, silversmith and enameller Eugène Feuillâtre obtained original effects from translucent enamelling on silver. Armand Point, at Haute-Claire, reconstituted a workshop along the lines of the old master craftsmen's corporations which turned out enamel work, pottery and embroidery. Georges Bastard introduced organic materials such as mother of pearl, horn, tortoiseshell and ivory, which he fashioned and sculpted with enormous skill into objets de luxe.

Hector Guimard 1867-1942 *Armchair* 1903 Pear-tree wood, original embossed leather upholstery 106 / 76 / 56 cm	Léopold Van Strydonck 1861-1937 *"The Struggle between Good and Evil", mounted elephant tusk* 1897 Ivory, bronze 76 / 70 / 35 cm	Hector Guimard 1867-1942 *Bench leg* 1905-1907 Cast iron 930 / 570 cm

Paul Hankar
1859-1901

Triple door for the painter Albert Ciamberlani's studio in Brussels (destroyed)
1897
Beech, mahogany, glass
345 / 244 cm

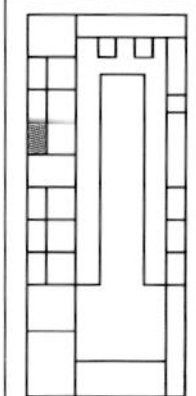

In 1899, Robert de Domecy, faithful patron of Redon's work, commissioned the latter to decorate the dining-room of his château, then in the final stages of building. This was a new undertaking for the artist who anxiously created a series of fifteen panels, peopled, he wrote, "with dream flowers, imaginary fauna; all in large panels treated with a little of everything, distemper, oil, even pastel..." The work was completed in October 1901 and the panels were hung over the sobre oak woodwork, while friezes framed windows and topped doors, lighting up the room with their glowing yellow and blue... This décor marked Redon's dazzling entrance into the world of colour and his lasting farewell to black and white; it was also a prelude to several other decorative projects, confirming the painter's commitment to the ideas of Art Nouveau: to contribute towards embellishing everyday surroundings, to pay the same attention to creating a décor as to painting a canvas on an easel.

Pottery took a major part in the general movement towards a rebirth of applied art. In the 1870's, potters reconsidered and analysed the technical processes of their craft, and effectively revive the whole concept of ceramic art. Ernest Chaplet was the first of a brilliant new generation of modern potters; inspired by the quality of Far Eastern pottery, he devoted himself to raw clay and glazed earthenware, which he covered in vivid red and blue glazes. Alexandre Bigot was also influenced by Chinese and Japanese sources. His rustic-looking creations are decorated with mat enamels in yellow, blue, green and brown tones. Around 1900, Bigot began manufacturing tiles and stoneware reliefs for architectural décors, in addition to reproducing the work of sculptors and architects such as Charpentier and Guimard.

Odilon Redon
1840-1916
Decorative panels
for the dining-room
of the château de
Domecy, in the l'Yonne
region
1901

III

The last decade of the century witnessed the development of a strong regional artistic centre at Nancy; what became known as the 'Ecole de Nancy' acquired its official letters patent as an 'Alliance Provinciale des Industries d'Arts' in 1901. Nancy was a town in full expansion; at the instigation of Emile Gallé, the local 'Alliance' of industrialists and craftsmen dedicated themselves to the principle of the 'unity of art', affirmed their faith in nature as the only inexhaustible source of renewal for the decorative arts, and acknowledged their duty to train and renew a highly-qualified workforce.

In 1901, François Vaxelaire founded a drapery and fancy goods store in the rue Raugraff at Nancy, and commissioned the architects Charles and Emile André to build it for him. Emile André, who was entrusted with the interior work, collaborated with the sculptor and cabinet-maker Eugène Vallin to create a décor dominated by sinuous Art Nouveaut woodwork, clematis motifs and stained glass designed by André and manufactured by Jacques Gruber.

The master cabinet-maker Louis Majorelle specialised in carved mahogany blended with naturalist marquetry decoration, the dynamic lines of which he adapted to the contours of his fitted furniture. He liked to embellish his pieces with gilded bronze waterlilies and stylized orchids, which he attached to angles in order to emphasise structure and reinforce balance and stability. The pieces of furniture exhibited at the Musée d'Orsay do not form an ensemble, though they are original Majorelle creations from 1905-1908. The light fixtures, also designed by Majorelle, were made with the collaboration of Daum and belong to the 'Lotus' and 'Water-lily' patterns he created around 1902.

Stained glass played an important part in the renewal of interior decoration, and for this architects looked to famous painters. Albert Besnard, who was both a painter and a decorator, displayed all his talent as a colourist in his *Cygnes sur le lac d'Annecy*, a French window which was executed by Henri Carot. On his return from a study tour of the United States in 1894, the dealer Siegfried Bing decided to promote Art Nouveau in his celebrated Paris gallery. Bing ordered ten stained glass windows from the American firm of Louis Comfort Tiffany, based on designs by the Nabi painters Bonnard, Denis, Vallotton and Vuillard, as well as by Toulouse-Lautrec *(Au nouveau Cirque).*

Louis Comfort Tiffany
1848-1933
and Toulouse-Lautrec
1864-1901
Au nouveau cirque, 1895
'American glass'
marbled and chenillé,
cabochons
120 / 85 cm

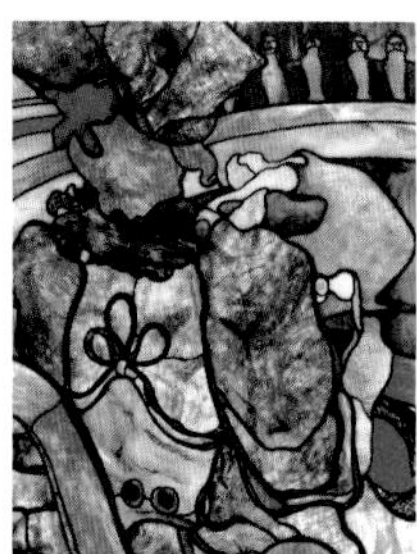

Louis Majorelle
1859-1926
"Orchid" desk
Circa 1905-1909
Mahogany amourette,
gilded bronze,
embossed leather
95 / 145 / 70 cm

Emile André
1880-1944
Eugène Vallin
1856-1922
Jacques Gruber
1870-1930
Door for fitting room at the Magasins François Vaxelaire et Compagnie, 1901
Mahogany, chenillé
'American' glass,
opalescent glass,
copper
198 / 182 / 65 cm

III

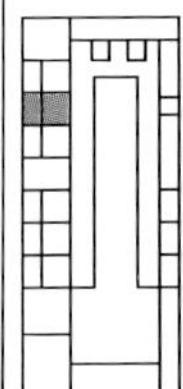

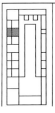

Glass and enamelwork processes were also renewed. Henri Cros, a sculptor and ceramist, received a commission in 1892 from the Ministry of Fine Arts for a pâte de verre polychrome fountain. This fountain was designed on the theme of the history of water, and was placed in the Musée du Luxembourg. Meanwhile, the glass maker and enameller Albert Dammouse created an extraordinarily refined process for pâte de verre decoration, while the work of François Décorchemont in the same field tended to be thicker and more transparent.

From the beginning of the Second Empire, the great dealers in fine crystal were consistent innovators. Rousseau, Léveillé and the Pannier brothers at *L'escalier de cristal* actively sought original processes for coloured glass. Abroad, Koepping was making his fragile corollas at the royal workshops in Berlin, while in New York Louis Comfort Tiffany perfected an original opalescent material in 1892. This material was the result of a number of processes, including irisation, filigree, gold and silver infusions; it became universally known as 'favrile glass'.

In the field of ceramics, as in glass, Emile Gallé took over from his father Charles, introducing new motifs based on regional flora. As an expert botanist, Gallé studied flowers and plants with particular attention to their colour and form; he also managed to produce a dense, refined, deep-toned glass paste, to which he applied opaque enamels, that glazed and adhered perfectly. Although Gallé continued to apply popular motifs to his work, he was inspired to more original designs, such as his *ornamental plate* in the Musée d'Orsay, by the Orient, China and Japan. The plate was a Japanese version of a work attributed to Bernard Palissy. Gallé even referred to Egyptian art for his *Jardinière* in the form of a Horus falcon, but in general nature itself was his preferred source.

Forms in Gallé glassware remained faithful to Western tradition and Western antiquity (*verres d'apparat*, between 1867 and 1876). But beginning in the mid-1870's, Japanese-influenced décors began to emerge, with forms and techniques suggested by Persia and Islam. Gallé's *Pique-fleurs* carries an unusual assembly of lightly-drawn Japanese motifs, insects, flowers and herbs, and European landscapes. The piece also combines the techniques of blown and craquelé glasswork with applications and painted, enamelled, gilded décor. The vase entitled *Liseron d'octobre (Autumn Convolvulus)*, 1891, in blown, double-layered crystal, bears both engraved and incorporated décor, while the cup 'Par une telle nuit' is handled like a cameo, with three layers of crystal tinted to produce a range of more or less profound blues, diffuse greens, and black; this piece also includes metallic

Emile Gallé
1846-1904
Pique-fleurs
(Flower Holder)
Pattern created circa 1878-1880
'Moonlight' glass crackled with applications, painted decor, enamelled and gilded
gilt bronze stand
24 / 22 cm

Emile Gallé
1846-1904
La main aux algues
et aux coquillages
Hand with Seaweed and Shells
1904
Engraved crystal,
inclusions and applications
33.4 / 13.4 cm

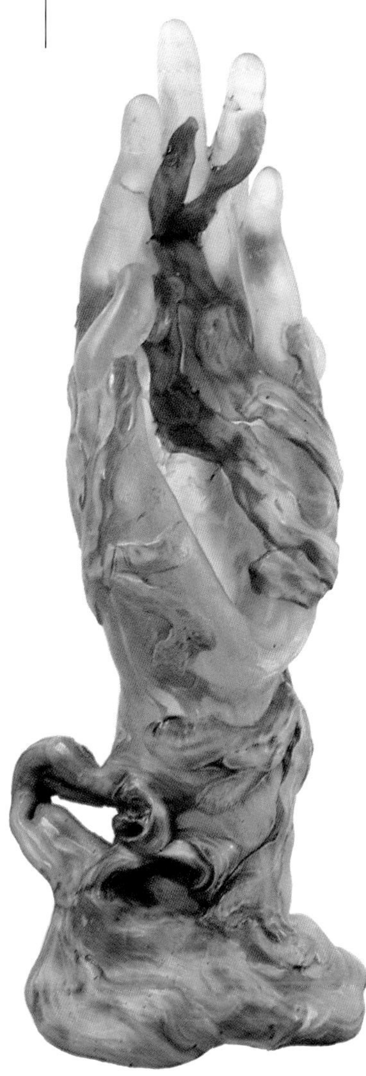

III

particles and engraved décor. Gallé was a master of such procedures, which were intended to reflect the primal, inexhaustible source of some poetic or musical endeavour. For example, 'Le Liseron d'Octobre' was inspired by a line from Verlaine: "Vous vous êtes penché sur ma mélancolie"; while the cup *Par une telle nuit (On such a Night as This)* evokes a passage from Berlioz' opera Les *Troyens*. The *Fleurs d'oignons* cornet, which was created for Gallés display at the 1900 Universal Exhibition, is a fine example of glass marquetry technique. Meadow flowers, exotic blooms, insects and marine fauna were soon to appear on Gallé cups and vases. Gallé's last creation in glass, *La main aux algues et aux coquillages (Hand with Seaweed and Shells),* appeals to the symbolism of underwater life, to the "enamels and cameos of the sea"... Reminiscent of antique votive offerings, of medieval relics or oriental cults, *La Main* appears above all as a poetic and mysterious "correspondence" with the marine world...

A long-standing interest in woodwork, along with his desire to see his ceramic and glass ware properly exhibited, eventually persuaded Gallé to become a manufacturer of "sculptured marqueté furniture". His "inlaid ware and small-scale, inexpensive pieces" were well-received, while his "luxury furniture" was sometimes violently criticized. The products were sold at prices geared to the value of the wood they contained and the relative quality of their finish; they included seats, sideboards, dessert trays and pedestal tables, and were often inspired by styles from the past to which Gallé applied his naturalist concepts. He used the shape of the poppy to make colonnettes, balusters and consoles; poppies were also featured in the marquetry of a suspended shelf (1890-1892), and as supports for the *Gardez les cœurs* tray-table, created in 1895. *La flore hivernale (Winter Flowers)*, a glass-fronted piece made for the 1889 Universal Exhibition, was conceived for a specific purpose, namely "... to contain the picture publications which appear around Christmas and the New Year". The glass is etched with landscapes and snowflakes, and the drawers are decorated with sprays of pine and holly.

Emile Gallé's ultimate creation, *La vitrine (Glass Cabinet)*, was commissioned in 1897 by the magistrate Henry Hirsch. In this piece, one of Gallé's favourite motifs, the dragonfly, is surprisingly used to impart monolithic heaviness and not, as one might expect, an airy quality.

Emile Gallé
1846-1904
Par une telle nuit
("On such a Night as This)
1894
Blown, triple-layered crystal, metal particles, engraved decor, partially gilded
13.3 ∅ 13.5 cm

Emile Gallé
1846-1904
Liseron d'octobre
(Autumn Convolvulus)
1891
Two-layered crystal, inclusions, engraved décor. Base of cut, engraved crystal
18.8 ∅ 9.8 cm

Emile Gallé
1846-1904
Vitrine aux libellules
(Glass Cabinet
with Dragonflies)
1904
Ironwood, oak, stippled mahogany, Brazilian rosewood, mother-of-pearl incrustations, patinated glass, cut stone, chiselled and patinated bronze
234 / 134 / 64.5 cm

III

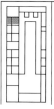

The principle of *unity in Art* which was fundamental to the aesthetic theory of Art Nouveau, asserted itself in France after the official abandonment of discrimination between 'major' and 'minor' arts. In 1891, the arts applied to industry were accepted at the annual Salon of the Société Nationale des Beaux-Arts, alongside painting and sculpture.

The Nabi painters participated in this unity of art when they demanded "walls, walls to decorate", with a view to embellishing everyday surroundings. With his four panels *Femmes au jardin (Women in the Garden)*, Pierre Bonnard created his first decorative ensemble that was presented at the 7th Salon des Indépendants. The sinuous graphic work familiar to Art Nouveau, the elongated format reminiscent of leaves in a screen, and the decorative plant motifs that break up the composition recall the painter's interest in Japanese art, which earned him the nickname "Nabi japonard".

A large number of sculptors contributed to the decorative arts. Alexandre Charpentier, Jean Baffier, Jean Dampt and Rupert Carabin were among those who 'converted' to decorative work, initiating a rehabilitation of the domestic arts and seeking a modern style which could be made available to all. Jules Baffier produced simple pewter crockery, while Jules Desbois, a pupil of Rodin, worked successfully in both silver and pewter. Jean Carriès, who was acclaimed as a sculptor by contemporary critics, discovered Japanese ceramics at the 1878 Universal Exhibition. He went on to master stoneware techniques, and exhibited a glass cabinet at the Société Nationale des Beaux-Arts in 1892 which won him much praise, including that of Gallé himself, who declared: "You are young and you have genius! Alone, you have revealed marvellous secrets of our ancient craft". A number of Carriès' objects in coloured, enamelled stoneware were bought for the national collection. The artist also exhibited several ceramic sculptures, among them *Le Grenouillard (Frog Man),*

Pierre Bonnard
1867-1947
Femme à la robe quadrillée
(Woman in a Checked Dress)
1891
Distemper on paper,
mounted on canvas
160 / 48 cm

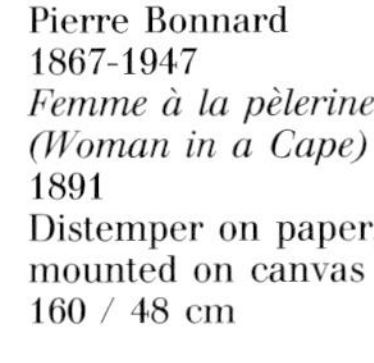

Pierre Bonnard
1867-1947
Femme à la pèlerine
(Woman in a Cape)
1891
Distemper on paper,
mounted on canvas
160 / 48 cm

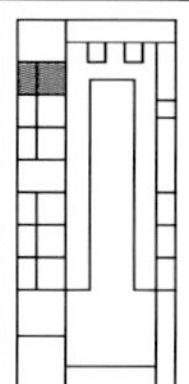

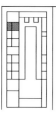

an anthropomorphic figure from the woods and marshes, conceived in solitude, the complete antithesis of his other more serene subject matter (see his series of heads of babies). Auguste Delaherches 'cabbage leaf' *Vase* in glazed stoneware depends for its decorative beauty on nothing more than the beauty of the material, complemented by the brightness and depth of the enamelling. Pierre-Adrien Dalpayrat and Alexandre Bigot preached the integration of ceramics and architecture; Bigot collaborated in the construction of many buildings. Inspired by folklore and popular themes of dancers and musicians, the Royal Porcelain Factory of Copenhagen brought out objects with simple forms, whose dazzling white enamelled porcelain served not only as the background, but was used as a colour for the snow-covered trees and ice crystals, conveying a sense of freshness evident in this *Vase*.

From an early date, Jean Dampt, Alexandre Charpentier and Rupert Carabin devoted their energies to making furniture ensembles. In March 1890, Carabin proudly unveiled his *Bookcase*, exhibited in the Gallé room, commissioned by the engineer Henry Montandon, only to see it refused by the Salon des Indépendants. In 1891, however, the same piece triumphantly represented the decorative arts at the Salon of the Société Nationale des Beaux-Arts. The symbolism of Carabin's figures are explained as follows by Gustave Geffroy: "Near the floor, the figures represent baseness, the passions that are the enemies of intelligence, which have been vanquished and enslaved by the Book. On one side is Ignorance; on the other are masks representing Vanity, Avarice, Intemperance, Anger, Stupidity and Hypocrisy... above are the three emblematic figures which give the work its full cerebral significance. Truth sits at the centre; and on the left and the right are two readers."

Dampt created a complete decoration for the drawing room (1900-1906) of the Comtesse de Béarn, with admirably controlled proportions and general harmonies. This rectangular salon, which was lit by a transparent central dome, was composed

Royal Porcelain Factory of Copenhagen Richard Bocher, decorator *Vase* 1919 Porcelain 46 cm	Jean Carriès 1855-1894 *Cache-pot* Circa 1891-1892 Glazed enamel, gold highlights 16 cm ∅ 16.8 cm	Auguste Delaherche 1857-1940 *Vase* 1892 Enamelled stoneware 37.7 cm ∅ 17.7 cm

François-Rupert
Carabin,
1862-1932
Book case
1890
Walnut and
cast iron
290 / 215 / 83 cm

III

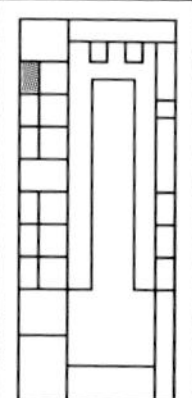

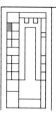

of oak, ash and elm panelling, sparsely decorated, since Dampt tended to rely on the knots of wood for decorative effect. As in Charpentier's dining room, functional elements are perfectly integrated (in this case, built-in library shelves). Above the boiseries, the walls were covered in pale painted stucco (green and yellow reseda) with a motif of ears of wheat and olive branches.

The simple décor of Dampt's boiseries and stuccos, for which all the motifs were taken from nature, the chimney-piece, topped by a marble bas-relief designed by the artist and featuring the *Chevalier de l'idéal (The Parfit Gentle Knight)*, the general play of forms and tones, every feature of this room was conducive to calm and reflection, in accordance with the client's original wish. Dampt designed this salon down to its smallest detail: andirons, tongs and shovel for the fireplace, the appliques for the electric lights, the writing table, the armchair with the curved back, the long wooden table, the gold-striped leather banquettes and even the curtains. Painter Lévy-Dhurmer also relied on oak and gnarled elmwood to create the interior decoration for industrialist Auguste Rateau's mansion in Paris. The work was completed in two parts – from 1908-1910 onwards, then after the war – and thus represents Parisian Art Nouveau's last creation. This long, drawing-room sofa illustrates late Art Nouveau trends: lower, more open form, rectilinear design curving slightly inwards at the corners, highly-stylized plant motifs concentrated at certain points on the piece.

Lucien Lévy-Dhurmer
1865-1953
and Edouard Collet
Sofa, from the large drawing-room of the Rateau mansion, 10, avenue Elisée-Reclus, Paris
Circa 1908-1910
Oak and gnarled elm
62 / 250 / 85 cm

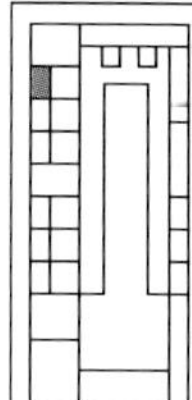

The sculptor and medallist Alexandre Charpentier learned many techniques — pewter-work, embossing, lithography, engraving, medal-making, cabinetmaking — with the generous aim of making his work available to the largest possible number of people. For many years, he led a somewhat rootless life, participating in Secessionist Salons like that of the Société Nationale des Beaux-Arts in Paris (from 1890 onwards), and the XX exhibitions in Brussels. His first great successes were had in Belgium.

Around 1900, the banker Adrien Bénard, wishing to redecorate his villa at Champrosay, commissioned Charpentier to design the dining room. Bénard was also one of the promoters of the Paris Metro, and it was thanks to him that the company chose Guimard to design its station entrances.

The space made available to Charpentier was cut in two by a heavy beam supported by two steel colonnettes. He responded to this problem with two carved wooden columns, supplemented by a purely ornamental, central wooden arch which gives the appearance of holding up the beam. The walls are covered by mahogany panels decorated with light, supple climbing plants; into these panels the artist has integrated two dessert sideboards, along with two silver cupboards and a flower basin by Bigot. A series of uprights curve upwards from the panelling, rising clear of the frieze of glazed tiles.

Charpentier designed all the furniture for this dining-room, of which only the table has survived. The 24 chairs, the chandelier and the electric wall-lights have unfortunately been lost. This ensemble constitutes one of the few complete Art Nouveau décors in existence, in which Charpentier achieves a perfect harmony through lightness of form and a subtle blending of colours and materials.

III

Alexandre Charpentier
1856-1909
Dining room of
Adrien Bénard's villa
at Champrosay
Circa 1900

Mahogany, oak and poplar,
gilded bronzes
Flower basin and glazed
tiles by Alexandre Bigot
(1862-1927)
346 / 1055 / 621 cm

III

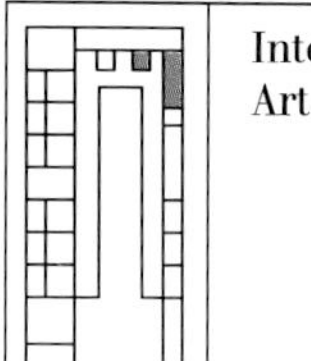

Art Nouveau ideas were spread in the early 1890s through exhibitions mounted by avant-garde groups (La libre esthétique, *Die Secession*, etc.) by illustrated magazines and decorators' catalogues. They quickly reached the great cities of Europe: Barcelona, Milan, Prague, Darmstadt, Vienna and Glasgow. Paris attracted the Czech designer Mucha (who decorated the Fouquet jewelry store and published his *Documents décoratifs),* the Italian Carlo Bugatti, who gained a reputation with his parchment-covered furniture, and the Englishman Hawkins, among others. As partisans of 'Art in Everything', these artists sought to impose their own ideal of a modern aesthetic, which they felt should be accessible to all.

In the 1850's Michael Thonet in Vienna had launched a factory to make light, bentwood furniture, and had developed a whole range for cafés, hotels and restaurants. Thonet furniture was cheap, strong, comfortable and simple, in contrast to the history-obsessed styles then in fashion. These features were neatly geared to the requirements of mass production. In 1869, Thonet's rival, J.J. Kohn, began using the same assembly procedures and sought to enlarge production to include domestic furniture. Kohn called in the architect Gustav Siegel, a pupil of Josef Hoffmann, to design the firm's stand at the Paris Universal Exhibition in 1900. Intrigued by the formal and technical quality of products which combined careful craftsmanship with industrial potential, Loos commissioned Kohn to design and manufacture the chairs of the Café Museum in Vienna (1898-1899) whose lightness and elegance echoed the first creations of Michael Thonet. Kohn also reproduced the bent beech and perforated plywood chairs designed by Joseph Hoffmann for the sanatorium he built at Purkersdorf (1904-1906), as well as his famous *Armchair with adjustable back.*

Koloman Moser designed drawing-room furniture for patron F. Waerndorfer's sister-in-law, Margarethe Hellman, that left priority to empty space, playing on slightly incurved lines with subtlety and refinement, and illustrated Viennese furniture's move towards simplicity and geometrical conciseness.

The Scotsman Mackintosh invented a chair for the Argyll Street Tearoom in Glasgow, with a distinctive high back topped by a pierced oval. The close ties between Hoffmann and Mackintosh, and Adolf Loos' discovery of the United States, brought about a Glasgow-Vienna-Chicago axis that favoured a return to straight forms and pure lines.

Thonet Frères Firm founded in Vienna, 1853 *Model No. 1* Bent beechwood, caning 90 cm 	Thonet Frères Firm founded in Vienna, 1853 *Model No. 2* Bent beechwood, caning 90 cm 	Thonet Frères Firm founded in Vienna, 1853 *Model No. 3* Bent beechwood, caning 90 cm 	Thonet Frères Firm founded in Vienna, 1853 *Model No. 4* Bent beechwood, caning 90 cm 
Adolf Loos, 1870-1933 *Model created* *for the Café Museum* Circa 1898 Bent beechwood, caning 87 / 42.5 / 51 cm 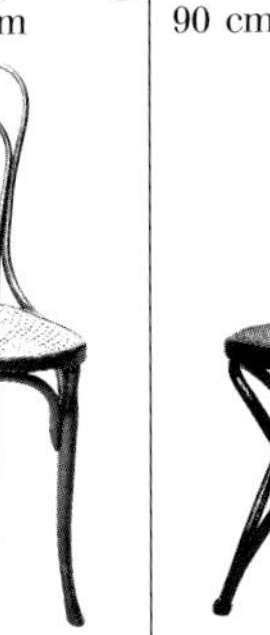	Thonet Frères Firm founded in Vienna, 1853 *Model No. 51* Circa 1888 Bent beechwood, caning 90 cm 	Joseph Hoffmann 1870-1956 *Chair* *'Purkersdorf'*, 1904 Bent beechwood perforated plywood imitation leather 99 cm 	Joseph Urban 1872-1933 Thonet Frères Firm founded in Vienna, 1853 *Chair* Circa 1905 Black varnished beechwood, dyed leather, brass 98.5/40/53cm 
Charles Rennie Mackintosh 1868-1928 *Chair for the Argyll* *Street Tearooms* 1897 Oak, horsehair 136.5 / 50 / 56 cm 	Koloman Moser 1868-1918 Manufactured by Wiener Werkstätter, from 1903 onwards *Armchair* Black varnished maplewood, modern upholstery 88 / 55 / 50 cm 	Otto Wagner 1841-1918 J. & J. Kohn *Armchair* (for the 'Die Zeit' newspaper offices) 1902 Bent beechwood, brass, caning 47 / 42 / 42 cm 	Carlo Bugatti 1856-1940 *Chair* Circa 1902 Mahogony and parchment pale wood filleting 114/45,3/50 cm 

III

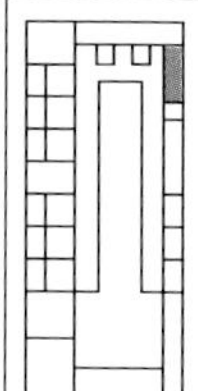

Vienna, Glasgow Chicago

Wagner, Moser, Hoffman, Mackintosh, Loos, Wright

In 1895, Otto Wagner, an Imperial councillor and professor at the Fine Arts Academy of Vienna, published his theories on modern architecture. In this work, Wagner proclaimed the need to abandon the styles of the past and promote a modern form of urban development better attuned to the needs of demographically and economically expanding cities. It is to Wagner that Vienna owes its Danube Canal and overhead Metro. In 1898, he rallied the Secessionist group (founded in 1897 by his pupils and followers, Olbrich, Hoffmann, Moser and the painter Klimt), to protest against the dominant trend of academic historicism. Koloman Moser was responsible for the design of the stained glass windows in the entrance porch of the church of St. Leopold at the Steinhof sanatorium near Vienna, built by Wagner between 1904 and 1907. For this porch, Moser chose the theme of *Paradise*, dedicating the side windows of the choir to *Works of Mercy*. Moser also drew some of the motifs of the central cupola, and his huge glass panels admit a special white and gold luminosity to the nave. The majestic, monumental shapes, the hieratic figure of God the Father, and the calm, contemplative angels and stylised motifs produce an overall effect of solemn austerity.

Well before 1900, Joseph Hoffman and Koloman Moser had planned an association of art professionals, along the lines of the English craftsmen's guilds. The 'Wiener Werkstätte' was founded in 1903, with the financial backing of Fritz Waerndorfer, an industrialist and art patron. In their manifesto, published in 1905, the group announced their programme and detailed their comprehensive activities in the crafts of silversmithing, coppersmithing, leatherworking and cabinet-making. The ambition of the 'Wiener Werkstätte' was to create a link between the designer, the craftsmen and the client, and to train highly qualified designers and craftsmen. Their aim was to create a form of luxury craftsmanship, which would counter the mediocrity of mechanically-produced objects. However, quality and the many hours they spent achieving it made their products very expensive.

Koloman Moser
Vienna 1868-1918
*Paradise,
sketch for window
of entry portico of
the church of
Saint Leopold
am Steinhof, Vienna*

1904
Distemper on paper
415 / 774 cm

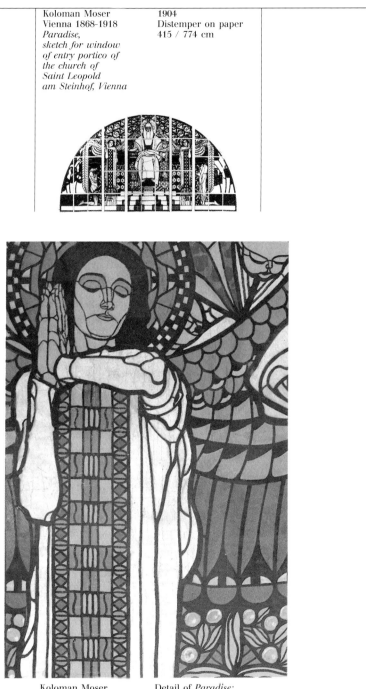

Koloman Moser
Vienna 1868-1918

Detail of *Paradise;
archangel*
1904
Distemper on paper

III

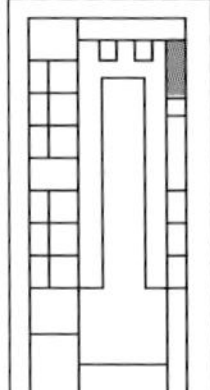

Reproduced in perforated or beaten metal, then silvered or white-enamelled, these objects matched interiors whose architectural organisation they reflected by their form and geometry. The artists of 'Wiener Werkstätte' utilised the ancient hammering technique for objects in silver or brass, whether polished or patinated.

Koloman Moser designed a huge *Music Cupboard*, in wide proportions, with protruding edges, refined decoration obtained solely from treated wood (oak brushed with white lead to highlight the natural grain), chased silver plaques, and delicate, gilded or silvered musical waves vibrating across the piece... This subtlety in choice of materials can also be found in the fragile *Casket*, created around 1904-1905, that combines silk, silver and agate with the finest workmanship.

This rigorous aesthetic had little appeal for the majority of people, who remained mesmerized by what they took to be symbols of wealth — namely, pastiches of bygone styles. But it did acquire a following of enlightened amateurs who appreciated modern trends.

After 1898, Secessionist artists such as Hoffmann, Moser and their pupils furnished patterns to industrial manufacturers with a view to mass production. Kohn produced large numbers of Hoffmann's *Swing-backed Armchair*, and the Joseph Böck ceramics factory reproduced Jutta Sik's tableware; Moser's glasses were mass-produced, by the Bakalowits glassworks. By the same token, when Wagner built the Post Office Savings Bank (1904-1906), he asked Thonet and Kohn to reproduce the furniture he had designed, among which were stools for the main hall and shelving for the director's offices in bent beech, perforated plywood and aluminium. These pieces are among the most successful prototypes of 20th century furniture in existence.

All these artists were motivated by the same wish to create utilitarian objects with simple, modern shapes. The resultant diffusion of industrially-produced objects contributed much more widely to making new ideas known to the general public, than did the relatively expensive, refined work done by the 'Wiener Werkstätte'.

Josef Hoffmann 1870-1956 Manufactured by Wiener Werkstätte	*Jardinière* 1904-1905 Silver plate 39.2 / 12.2 / 11 cm	Koloman Moser 1868-1918 Manufactured by Wiener Werkstätte	*Encrier et plateau (Inkpot and dish)* 1903-1904 Silver, glass Tray: 7 / 22.7 / 15.4 cm

III

Koloman Moser
1868-1918
Produced by Wiener Werkstätter from 1903 onwards
Music Cupboard
Circa 1904
Oak treated with white lead and varnished in black; carved and gilded wood; silver-plated, chased metal; white metal, glass
119.5 / 200.5 / 65.5 cm

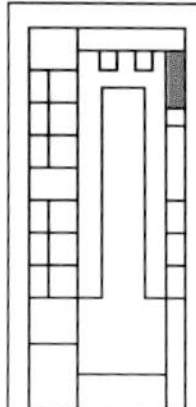

The Glasgow school, centred around Charles Rennie Mackintosh, Margaret and Frances MacDonald and Herbert MacNair, was born of the great social and technological changes wrought by industrial development in the late 19th century. Its work covered a variety of different fields – architecture, decoration, furniture, objets d'art, textiles, bookbinding and poster design – and was exhibited all over Europe; at the Bing Gallery in Paris (1895), at the Secession Exhibition in Munich in 1894, at Vienna in 1900 and at Turin in 1902. All these venues were important as points of exchange and diffusion for the new Glasgow aesthetic, with its emphasis on functional as opposed to decorative values.

Mackintosh himself was a rationalist, staunchly attached to local traditions, who sought to enclose the symbolism of Art Nouveau within a rigid framework of vertical and horizontal forms. He designed a number of apartments and houses, but became known mainly for his public work projects, offices, schools (Glasgow Academy of Fine Arts, 1898-1899), churches and tearooms (Argyll Street Tearooms, 1897, Ingram Street Tearooms, 1900, etc.).

When Mrs Cranston, one of his principal clients (for whom he had already built four tearooms) asked Mackintosh to convert her home, Houshill, at Nitshill near Glasgow (circa 1904), he had already rejected symbolism in favour of a more austere, abstract-oriented style. His white-painted furniture for the double guest bedroom was rigorously simple, with decoration reduced to squares and perforated rectangles with pastel-coloured glass incrustations and mother-of-pearl drawer handles. Naturalist motifs were relegated by Mackintosh to the mural decoration, textiles and light fixtures, now lost.

Adolf Loos was an eager partisan of modernity and functionalism as practised in the United States, and hence was somewhat aloof from the Secession group, whose strict approach he condemned. As an individualist he was opposed to 'total' art; according to him, every building should have its own specific style, matching that of its occupants. The architect should assist, advise, suggest and finally construct simple, forthright furniture.

Charles Rennie Mackintosh
1868-1928

Dressing table and looking glass
from Houshill, Glasgow
1904

Painted wood, ebony, mother-of-pearl, glass, silver-plated bronze
79.6 / 101.6 / 45.7 cm

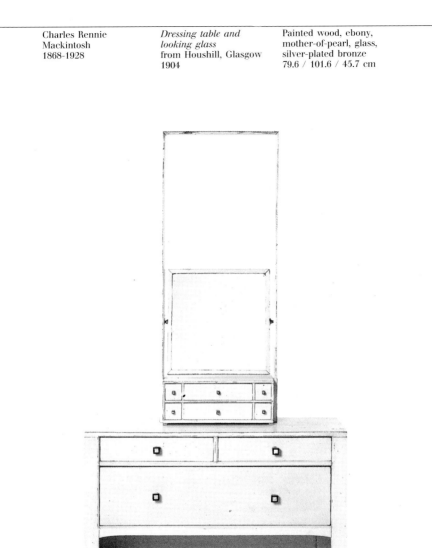

III

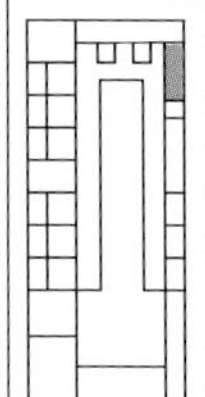

For Gustave Turnowsky's apartment in Vienna, Loos opted for a copper-framed bed and practical, traditionally-shaped chairs with Biedermeier upholstery. In the bedroom of Mrs Turnowsky, the arrangement of woodwork and furniture was adapted to ordinary daily requirements; sleep and toilet were consigned to one side of the room, work and relaxation to the other. The central partition, with its bevelled glass panels and mirror screen, contribute to this transparent, reflective fragmentation of space. Loos knew how to use material such as white maple, brass, marble and blue-grey silk, to create a refined ambiance.

In the early 1900's, the Chicago-based Frank Lloyd Wright embarked on his famous series of 'houses for the prairie', which were characterized by a break-up of traditional house design with wings and levels developing freely vis-à-vis a central nucleus. Wright also used natural, unmasked wood, brick and stone as a means to harmonized his buildings with their sites and surroundings; this concept owed much to Japanese architecture, with its low, wooden, horizontal structures and sense of pure decoration.

In Wright's designs, chairs play an important part in breaking up space; see the chairs he created for Isabel Roberts' house (1908), which belong to a series whose barred backs were intended to serve as screens and interior partitions.

A comparison of the stained glass on display shows how these elements evolved toward a spare, abstract style. For example, the glass door designed for the house of Darwin D. Martin (built between 1903 and 1905) is dominated by the hues of trees in autumn, while the windows for Avery Coonley's residence (1908) with its simple play of horizontal lines punctuated by coloured areas, made Wright one of the pioneers of pure abstract art well before he discovered the work of the European avant-garde.

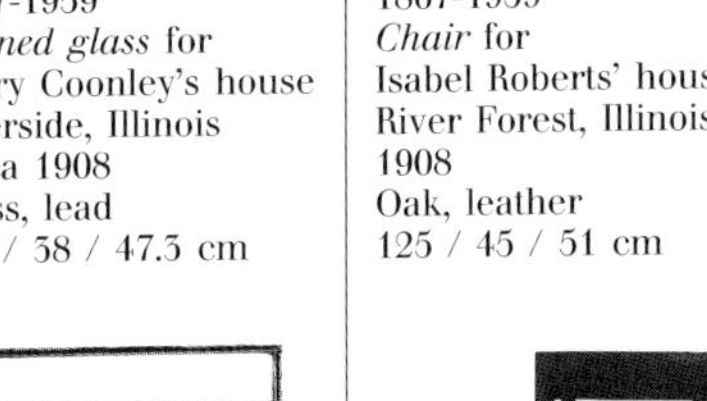

Frank Lloyd Wright
1867-1959
Stained glass for
Avery Coonley's house
Riverside, Illinois
Circa 1908
Glass, lead
101 / 38 / 47.5 cm

Frank Lloyd Wright
1867-1959
Chair for
Isabel Roberts' house,
River Forest, Illinois
1908
Oak, leather
125 / 45 / 51 cm

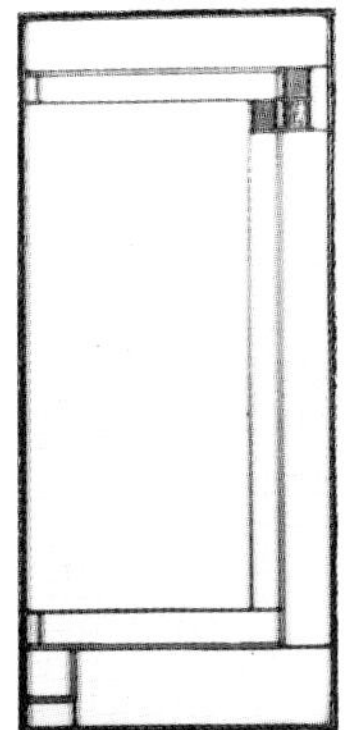

Adolf Loos
1870-1933
Chest of drawers
with doors
from the apartement of
G. Turnowsky, Vienna
Circa 1902
Maplewood, brass,
marble
74 / 112.5 / 56 cm

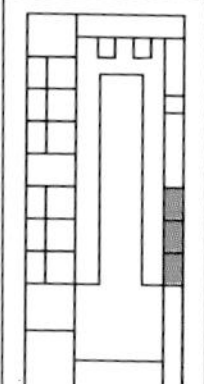

United in their decision to rediscover purity in art, exalted by Gauguin's testament transmitted by Sérusier *(The Talisman*, 1888, see small paintings' room), the Nabis, "prophets" of a new art, chose to abandon traditional rules of painting and looked towards "medieval stained glass windows, Japanese engravings, Egyptian painting", in the words of Maurice Denis, the group's theorician. From these few common ideas, each artist was to develop his own style; Pierre Bonnard, rightly called the "Nabi japonard", favoured a screen-like, elongated format, a gentle humour and intimist atmosphere in his *L'Enfant au pâté (Mud Pies)*, which shows one of his nephews, dressed in a kimono and his nape bared, playing on the Dauphiné property belonging to the artist's family. This same garden was the setting for *La partie de croquet (The Croquet Game)*, which depicts the various members of Bonnard's family, who appear as decoratively-outlined silhouettes filling several perspectives. A few years later, *Le grand jardin (The Garden)*, 1894, used the same surroundings, but in a symphony of lighter greens. *L'indolente (Lazy Nude)* is one of his first nudes; later, this theme became a favourite with him, handled in darker, cameo colours. The bird's eye angle of vision has the effect of tilting the space, which fills the entire canvas; at this stage, Bonnard and Vuillard were aesthetically closer than ever before or since.

When he began painting, Edouard Vuillard was perhaps the most Nabi painter of them all, as proved by *Au lit (In Bed)*. This familiar, intimate subject is arranged with astonishing daring; layers of superimposed colour, without depth, are set against a range of similar beige tones. The long, sinking line of the body, with its interconnected curves, evokes the atmosphere of sleep, while Vuillard's arbitrary deformation of the human figure produces a robust form of stylisation that is all his own.

Towards 1890 the Nabis demanded "walls, walls to decorate", with a view to embellishing the ordinary day-to-day framework of existence: this, in any case, was one of the foremost concerns of all Art Nouveau. *La nature morte à la salade (Still Life with Salad)*, with its discreet, nacreous tones, was probably part

Pierre Bonnard
1867-1947
Femme assoupie sur un lit
ou *L'indolente*
(Woman asleep on a Bed
or *Lazy Mude)*
1899
Oil on canvas
96 / 106 cm

Pierre Bonnard
1867-1947
L'enfant au pâté
(Mud Pies)
Glue distemper
on canvas
162 / 50 cm

Pierre Bonnard
1867-1947

La partie de croquet
(The Croquet Game)
1892
Oil on canvas
130 / 162 cm

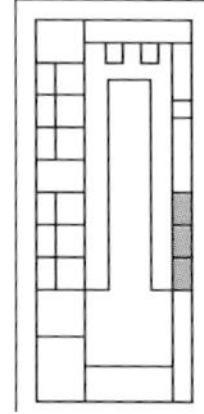

Edouard Vuillard
1868-1940
Jardins publics
(Public Gardens)
Panels for
Alexandre Natanson's
dining room:
glue-based
paint on canvas

Fillettes jouant
(Girls Playing)
215 / 88 cm

L'interrogatoire
(The Interrogation)
215 / 92 cm

Les nourrices
(Nannies)
212 / 80 cm

La conversation
(The Conversation)
212 / 152 cm

L'ombrelle rouge
(The Red Umbrella)
212 / 80 cm

III

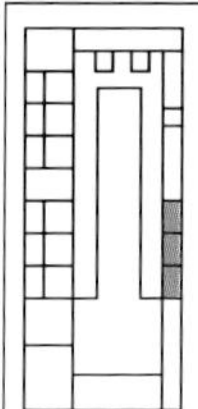

of a series painted by Vuillard between 1887 and 1888 as decoration for his dining room. But Vuillard's decorative work is best illustrated by his *Jardins publics (Public Gardens)*, 1894, of which five out of nine panels are shown in the Musée d'Orsay at the same angle as they were originally displayed in Alexandre Natanson's townhouse. (The other sections are in the Museums of Brussels, Cleveland and Houston.) Director of the *Revue Blanche*, Natanson actively supported the young, avant-garde painters, published their engravings and exhibited their works. The arbitrary arrangements of these five compositions, influenced by Japanese art, produce an extraordinary effect of foreshortening, while the glue-based paint creates a special surface relief of broad simplified masses, which are intended to be viewed from a distance. The slightly asymmetrical rhythm of the panels offsets that of the figures, while the delicate balance of colours and subtle tones is worked in a minor key. The overall effect is one of charming gravity and serenity.

The Swiss painter Vallotton came to live in Paris in 1882; the funny and ingenious composition of *Le Ballon (The Ball)*, 1899, lays emphasis on the concise style and flat coloured tints which characterize the Nabi movement. The realism and meticulous treatment of *Dîner, effet de lampe (Dinner, Effect of Lamplight)*, 1899, captures the artist's family in a fashion approaching caricature. They are depicted under a strong light, in shiny, contrasting tones; the hard graphics of this painting are a foretaste of expressionism and even surrealism.

Aristide Maillot (1861-1944) started out as a painter, not a sculptor, and joined the Nabi group whose preoccupations he shared. His decorative, crisply-profiled *Femme à l'ombrelle (Woman with Umbrella)*, circa 1895, stands out against a simple background resembling the tapestries he was creating at the same time. His subject matter, like his colours, aligned him with the Impressionists.

Maurice Denis was the theorist of the group; his famous definition of a painting as "essentially a flat surface covered in colours that have been assembled in a certain order", could be applied to any Nabi work, especially his own early painting, and his *Muses (The Muses)*, 1893. Denis' colours are deep and mat, suiting his work to vigorous simplification and emphasising its decorative character. The stylisation of forms and

Maurice Denis
1870-1943
Les muses
(The Muses)
1893
Oil on canvas
168 / 135 cm

Félix Vallotton
1865-1925
Le ballon
(The Ball)
1899
Oils thinned with turpentine
and gouache on cardboard
49.5 / 61.9 cm

Edouard Vuillard
1868-1940

Au lit
(In Bed)
1891
Oil on canvas
74 / 92 cm

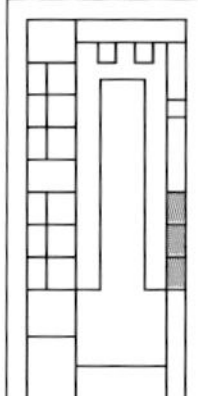

the use of arabesques in his depiction of foliage creates an unreal, poetic atmophere, not unlike that of the symbolists; *Les muses* constitutes a kind of redefinition of Puvis de Chavannes' *Bois sacré (Sacred Wood).* Denis and his friends greatly admired Cézanne, Gauguin and Redon, whom they considered as their 'initiators'. This admiration was expressed in *L'hommage à Cézanne,* 1900. In the spirit of Fantin-Latour's *Hommages*, Denis painted a group of the foremost Nabis, around a still life by Cézanne that had belonged to Gauguin (from left to right: Redon, Vuillard, Mellerio, Vollard, Denis, Sérusier, Ranson, Roussel, Bonnard and Marthe Denis). The scene is set in Vollard's gallery, in the presence of Redon and the critic André Mellerio. This work is historically and iconographically important, in that it includes the portraits of all the Nabis and affirms the group's cohesion until nearly 1900.

At the turn of the century, a perceptible change affected many of the Nabi painters. They began to move away from the flat tints of their youth, while at the same time abandoning simplifications and softening colours.

Maurice Denis had been one of the first to understand Cézanne, well before the great retrospective of the 1907 Salon d'Automne at which Cézanne was finally recognised as the master of the new generation of artists. Since his childhood visits to the Louvre and a first trip to Fiesole in 1895, Denis developed a passion for the Italian primitives, in particular Fra Angelico; a second stay in Florence and Rome in 1897-1898, and his encounter with André Gide, reinforced his desire to combine the individual with universal harmony. Thus when he paints scenes of simple contentment such as *Bretonnes sous la treille* or *Le paradis (Breton Women under a Pergola,* or *Paradise)*, a 1908 image of the flower garden of his house at Perros Guirec, Denis suggests a 'golden age' which is within the reach of every human being. His 'Maquette' for the dome of the Theatre des Champs Elysées, which was executed in 1911 for the art patron and Theatre Company chairman Gabriel Thomas, shows how he employs symbols to spark emotion, while at the same time using logic to reduce the effort of understanding required of the viewer to a minimum. In four panels, he evokes four different themes: The Dance, The Opera, The Symphony and The Lyrical Drama. In the second half of his life, Maurice Denis, known as the "Nabi of the beautiful icons", executed numerous religious painting as his many decorative works testify.

Edouard Vuillard
1868-1910
La chapelle du château de Versailles (The Chapel at Versailles)
Oil on canvas
96 / 66 cm

Maurice Denis
1870-1943
Maquette du plafond du théâtre des Champs-Elysées (Maquette for the Ceiling of the Theatre des Champs-Elysées)
1911
Distemper on reinforced plaster
∅ 240 cm

III

After the 1900 Universal Exhibition had consolidated the triumph of Impressionism and Symbolism, the disappearance in 1903 of the Natanson brothers' *Revue Blanche*, which had supported the Nabis, led to the breakup of the group. Although solid ties of friendship existed between its members, their differences and particularities about painting itself became too acute. Nonetheless, the place of honour accorded to Bonnard, Vuillard, Roussel and Vallotton at the 1905 Salon d'Automne was conspicuous; all these painters remained deeply influenced by their Nabi beginnings.

Vuillard's work came to prominence from 1900 onwards, in small exhibitions organised at the Bernheim brothers' gallery. In 1904, Camille Mauclair described Vuillard as "an intimist of rare delicacy, one of those whose modesty we almost regret,... given his remarkable gifts". Vuillard's *Chapelle du Château de Versailles (Chapel at Versailles),* behind an apparent concern for descriptive quality, reveals the painter's great virtuosity; amid a severe architectural setting, we perceive the opulent hair of a woman, viewed from behind. *La bibliothèque (The Library),* a large decorative panel executed by Vuillard in 1911 for Princess Bassiano, shows the painter's power to create a 'warm, quiet unity', with great decorative facility and muted, intense tones. Among his society portraits, that of *Mme de Polignac* (1930) testifies to Vuillard's skill at capturing space and the play of light.

Roussel's themes are usually taken from mythology, especially those of his commissioned décors. *L'enlèvement des filles de Leucippe (The Abduction of the Daughters of Leucippe)* illustrates the painter's skill in blending this mythological episode into a real landscape.

L'après-midi bourgeoise (Bourgeois Afternoon) marks a turning point in Bonnard's work. With it he abandons his early Japanesque and Art Nouveau tendancies; the decorative arrangement and humouristic distortion are still present, but this large canvas, with its strange, fixed character, is new in the artist's inspiration.

Edouard Vuillard
1868-1910
La bibliothèque
(The Library)
1911
Oil on canvas
400 / 300 cm

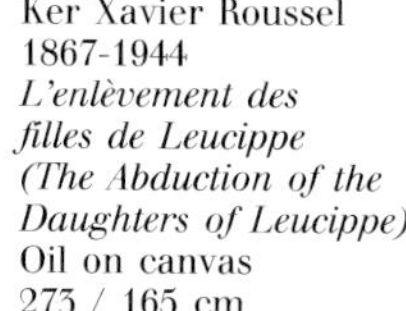

Ker Xavier Roussel
1867-1944
L'enlèvement des filles de Leucippe
(The Abduction of the Daughters of Leucippe)
Oil on canvas
273 / 165 cm

Pierre Bonnard
1867-1947
En barque
(In the Boat)
Circa 1907
Oil on canvas
278 / 301 cm

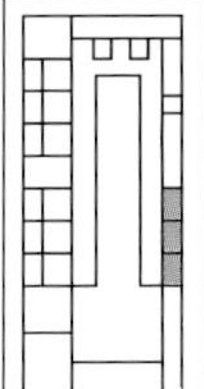

La femme au chat (Woman and Cat), 1912, contains three of Bonnard's favourite themes; his mistress Marthe, a cat, and a laid table. In this painting he discards his earlier taste for sombre tints in favour of vivid colours, which have the effect of plunging Marthe into a kind of soft shadow. There are Nabi overtones here, in the Japanese-style freedom and mastery of rhythm with which Bonnard handles perspective; thus he opposes curves (face, table, plates, shoulders) with straight lines (chimneypieces, wall, chair), the cat serving as a liaison.

"All my life", Bonnard told George Besson, "I have been drifting between intimist and decorative work". His *En Barque (In the Boat)* is a perfect illustration of this ambivalence, with its juxtaposition of an intimate scene in the foreground with a solid decorative landscape at rear. When he began painting, Bonnard, like most of his contemporaries, challenged the precepts of Impressionism; but here we can sense both its influence, and the progress made by Bonnard to escape that influence. Bonnard in this painting is not working in the open air; nor does he attempt to capture the mobility of light. His concern is to dominate his subject. Bonnard's perception of space and his blazing colours justify André Lhote's remark that his works "... bring out the purest values of painting, at the expense of immediate reality".

La loge (The Box), a commissioned work, depicts the two Bernheim-Jeune brothers, close friends of Bonnard, together with their wives. This theme, already treated by Renoir, Mary Cassatt and Toulouse-Lautrec, allows the painter to execute a very free composition, in which the central figure only features incompletely, the face being cut off at eye level. The flamboyant colours are unable to dissipate the atmosphere of "distinguished boredom" that emanates from this canvas.

The *Frères Bernheim de Villers (Bernheim de Villers Brothers)* are also represented in their gallery on the boulevard de la Madeleine. The innovative daring of this work lies in its stunning colours, bold arrangement and binary composition (two doors, two paintings, two figures, two light sources). Its rhythm is derived from the severity of its lines and right angles, which alone break the oblique angles of the two, dark, hieratic silhouettes.

Pierre Bonnard
1867-1947
La loge (The Box)
1908
Oil on canvas
91 / 120 cm

Pierre Bonnard
1867-1947
Portrait des frères Bernheim (Portrait of the Bernheim Brothers)
1920
Oil on canvas
165.5 / 155.5 cm

III

The Birth of Cinematography
The Birth of the Phonograph

In the cultural effervescence of the last years of the 19th century, the cinema gave the impression of being both a fortuitous discovery, and an invention that the whole world had been waiting for. In a sense, its advent was pure luck, generated by necessity. At first sight its development seems entirely linear, a process leading from rudimentary optical entertainment to films projected before large audiences. As far as expressive syntax is concerned there is about as much difference between a magic lantern and *La promenade en barque*, by the Lumière brothers, as between a box of colours and a pastel by Degas.

The cinema was the child of scientific research, born of a belated marriage between science and art which had been only partly consummated by photography. But in terms of structured spectacle, the cinema derived its power from a whole range of expressive tensions which profoundly affected turn-of-the-century culture: in other words, its development was not an isolated phenomenon.

The advances of photography produced a kind of cadastral survey of the world, the reverse of the normalisation process which colonialist Europe was imposing on the planet. Whether it concerned portraits, exotic scenes, monuments or landscapes — given relief and depth by *stereoscopic* techniques —the demand for knowledge of the outside world and for possession of reality could only be met by a complete mastery of panoramic vision. Added to this was the contemporary trend towards total art; Wagner is said to have prophesied the cinema when he dreamed of a form of art that would combine song, declamation, pantomime and fantasmagoria. Moreover, the perfecting of artificial scenery and an insatiable thirst for the marvellous and mysterious, also pointed straight to the cinema, by way of Reynaud's optical pantomimes and the *Chat Noir* shadow theatre.

It was thus perfectly normal that this new language should borrow its first cadences from the established plastic arts. Despite public resistance to novelty, Impressionist and post-Impressionist painting had already proved receptive to the suggestions of photography and Japanese art, and had gradually accustomed people to a more mobile appreciation of space and light, along with variable perspectives and compositions geared to the fleeting instant: in general, to a more dynamic reconstitution of reality. On the other hand, the people who flocked to the Salons sought in 'Pompier' art the same exquisite feeling of removal from their usual surroundings that later generations were to discover in the epic films of Pastrone, Griffith or Cecil B. de Mille.

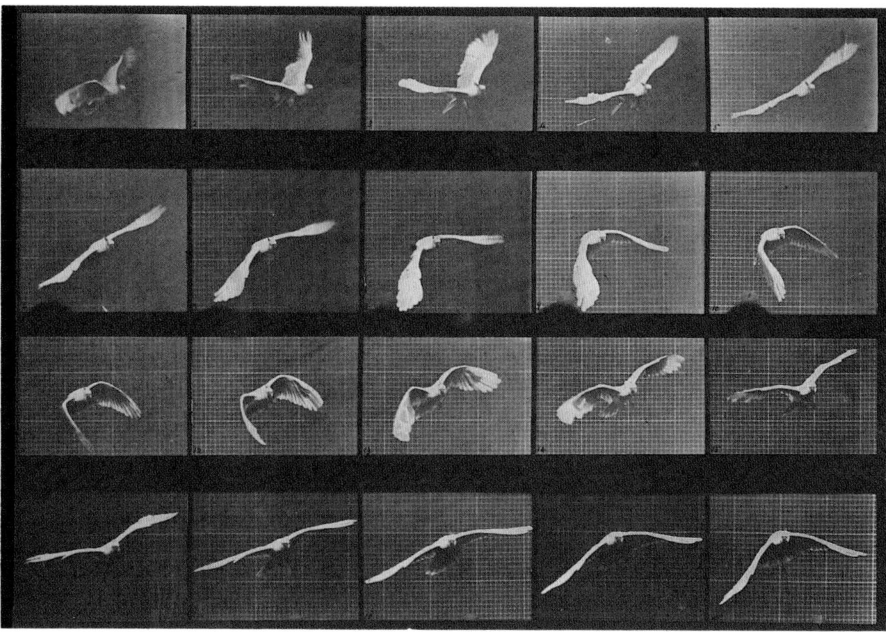

Eadweard Muybridge
1830-1904
Animal locomotion
1872-1885
Published in 1887

Facsimile of a plate from the album donated by the Kodak-Pathé foundation
1983

III

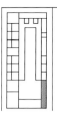

The scientific verification of movement served as a trigger for the new technique. In 1878, using a battery of cameras placed at regular intervals along a track, Eadweard Muybridge managed to capture the different phases in the action of a galloping horse; and in 1882 the physicist E.J. Marey dissected the flight of a seagull with his *chronophotography* procedure. In both cases, photography was being used for scientific research but, in fact, resulted in the first *photograms* of action on film. In order to reconstruct that action within a given time-span, both researchers had the idea of joining up their still shots in a reel, which they then passed through projection machines (notably, the *zoopraxinoscope*). The cinema proper was just around the corner. In 1889, T.A. Edison invented the perforated film roll, going on to shoot small motion pictures which could be viewed by one spectator at a time, with the aid of a large box and a magnifying glass which enlarged the image as it unrolled at a given speed. This projector was baptised the *kinetoscope*.

With the brothers Louis and Auguste Lumière, the decisive step was taken. By comparison with Edison, their progress was minimal; yet they accomplished something immense in terms of civilisation by transforming the motion picture from a fairground attraction to a codified art. Not only was the projection turned into a real collective spectacle, but the artistic sensitivity of the Lumière brothers and their creative complicity enabled them to film absolute masterpieces of the Seventh art almost immediately. In *L'arrivée du train en gare de La Ciotat (Train arriving at La Ciotat). La sortie des usines Lumière (Gates of the Lumière Factory)* and *La démolition d'un mur (Knocking down a Wall),* Lumière explored with deceptive ease virtually every possibility afforded by instantaneous recorded motion, depths of fields of visibility and camera mobility, using equipment that was nothing short of prehistoric. The cinema imposed a completely new concept of time and space, along with a new expressive dimension.

From the day of their first projection at the Grand Café in Paris (28 December, 1895), the success of the Lumière brothers was phenomenal. They opened theatres all over Paris and in the provinces, drawing huge crowds to see their 'animated photograhs' that had to be kept in order by squads of police.

Georges Méliès diverged from the Lumière brothers' naturalist approach to invent a two-dimensional world of hysterical sleight of hand, enchantment, fantasy and scathing humour, entirely fabricated in his glass-roofed studio at Montreuil. But producers quickly understood that the public wanted more

Entrance to a cinema projection theatre	Louis Lumière 1864-1948 *Entrée d'un train en gare de La Ciotat (Train arriving at La Ciotat)*

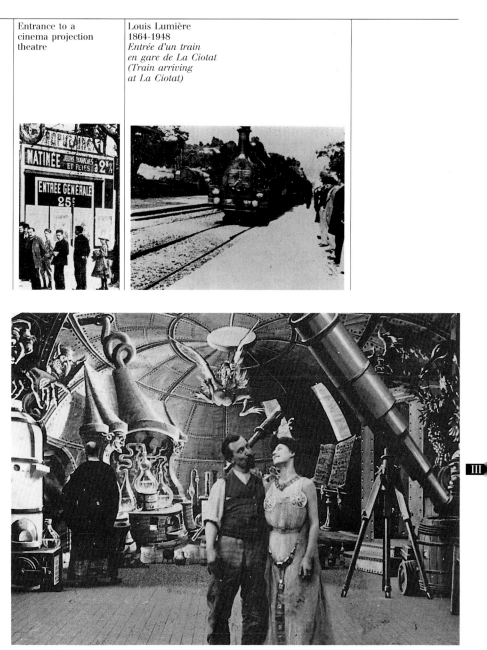

Georges Méliès
(1861-1938)
in one of his films

III

sophisticated direction. This presupposed rational production and large budgets supplied by heavyweight financial institutions, if the cinema were to handle 'noble' cultural themes (such as *L'assassinat du Duc de Guise – Assassination of the Duc de Guise)*, Films d'Art, 1908. In the USA, American cinema left New York for California, with its constant sunshine (1908); in France, meanwhile, the star system began to take shape (Sarah Bernhardt, Max Linder), and the great movie empires of Pathé and Gaumont were founded. Cinema's amateur era was gone forever.

The visit ends with a few showcases recalling the birth of the phonograph: one of the great inventions of the century that is owed simultaneously to Charles Cros for the principle (April 1877) and to Thomas Edison for its applicaion (December 1877).

Various phonographs, posters, wax cylinders and records trace the evolution of these "talking machines", from the modest apparatus with tinfoil to the grand horned instrument of the 1900s, not forgetting the first attempts at combining the phonograph and the cinema: Phono-Cinema-Theatre at the 1900 Universal Exhibition or Léon Gaumont's Chronophone (c. 1910). The latter left us precious documentary evidence of our acoustic and visual history, such as *Cyrano de Bergerac's* tirade recited by actor Coquelin Sr. in 1900.

Eadweard Muybridge
1830-1904
Animal locomotion
1887
Facsimile of a plate
from the album donated by
The Kodak-Pathé foundation
1983

III

Index

• illustrations

A

B

C

D

D

• illustrations

G

• illustrations

E

• illustrations

F

• illustrations

H

• illustrations

I - J - K

• illustrations

L

• illustrations

M

• illustrations

N - O

• illustrations

M

• illustrations

P - Q

R

• illustrations

T - U

• illustrations

V

S

• illustrations

• illustrations

W - Z

• illustrations

Contents

I ground floor first part of the visit

Floor Plans of the Museum's three Principal Levels

I
Ground floor, first part of the visit

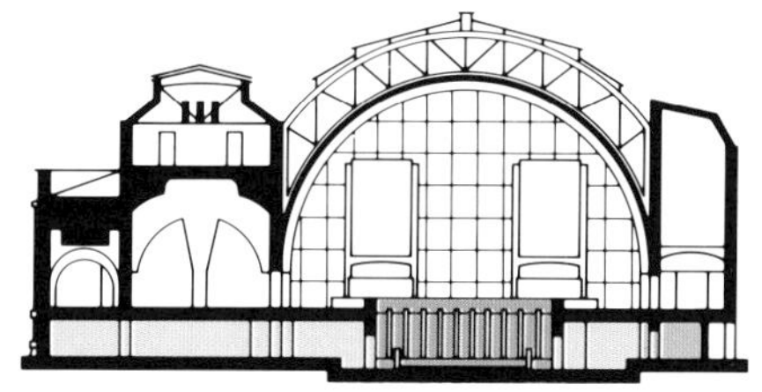

Sculpture 1850-1870

Paintings

A Ingres and 'Ingrisme', Delacroix, Chassériau, History Painting and the Portrait 1850-1880

B Daumier, Chauchard Collection Millet, Rousseau, Corot, Daubigny, Realism, Courbet

C Puvis de Chavannes, Gustave Moreau, Degas pre-1870

D Manet, Monet, Bazille and Renoir pre-1870, Fantin-Latour Outdoor Landscapes, Personnaz Collection, Eduardo-Mollard Collection Realism, Orientalism

Decorative Arts 1850-1880

Architecture

E The Paris Opéra

F Pavillon Amont: Architecture 1850-1900 Viollet-le-Duc, Pugin, Morris, Webb, Mackmurdo, Jeckyll, Godwin, Sullivan, Dossier 4

Temporary exhibitions

G Dossier 1

H Dossier 2

I Dossier 3

J Dossier 3

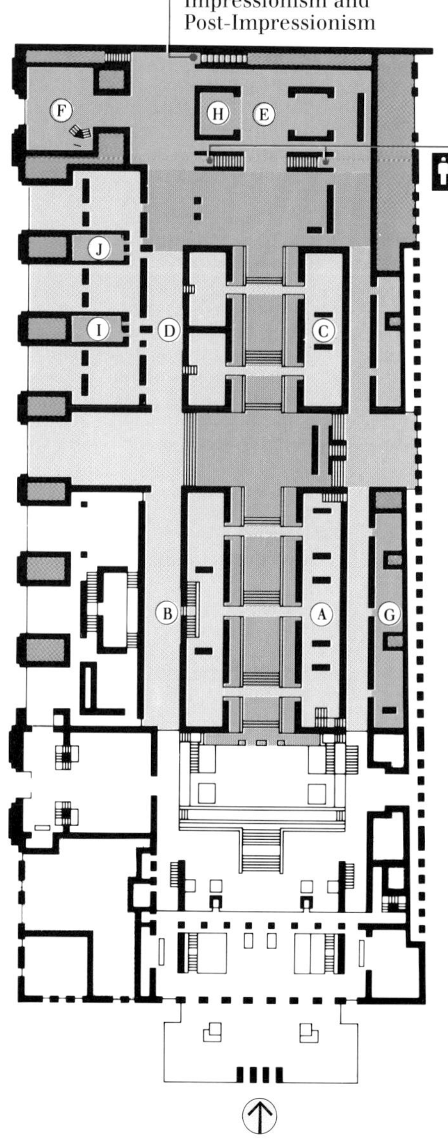

II
Upper level second part of the visit

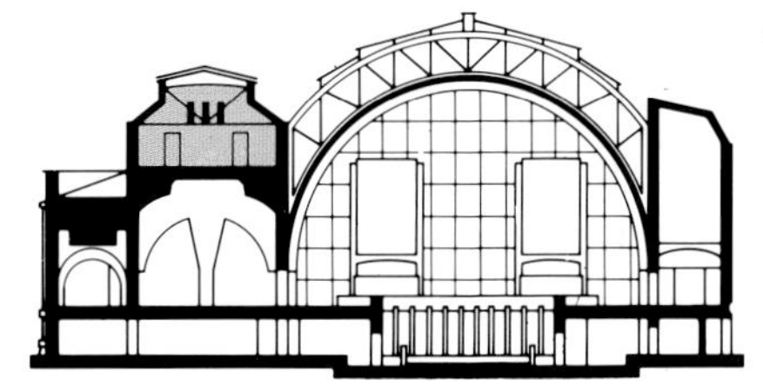

Painting

K Impressionism:
Moreau - Nélaton Collection
Whistler, Morisot, Caillebotte,
Degas, Manet post-1870,
Monet, Renoir, Pissarro and
Sisley pre-1880,
Monet post-1880,
Renoir, Pissarro post-1880,
Cézanne
Pastels: Degas

L Van Gogh
Gachet Collection
Redon, pastels

M Douanier Rousseau
Pont-Aven School:
Gauguin, Bernard, Sérusier.
Neo-Impressionism:
Seurat, Signac, Cross, Luce,
Toulouse-Lautrec.
Small paintings

Temporary exhibitions

N Dossier 4
way down to the middle level

Rooftop café

O Documentation room above
the Rooftop café: videos,
computers, catalogues

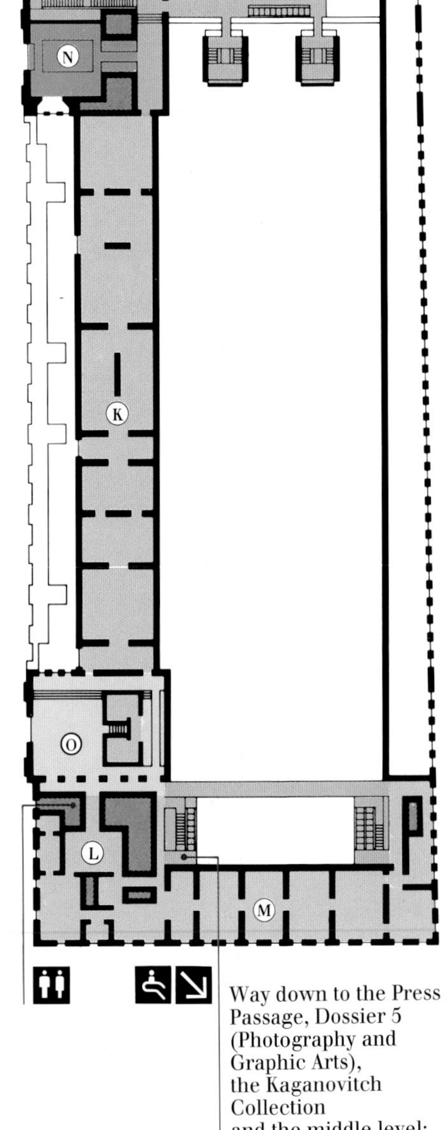

Way down to the Press Passage, Dossier 5 (Photography and Graphic Arts), the Kaganovitch Collection and the middle level: last part of the visit.

III
Middle level last part of the visit

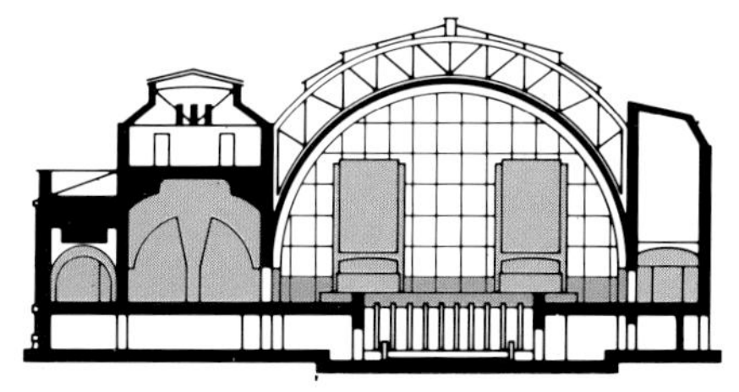

Sculpture

P Decorative Arts of the IIIe République

Q Fremiet, Gérôme, Rodin

R Desbois, Rosso, Bartholomé, Bourdelle, Maillol, Joseph Bernard

Painting

S Painting at the Salon 1880-1900, Naturalism, Foreign schools, Symbolism

T The Nabis: Bonnard, Denis, Vallotton, Vuillard, Roussel.

Art Nouveau

U France, Belgium, Holland, Germany, Scandinavia, Redon The Nancy School, Gallé Carabin, Charpentier, Dampt

V Tour amont

W International Art Nouveau

X Vienna, Glasgow, Chicago

Birth of the Cinema and the Phonograph

Temporary exhibitions

Y Dossier 6

Z Dossier 7

Restaurant

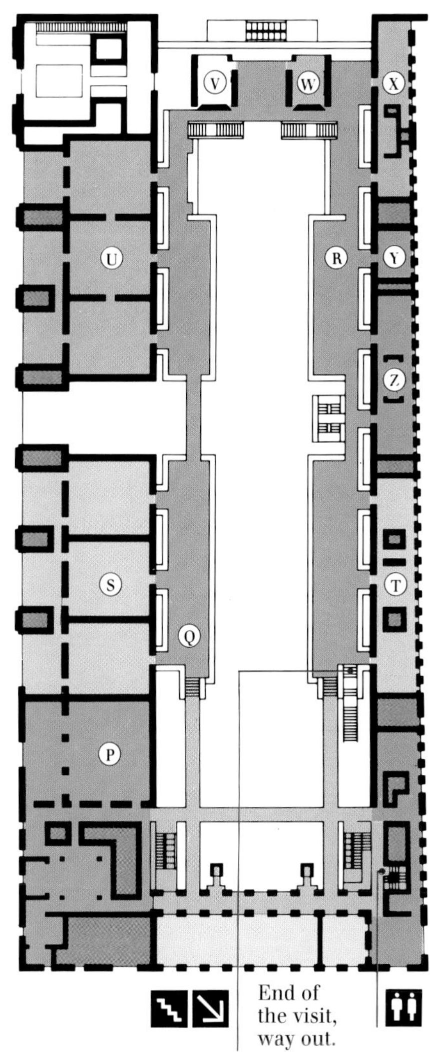

Caroline Mathieu wishes to convey her warmest thanks to M. Michel Laclotte and Mme Françoise Cachin, who entrusted her with the writing of this Guide, and to the staff of the Musée d'Orsay, who have supplied her with constant help and advice: especially Marc Bascou, Guy Cogeval, Chantal Georgel, Antoinette Le Normand-Romain, Monique Nonne, Claude Pétry and Anne Roquebert. She would also like to express her gratitude to Françoise Fur, Frédéric Lemercier and Marie Lionnard for their invaluable assistance.

Architectural Models

The maquette of the Opera quarter exhibited in the *Salle de l'Opéra* (p. 103) was created by Rémy Munier, with the assistance of Eric de Leusse.
The maquette of the side section was made in Rome by L'Atelier, under the direction of Richard Peduzzi.

Architectural scale modelling: Ercole Borsani: sculpture: Gianni Gianese; ornamental decoration, architecture: Bruno Fioeetti; painting: Amedeo Brogli; mouldings: Romolo Felici; carpentry work: Lorenzo Lodi, with the assistance of Epifania Imperiali, Claudia Scodina and Pasquale Gizzi; painted skies: Jean-Marc Misiaszek, Alain Tchillinguirian.

The plaster reliefs in the 'Pavillon Amont' (pages 106-113) were made in Rome by Enzo Bellardelli; the reliefs and painted canvases were executed in the Nanterre-Amandiers studios by Alwyne de Dardel, Alexandra Katzeflis, Astrid de Montalembert, Mario Rechtern, Marie Potvin and Xavier Morange, under the Direction of Richard Peduzzi.

Photography credits

The photography section of the RMN: D. Arnaudet, G. Blot, C. Jean, J.P. Lagiewski, H. Lewandowski, J. Schormans.

The photography section of the Musée d'Orsay: Jim Purcell, Jean-Jacques Sauciat, Patrice Schmidt.

Exterior Services: Pierre Joly, Véra Cardot (p. 11); Roger Viollet, Paris (p. 9); Bibliothèque Nationale, Paris (p. 28, 50, 86, 142 180, 183, 185).

Catalogue

Printed at the Imprimerie Aubin Poitiers.
Layout by Visuel Design, Jean Widmer, Gérard Plénacoste, Théa Sautter, Frédéric Lemercier.

Typesetting by Composition nancéienne, in Walbaum type
Illustrations engraved by Haudressy, Paris.

Premier dépôt légal : mars 1993
Dépôt légal : nov. 2000
French edition
ISBN : 2.7118.2714.3
English edition
ISBN : 2.7118.2781.X
GG. 20. 2781